STEP-BY-STEP ARABIC LANGUAGE

Beginner and Intermediate Learning

Nisreen Neqresh Beshqoy

Step-By-Step Arabic Language
Copyright © 2022 Nisreen Neqresh Beshqoy

Edits by Natalia Beshqoy and Noor Beshqoy
Book cover designed by Noor Beshqoy
Published by Nisreen Neqresh Beshqoy

Paperback ISBN: 979-8-218-06102-9
Library of Congress Control Number: 2022909739

Tables of Contents

Introduction

Nisreen Beshqoy is an author and former professor of Arabic Language and Arab Culture at Saddleback College in Southern California. She graduated from the University of Jordan with a degree in Law and she has also received an honorary achievement award from the Ministry of Education of Jordan for achieving the highest exam score in the country for the Arabic language. With many years of experience teaching all levels of Arabic, she has developed her own unique method of teaching the language, which follows a step-by-step approach. Her textbook, "Step-by-Step Arabic Language," is designed to guide Arabic students from beginner to intermediate levels of learning.

During her experience teaching Arabic language to college students, Nisreen identified several deficiencies in the conventional teaching system and the college textbooks that were being used. Her methodology aims to create a system that makes learning Arabic simple and easy, with a focus on independent learning. Her approach involves teaching students the rhythmic patterns inherent to the Arabic language and how words can be grouped into families that share a common root word, indicative of their meaning. The "Step-by-Step Arabic Language" textbook is intended to introduce a new style of learning Arabic based on Nisreen's approach.

The Arabic language is a beautiful and sophisticated language, with each word capable of conveying multiple meanings and dimensions of understanding. It has had a significant impact on the world, emerging in the 5th century and flourishing between the 7th and 14th centuries. Today, Arabic is widely used throughout the world, and Nisreen hopes to create a simplified way of learning the language through her approach. "Step-by-Step Arabic Language" teaches modern and formal spoken Arabic, which is the most commonly used form of the language in all Arab countries.

Nisreen Beshqoy hopes that "Step-by-Step Arabic Language" can be a valuable learning resource for students interested in learning and expanding their knowledge of the Arabic language. The textbook can be used in colleges and universities or by independent learners studying at home. It includes all the essential grammar rules required for building Arabic words and constructing sentences, with many examples provided for illustration.

The English Pronunciation System
Used in This Textbook

- The English pronunciation of the Arabic letters used in this book is provided to help you build vocabulary without having to wait until you have mastered all the Arabic letters.

- The uppercase English letters are used to represent the Arabic deep sound letters, while the lowercase English letters represent the Arabic frontal light sound letters. For example, the letter ع has no exact equivalent in English, but it is pronounced as a very deep "A". An apostrophe will be used with uppercase A' to distinguish its pronunciation from the regular "a".

- When you encounter vowels (a-o-i), they represent the Arabic short vowels, and when you see vowels written in a double format (aa-oo-ee), they represent the Arabic long vowels.

- The shadda symbol in Arabic ّ is used to double the sound of a letter. In this textbook, I have doubled the English letters to represent the shadda symbol in Arabic.

- The ending (an-on-in) in a word represents the doubling of the three Arabic short vowels.

- The comma (,) before the short vowels (,a ,o ,i) or at the end of a word in the English pronunciation represents the symbol 'hamza' ء in Arabic, which sounds like a sudden breath or a sudden stop.

- This English pronunciation system is meant to be temporary and transitional until you learn all the letters. Once you have learned all the Arabic alphabets, you should start practicing reading without relying on the English pronunciation and use it only when you need extra help in reading.

- I intentionally wrote the Arabic letters disconnected in the first few lessons to make the content of the words clear. However, this is not how Arabic words are written.

- The vowels at the end of words are not always necessary for pronunciation or understanding the context. You can read and understand the context without them. Therefore, the examples used in the book are not voweled at the end, in order to focus on other important grammar rules introduced in the lesson.

- This book teaches Modern Standard Arabic (MSA), which is the standard and spoken form of Arabic used in all Arab countries. However, you may also encounter some informal Arabic words that are commonly used in the Middle East.

Lesson One
The Arabic Alphabet

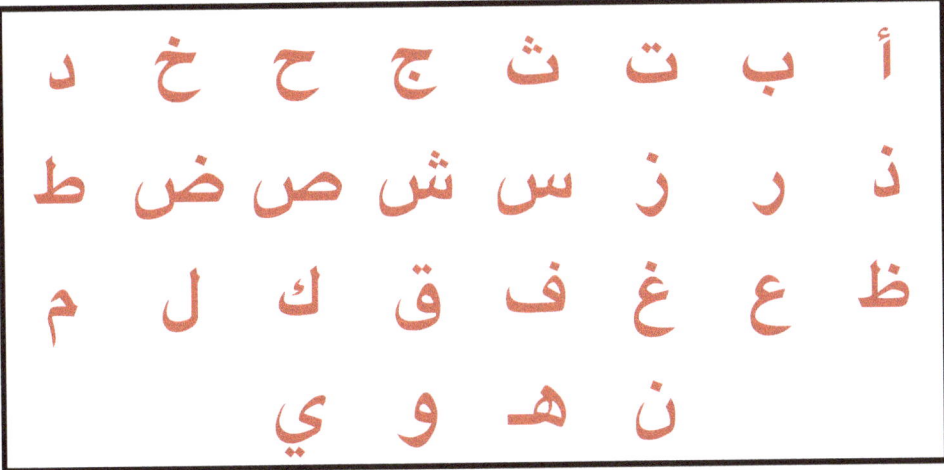

The Arabic alphabet is made up of 28 consonant letters. To produce complete sounds, vowels are essential and are represented by additional letters that follow the alphabet, as well as symbols placed above or below the consonants. Furthermore, Arabic script is cursive, meaning that the letters are joined together in a flowing manner. The Arabic language is read and written from right to left, in contrast to languages that follow a left-to-right writing direction. Below is a table summarizing the names and pronunciations of each letter:

- Note: The use of capitalized letters in the English pronunciation represents the letters pronounced deep in the throat (as explained on page 6).

Name of the letter	Pronunciation of the letter	Arabic form	Equivalence in English
alif	a	أ	a, as in "athletic" and "academic"
baa	b	ب	b, as in "bag" and "big"
taa	t	ت	t, as in "tank" and "took"
thaa	th	ث	Pronounced like the English sound of 'th', as in "thanks" and "think"

Name of the letter	Pronunciation of the letter	Arabic form	Equivalence in English
jeem	j	ج	j, as in "jacket" and "Juice"
Haa	• very deep H	ح	No equivalence in English. Pronounced deep down the throat, similar to clearing the bottom part of the throat or coughing
KHaa	• very deep KH	خ	No equivalence in English. Pronounced deep in the throat, similar to clearing the top part of the throat
daal	d	د	d, as in "dance" and "deer"
dhaal	dh	ذ	Pronounced like the English sound of 'th', as in "the", "that", and "this"
raa	r	ر	r, as in "ran" and "room"
zay	z	ز	z, as in "zip" and "zoo"
seen	s	س	s, as in "sand" and "soon"
sheen	sh	ش	sh, as in "shark" and "should"
SaaD	• S	ص	S, as in "sun" and "subway"; with more emphasis and tongue stress on the S
Daad	• D	ض	D, as in "done" and "double"; with more emphasis and tongue stress on the D
Taa	• T	ط	T, as in "cut" and "but"; with more emphasis and tongue stress on the T

Name of the letter	Pronunciation of the letter	Arabic form	Equivalence in English
DHaa	• DH	ظ	Pronounced like the English sound 'TH', as in "mother" and "father"; with more emphasis and tongue stress on the TH
A'ayn	• Very deep A'	ع	No equivalence in English. Start vocalizing letter 'A' then push your tongue downward.
GHayn	• GH	غ	No equivalence in English. The sound stems from the deep upper throat; it resembles the sound of a gargling, similar to French 'r'.
faa	f	ف	f, as in "fat" and "food"
Caaf	• C	ق	C, as in "come" and "column"; with more emphasis and tongue stress on the C
kaaf	k	ك	k, as in "keep" and "kitten"
laam	l	ل	l, as in "land" and "lesson"
meem	m	م	m, as in "mad" and "miss"
noon	n	ن	n, as in "nap" and "neck"
haa	h	ه	h, as in "hand" and "hint"
waaw	w	و	w, as in "was" and "when"
yaa	y	ي	y, as in "yes" and "you"

The Arabic Language Specifications

Understanding the unique characteristics of the Arabic language is crucial when beginning to learn it. By understanding these specifications, learners can lay a strong foundation for their Arabic language studies. Here are some essential points to consider:

1. **Arabic is built on a unique system called the three-letter root:** This means that many words in Arabic are formed from a set of three consonant letters that carry a basic meaning. By adding different vowels and additional letters to these roots, new words can be created. This structure allows for a wide variety of vocabulary to be derived from a limited number of roots. It makes Arabic an interesting and logical language to learn, as you can understand and generate many words by recognizing and manipulating these root patterns.

2. **Arabic words rhyme because they follow a special pattern:** Words belonging to the same category, like nouns, verbs, or adjectives, have similar endings or vowel patterns. This makes the language sound musical and rhythmic. It also helps us remember words easily. The rhyming patterns in Arabic make the language expressive and allow for the creation of beautiful poetry and songs.

3. **Arabic Script**: The Arabic script is written in a flowing manner called cursive. When writing, the letters are connected to form words, creating a smooth appearance. Unlike English or other left-to-right languages, Arabic text is read from right to left. This right-to-left direction is a key feature of Arabic writing.

4. **Connected Letters:** In Arabic, all letters are connected when writing words. However, there are six letters known as one-way connectors. These letters join with the preceding letter in a word but do not connect to the letter that follows. These one-way connector letters are:

و	ز	ر	ذ	د	ا
w	z	r	dh	d	a

Here are examples of words that include the six one-way connector letters in Arabic:

مَوْعِد	عَزِيز	بَرِيد	لَذِيذ	مَدِينَة	جَمَال
mawA'id	A'azeez	bareed	ladheedh	madeena	jamaal
Date	Dear	Mail	Delicious	City	Beauty

وَزير	زَفير	فَريق	بُذور	صَديق	مال
wazeer	**zafeer**	**fareeC**	**bodhoor**	**SadeeC**	**maal**
Minister	Exhalation	Team	Seeds	Friend	Money

5. **In the Arabic alphabet, there are 9 letters that have deep sounds.** These deep sound letters are pronounced from the depth of the throat. For each sound in Arabic, whether it is light or deep, there is a special letter that represents it. Pronouncing the deep letters correctly may require training your tongue with repetition, especially since the majority of sounds in English are predominantly frontal.

Here is a table displaying the 9 deep letters of the Arabic alphabet along with their English equivalent sounds:

The Deep Letters

Very deep 'H' (no equivalence in English): Pronounced deep in the throat, as if clearing the bottom part of the throat or coughing.	ح
Very deep 'KH' (no equivalence in English): Pronounced deep in the throat, as if clearing the top part of the throat.	خ
'S': Pronounced as 'S' in words like "sun" and "subway," with more stress and emphasis on the tongue.	ص
'D': Pronounced as 'D' in words like "done" and "double," with more emphasis and stress on the tongue.	ض
'T': Pronounced as 'T' in words like "ton" and "but," with more emphasis and stress on the tongue.	ط
'DH': Pronounced like the English sound 'TH,' as in "mother" and "father," with more emphasis and stress on the tongue.	ظ

The Deep Letters

Very deep 'A' (no equivalence in English): Start vocalizing the letter 'A' and then push your tongue downward.	ع
'GH' (no equivalence in English): The sound originates from the deep upper throat and resembles the sound of gargling.	غ
'C': Pronounced as 'C' in words like "come" and "column," with more emphasis and stress on the tongue.	ق

6. **In Arabic, words are classified as either masculine or feminine**. One common way to identify feminine words is through the presence of the feminine sign, which is a closed 't' (ة). This feminine sign is derived from the regular 't' (ت) and is used as an indicator of femininity. Masculine words, on the other hand, do not have any specific signs associated with them.

7. **The Arabic language encompasses two distinct styles:**

A. **Formal Classical Arabic, known as "fusHa,":** This style is employed in television news broadcasts, social programs, newspapers, radio, and formal discussions among educated individuals. It is also the form taught in schools from elementary to university level across all Arab countries. Formal Arabic is used in all types of books, ranging from educational textbooks to social, scientific, economic, religious, and political literature.

B. **Informal or Dialectal Arabic:** This style is used in everyday social interactions. With 19 Arab countries, each region has its own dialect, and even within each country, multiple dialects exist. However, as you expand your Arabic knowledge, you will notice that a majority of words and expressions are shared between formal Arabic and the various spoken dialects. It is important to note that informal Arabic does not adhere to the strict rules of grammar and sentence structure. Therefore, it is advisable to focus on studying the spoken formal Classical Arabic first. This will provide a solid foundation, making it easier to incorporate and learn informal words and expressions later on.

- **Formal Classical Arabic, known as "fusHa,"** has two levels of formality. The degree of formality is evident in the pronunciation of vowels, especially at the end of words, when writing, reading, or speaking. In the First Level, Arabic is fully voweled, representing old classical or very formal Arabic. The Second Level of formal Arabic is characterized by the omission of vowels, particularly at the end of words. This style, known as modern classical Arabic, spoken classical Arabic, or standard Arabic, is more commonly used among Arabic speakers. In this book, our focus is on spoken Modern Standard Arabic (MSA), as it is the most widely used and common style across Arab countries.

8. **In Arabic, the presence of vowels at the end of each word is not necessary** to convey meaning. It is possible to pause at the end of each word at any desired moment. This approach helps avoid errors in choosing the correct vowel.

9. **Arabic has three unique letters with distinct roles:**

'Alif' ا, 'Waw' و, **and** 'Yaa' ي are considered special letters as they serve three functions within a word.

- **The first function** of the letters 'a' (alif) أ, 'w' (waw) و, and 'y' (ya) ي they work as long vowels. These letters have the ability to lengthen the sound of other letters that precede them, under certain conditions. Specifically, this occurs when these letters are not marked with any of the three short vowels (fatha, kasra, and damma), and when they are not used as seats for the symbol 'hamza' ء. When the letter 'alif' أ is used as a long vowel (aa) ا, it must lose the 'hamza' ء on top, which is usually marked with it. In this case, the 'alif' ا functions solely as a long vowel and does not carry the 'hamza' symbol.

- **The second function** of the letters 'a' (alif) أ, 'w' (waw) و, and 'y' (ya) ي is their ability to function as regular consonants. This occurs when these letters are marked with any of the three short vowels: 'fatHa' , 'Dammeh' , or 'kasrah' . When these letters are marked with a short vowel, they are treated as consonants and do not elongate the sound of the preceding letters. Instead, they maintain their consonant sound and are pronounced accordingly based on the specific vowel marking present.

By using the appropriate short vowel mark, whether it's 'fatHa', 'Dammeh', or 'kasrah', these three letters can be distinguished as consonants rather than functioning as long vowels.

- **The third function** of the letters 'a' (alif) أ, 'w' (waw) و, and 'y' (ya) ي is their ability to act as seats for the symbol 'hamza' ء. The letter 'alif' ا uses the 'hamza' symbol ء on top of it, referred to as 'alif hamza' أ, in order to function as a consonant. However, the 'hamza' symbol can also appear on top of the letters 'waw' ؤ and 'ya' ئ, using them as seats and transforming them from long vowels or regular consonants into mere carriers for the 'hamza'. In this case, these letters do not have sounds of their own and solely serve as carriers for the 'hamza'.

- It is important to note that the 'hamza' symbol ء can sometimes appear on the line without any carrier. Additionally, the letter 'alif' ا at the beginning of a word always functions as a consonant, regardless of whether the 'hamza' symbol is visibly present or not. Furthermore, when the letter 'ya' ي functions as a seat for the 'hamza' ئ, it loses its two dots. This alteration occurs to indicate its role as a carrier for the 'hamza'.

- In this book, I recommend focusing on recognizing the seats of the 'hamza' symbol ء without delving into the intricate rules surrounding them, as some of these rules may be too complex for beginners. It is more important to familiarize yourself with identifying and understanding the usage of these seats. It is worth noting that the sound of the 'hamza' symbol ء can be likened to a sudden exhaling breath. This understanding will aid in recognizing and pronouncing the symbol accurately.

By emphasizing recognition and the basic concept of the 'hamza' seats, this book aims to provide a solid foundation for beginners without overwhelming them with complex rules surrounding this aspect of the Arabic language.

- Here are some examples of words that contain one of the three seats for the 'hamza' (ء):

On the line	On top of 'y' ئ	On top of 'w' ؤ	On top of 'a' أ
ذَكَاء	طَوارِئ	سُؤَال	أَمَل
dhakaa,	Tawaari,	so,aal	amal
Intelligence	Emergency	Question	Hope

10. The letter "alif" ا in Arabic has four different shapes:

- **The first shape** is a regular vertical stroke that is written from top to bottom ا . Here are some examples of words containing this form of the letter "alif":

حَمْراء
Hamraa,
Red

دار
daar
House

هَواء
hawaa,
Air

- **The second shape** for the letter "alif" ا is similar to the letter "yaa" ى without the two dots at the bottom. This shape is known as the "broken alif" and is commonly found in feminine names. It serves as a feminine gender sign for the word and is typically used at the end of a word. In feminine names, the "broken alif" is used to indicate the feminine gender and distinguish it from masculine names or words. Here are some examples of words or names where the "broken alif" is used:

15

mostashfaa
Hospital

salwaa
(Female name)

Halwaa
Dessert

• **The third shape** for the letter "alif" ا is called the "stretched alif" آ. It is a symbol used to avoid repeating the letter 'a' twice in writing. Instead of writing two separate 'alif' letters, it is replaced with the "meddeh sign" ‒ placed on top of the 'alif' آ.

This occurs when an "alif hamza" أ is followed by another "alif hamza" أأ or by a long vowel 'alif' أا. The pronunciation of this 'stretched alif' آ is lengthened 'aa' in the words that contain them. The "stretched alif" is pronounced as a lengthened 'aa' sound in words where it is used. It represents an elongated vowel sound similar to the sound in the English word "car." It is important to note that the "stretched alif" only affects the pronunciation and does not change the meaning of the word.

Here are some examples of words containing the "stretched alif":

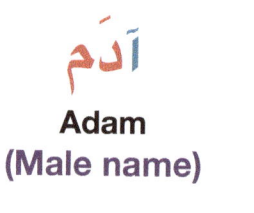

aaraa,
Opinions

aameen
Amen

Adam
(Male name)

- **The fourth shape** of the letter "alif" ‏ا‏ is an old symbol used in ancient Quranic writings. It looks like a small vertical stroke placed on top of the letter. This old symbol is not commonly used in modern Arabic script, except for a few words. It is mainly associated with preserving the beauty and authenticity of Quranic manuscripts. While its usage is specific to ancient calligraphy styles, it holds cultural and historical significance in the context of Quranic script.

haathihi
This (for feminine)

haatha
This (for masculine)

laakin
But

11. **Arabic has three long vowels and three short vowels.** The short vowels, referred to as "Harakat" (meaning movements), are diacritical marks that are placed above or below the consonants. These markings indicate the movement or sound of the vowels, assisting in the accurate and a full pronunciation of the letters. Additionally, Arabic includes three long vowels that are pronounced twice as long as the short vowels. The following table shows the long and the short vowels that corresponds:

Pronunciation	Short Vowels	Pronunciation	Long Vowels
a	◌َ	aa	‏ا‏
	fatHa		alif
o	◌ُ	oo	‏و‏
	Dammeh		waaw
i	◌ِ	ee	‏ي‏
	kasra		yaa

17

Note: The short vowel signs in Arabic are pronounced with equal length, similar to the vowels in English. It is important to mention that the short vowels in Arabic are represented by small symbols, unlike in English where vowels are expressed by letters.

12. **Arabic has other derived vowel signs** formed by doubling the original short vowel signs, a feature known as "tanween." When the three short vowels are doubled, they create the sound of "n" at the end of the word. In this book, you will explore and learn more about these derived vowel signs. Here are the specific forms:

Tanween kasra	Tanween Dammeh	Tanween fatHa
ﹴ	ﹲ	ﹰ
Symbol represents the doubling of the vowel 'kasrah', which produces the sound 'in'. It is placed at the end of a word.	Symbol represents the doubling of the vowel 'dammah', resulting in the sound 'on'. It is placed at the end of a word.	Symbol represents the doubling of the vowel 'fatḥah', producing the sound 'an'. It is placed at the end of a word.

13. **The short vowels are often omitted** in magazines, newspapers, and most books in Arabic. Native Arabic readers are accustomed to reading without the short vowels. Once you have developed a solid vocabulary and become familiar with Arabic word patterns and structures, you will be able to read without relying on the short vowels. You will learn to accurately read words without vowel markings. However, it's important to note that certain textbooks, such as elementary school textbooks and religious texts like the Quran, are fully voweled, providing the vowel markings for easier reading and pronunciation.

I have purposely included written vowels throughout this book based on my experience teaching college students at the elementary level. I have found it to be crucial and beneficial for building students' confidence in pronouncing words correctly at this stage. It helps establish a strong foundation in becoming familiar with the patterns of the Arabic language, which are heavily influenced by short and long vowels. However, I have omitted vowels at the end of words since it is uncommon to pronounce or write them in spoken Modern Standard Arabic.

14. **Arabic has other pronunciation symbols and grammatical endings** that you will learn in detail throughout this book.These symbols play significant roles in Arabic pronunciation and grammar, and throughout this book, you will learn more about their usage and functions. Some of these symbols include:

hamzat al-waSl	sukoon	shaddeh
ٱ	ْ	ّ
Symbol is used above the letter 'alif' instead of the regular 'hamza'. It signifies the skipping of pronouncing the 'hamza' and instead emphasizes the connection between two letters.	Symbol represents a stillness or absence of a vowel sound on a letter. It indicates that the letter is not pronounced with a vowel.	Symbol signifies intensity and denotes the doubling of the sound of the Arabic letter. It emphasizes the pronunciation of the letter with doubled intensity.

- To differentiate between when to use the regular 'hamza' ء on top of the 'alif' ا and when to use 'hamzat al-wasl' ٱ, you can follow this approach:

A. If the 'alif' ا is not preceded by a letter or a word, add the letters و (waaw) before the 'alif' ا and try to pronounce the 'alif hamza' أ. If you are able to smoothly pronounce it, then use the 'alif hamza' أ, as in the word 'mother' وَأُم.

B. However, if it is difficult to pronounce the 'hamza' ء and it is easier to skip the 'alif hamza' أ and directly pronounce the next letter, then use 'hamzat al-wasl' ٱ instead of the regular 'hamza' on top of the 'alif'. An example of this is the word 'night' وٱلّيل. By applying this approach, you can determine whether to use the regular 'hamza' or 'hamzat al-wasl' based on pronunciation ease and smoothness.

Lesson Two
The Shapes of the Letters

The Arabic alphabet is cursive, meaning that the letters are connected to one another when forming words. When the letters are combined, their shapes may differ from when they are written independently. Additionally, the appearance of the letters can vary depending on whether they are used at the beginning, middle, or end of words. By understanding the different shapes and positions of Arabic letters, you will be able to read and write words more accurately.

In this lesson, we will explore the shape variations of letters in spoken Modern Standard Arabic. It's essential to understand that Modern Standard Arabic generally does not include full vowel markings, particularly the vowel marking for the last letter in a word, which is often not pronounced or written.

In written Modern Standard Arabic, there are mostly consonants, and vowels are often indicated by diacritic marks or understood from the context. However, when speaking Arabic, the pronunciation of vowels can change depending on regional accents, local dialects, and personal preferences. Here are examples of words for each letter of the Arabic alphabet in all positions:

The letter "alif" أ in all positions: In Arabic, the letter "alif" is represented by a straight

vertical line that resembles a long stick. It has a symbol on top that looks like a small "c" shape with a tail. The "alif" does not have any dots or curves. It is written from top to bottom. Regardless of its position within a word, the "alif" maintains its basic straight vertical shape. It can be found at the beginning, middle, or end of a word, without any significant changes to its form.

• Please note that this letter is part of a group of six letters known as "one-way connectors" in Arabic. This means that it connects with the preceding letter in a word, but it does not connect with the following letter.

End	Middle	Beginning	Independent
ـأ	ـأ	أ	أ
خَطَأ	كَأس	أَمَل	أ
KHaTa,a	ka,as	,amal	A
Mistake / Fault	**Cup**	**Hope**	

Examples of letter 'b' ب in all positions:

The letters ب (ba), ت (ta), and ث (tha) in Arabic have a similar shape, but they differ in the number and placement of dots. The letter "ب" has one dot below, "ت" has two dots above, and "ث" has three dots above. These dots help distinguish between the letters.

End	Middle	Beginning	Independent
ب	ـب	بـ	ب
حَليب	لَبَن	بَيْت	ب
Haleeb	laban	bayt	b
Milk	Yogurt / Milk	House	

Examples of letter 't' ت in all positions:

End	Middle	Beginning	Independent
ـت	ـتـ	تـ	ت
بَيْت	كِتاب	تاج	ت
bayt	kitaab	taaj	T
House	Book	Crown / Tiara	

Examples of letter 'th' ثُ in all positions:

End	Middle	Beginning	Independent
ثـ	ـثـ	ثـ	ث
غَيْثْ	مَثَل	ثَلاثَة	ث
GHayth	mathal	thalaatha	th
Rain	Example	Three	

Examples of letter 'j' جـ in all positions:

The Arabic letters "jeem" جـ, "ha" حـ, and "khah" خـ have a similar shape. However, "Jeem" has a single dot in the middle, "ha" has no dots, and "khah" has a one dot above.

End	Middle	Beginning	Independent
ـج	ـجـ	جـ	ج
خَليج	سِنْجاب	جَبَل	ج
KHaleej	sinjaab	jabal	J
Golf	Squirrel	Mountain	

Examples of letter 'H' ح in all positions:

- Please note that this letter belongs to a group of nine letters pronounced with a deep throat sound in Arabic.

End	Middle	Beginning	Independent
ج	ح	ح	ح
بَلَح	سَحاب	حَرْب	ح
balaH	saHaab	Harb	H
Dates 'fruit'	Clouds	War	

Examples of letter 'KH' خ in all positions:

- Please note that this letter belongs to a group of nine letters pronounced with a deep throat sound in Arabic.

End	Middle	Beginning	Independent
خ	خ	خ	خ
فَرْخ	مَخْرَج	خَبَر	خ
farKH	maKHraj	KHabar	KH
Chick	Exit	News	

23

Examples of letter 'd' د in all positions:

The letter "dal" د and the letter "dh" ذ have a similar shape, but the main difference is that "dh" ذ has a single dot above, while "dal" د has no dots.

- Please note that the Arabic letters "dal" (د) and "dh" (ذ) are part of a group of six letters known as "one-way connectors" in Arabic. This means that these letters connect with the preceding letter in a word but do not connect with the following letter.

End	Middle	Beginning	Independent
ـد	ـد	د	د
حَديد	مَدْخَل	دولاب	د
Hadeed	madKHal	doolaab	D
Iron	Entrance	Wheel	

Examples of letter 'dh' ذ in all positions:

End	Middle	Beginning	Independent
ـذ	ـذ	ذ	ذ
لَذيذ	بُذور	ذَنْب	ذ
ladheeth	bodhoor	dhanb	dh
Delicious	Seeds	Sin / Guilt	

Examples of letter 'r' ر in all positions:

The Arabic letters "ra" ر and "za" ز have a similar shape. The difference between them is that "ra" has no dots, while "za" has a single dot above it.

- Please note that the Arabic letters "ra" ر and "za" ز are part of a group of six letters known as "one-way connectors" in Arabic. This means that these letters connect with the preceding letter in a word but do not connect with the following letter.

End	Middle	Beginning	Independent
ـر	ـر	ر	ر
أَمِير	تُراب	رَبِيع	ر
ameer	toraab	rabeeA'	R
Prince	Dirt	Spring	

Examples of letter 'z' ز in all positions:

End	Middle	Beginning	Independent
ـز	ـز	ز	ز
عَزِيز	مَزاد	زَنْبَق	ز
A'azeez	mazaad	zanbaC	Z
Dear	Auction	Lily	

Examples of letter 's' س in all positions:

The Arabic letters "seen" س and "sheen" ش have a similar shape, but they differ in the presence and placement of dots. "Seen" has no dots, while "sheen" has three dots above it.

End	Middle	Beginning	Independent
ـس	ـسـ	سـ	س
شَمْس	مُسْلِم	سَمَك	س
shams	moslim	samak	S
Sun	Muslim	Fish	

Examples of letter 'sh' ش in all positions:

End	Middle	Beginning	Independent
ـش	ـشـ	شـ	ش
حَشِيش	مِشْمِش	شعور	ش
Hasheesh	mishmish	shoA'oor	sh
Grass	Apricot	Feelings	

26

Examples of letter 'S' ص in all positions:

The Arabic letters "SaD" ص and "DaD" ض have a similar shape, but they differ in the presence and placement of dots. "S" has no dots, while "D" has one dot above it.

- Please note that this letter belongs to a group of nine letters pronounced with a deep throat sound in Arabic.

End	Middle	Beginning	Independent
ﺺ	ﺼ	ﺻ	ص
لِصّ	عَصير	صَيْد	ص
liSS	A'aSeer	Sayd	S
Robber	Juice	Hunting	

Examples of letter 'D' ض in all positions:

- Please note that this letter belongs to a group of nine letters pronounced with a deep throat sound in Arabic.

End	Middle	Beginning	Independent
ﺾ	ﻀ	ﺿ	ض
مَريض	مُضِر	ضِرْس	ض
mareeD	moDir	Dirs	D
Sick	Harmfull	Molar / Tooth	

27

Examples of letter 'T' ط in all positions:

The Arabic letters "Ta" ط and "DH" ظ have a similar shape, but they differ in the presence and placement of dots. "T" has no dots, while "DH" has one dot above it.

- Please note that this letter belongs to a group of nine letters pronounced with a deep throat sound in Arabic.

End	Middle	Beginning	Independent
ط	ط	ط	ط
بَطّ	مَطار	طَيْر	ط
baT	maTaar	Tayr	T
Ducks	Airport	Bird	

Examples of letter 'DH' ظ in all positions:

- Please note that this letter belongs to a group of nine letters pronounced with a deep throat sound in Arabic.

End	Middle	Beginning	Independent
ظ	ظ	ظ	ظ
لَفْظ	مُظْلِم	ظُهْر	ظ
lafDH	moDHlim	DHohr	DH
Pronunciation	Dim	Noon	

Examples of letter 'A' ع in all positions:

The Arabic letters "Aayn" ع and "GHain" غ have a similar shape, but they differ in the presence and placement of dots. "A'" has no dots, while "GH" has one dot above it.

- Please note that this letter belongs to a group of nine letters pronounced with a deep throat sound in Arabic.

End	Middle	Beginning	Independent
ع	ـعـ	عـ	ع
نَبْع	طَعْم	عِلْم	ع
nabA'	TaA'm	A'ilm	A'
Spring water	Taste	Knowledge	

Examples of letter 'GH' غ in all positions:

- Please note that this letter belongs to a group of nine letters pronounced with a deep throat sound in Arabic.

End	Middle	Beginning	Independent
ـغ	ـغـ	غـ	غ
صِبْغ	مُغَامَرَة	غَريب	غ
SibGH	moGHaamara	GHareeb	GH
Dye	Adventure	Strange	

Examples of letter 'f' ف in all positions:

End	Middle	Beginning	Independent
ـف	ـفـ	فـ	ف
خَفيف	قَفَص	فَرْخ	ف
KHafeef	CafaS	farKH	f
Light weight	Cage	Chick	

Examples of letter 'C' ق in all positions:

- Please note that this letter belongs to a group of nine letters pronounced with a deep throat sound in Arabic.

End	Middle	Beginning	Independent
ـق	ـقـ	قـ	ق
رَفيق	فَقير	قَلَم	ق
rafeeC	faCeer	Calam	C
Companion	Poor	Pencil / Pen	

Examples of letter 'k' كـ in all positions:

End	Middle	Beginning	Independent
كـ	ـكـ	كـ	ك
فَلَك	سُكَّر	كَوْن	ك
falak	sokkar	kawn	k
Space / Astron-omy	Sugar	Cosmos	

Note: The letter 'k' has a distinct shape at the beginning and within the middle of a word, resembling a zig-zag pattern descending from top to bottom (كـ).

Examples of letter 'l' ل in all positions:

End	Middle	Beginning	Independent
ـل	ـلـ	لـ	ل
لَيْل	مِلْح	لَوْن	ل
layl	milH	lawn	L
Night	Salt	Color	

31

Examples of letter 'm' مُ in all positions:

End	Middle	Beginning	Independent
ـم	ـمـ	مـ	م
حاكِم	ثَمين	مال	م
Haakim	thameen	maal	m
Ruler	Valuable	Money	

Examples of letter 'n' ن in all positions:

End	Middle	Beginning	Independent
ـن	ـنـ	نـ	ن
فَنّ	كَنْز	نور	ن
fann	kanz	noor	N
Art	Treasure	Glow/light	

Examples of letter 'h' **هـ** in all positions:

End	Middle	Beginning	Independent
ه / ـه	ـهـ	هـ	هـ
قِصَّه	مَفْهوم	هام	هـ
CiSSah	mafhoom	haam	H
Story	Understandable / Concept	Important	

Examples of letter 'w' **و** in all positions:

- Please note that this letter is part of a group of six letters known as "one-way connectors" in Arabic. This means that it connects with the preceding letter in a word, but it does not connect with the following letter.

End	Middle	Beginning	Independent
ـو	ـو	و	و
دَلو	قَوْل	وَطَن	و
daloo	Cawl	waTan	W
Bucket / Pail	Say / Saying	Homeland	

Examples of letter 'y'  in all positions:

End	Middle	Beginning	Independent
ـي	ـيـ	يـ	ي
حَيّ	سَيْل	يَوْم	ي
Hayy	sayl	yawm	Y
Neighborhood / Alive	Stream / Torrent	Day	

- **Keep in mind that while practicing reading Arabic, it is important to remember that Arabic is a cursive script and is read and written from right to left.**

The table below presents the forms of all letters in each of the four positions: beginning, middle, end, and standalone.

Pronunciation	End	Middle	Beginning	Independent
a	ـأ	ـأ	أ	أ
b	ـب	ـبـ	بـ	ب
t	ـت	ـتـ	تـ	ت
th	ـث	ـثـ	ثـ	ث
j	ـج	ـجـ	جـ	ج
H	ـح	ـحـ	حـ	ح

34

Pronunciation	End	Middle	Beginning	Independent
• KH	خ	ـخـ	خـ	خ
d	ـد	ـد	د	د
dh	ـذ	ـذ	ذ	ذ
r	ـر	ـر	ر	ر
z	ـز	ـز	ز	ز
s	ـس	ـسـ	سـ	س
sh	ـش	ـشـ	شـ	ش
• S	ـص	ـصـ	صـ	ص
• D	ـض	ـضـ	ضـ	ض
• T	ـط	ـطـ	طـ	ط
• DH	ـظ	ـظـ	ظـ	ظ
• Very deep A'	ـع	ـعـ	عـ	ع
• GH	ـغ	ـغـ	غـ	غ
f	ـف	ـفـ	فـ	ف
• C	ـق	ـقـ	قـ	ق
k	ـك	ـكـ	كـ	ك

Pronunciation	End	Middle	Beginning	Independent
l	ـل	ـلـ	لـ	ل
m	ـم	ـمـ	مـ	م
n	ـن	ـنـ	نـ	ن
h	ـه	ـهـ	هـ	هـ
w	ـو	ـو	و	و
y	ـي	ـيـ	يـ	ي

Below is a table showcasing words that serve as examples for the different shapes of each letter when they appear at the beginning, middle, and end of words:

English	End		Middle		Beginning		Alone
a	news	نَبَأ	cup	كَأْس	hope	أمَل	أ
b	dog	كَلْب	race	سِباق	door	باب	ب
t	house	بَيْت	book	كِتاب	figs	تين	ت
th	rain	غَيْث	example	مَثَل	three	ثَلاثَة	ث
j	golf	خَليج	squirrel	سِنْجاب	beautiful	جَميل	ج
· H	dates 'fruit'	بَلَح	clouds	سَحاب	milk	حَليب	ح

Eng-lish	End		Middle		Beginning		Alone
• KH	chick	فَرْخ	palm-tree	نَخيل	bread	خُبْز	خ
d	iron	حَديد	entrance	مَدْخَل	wheel	دولاب	د
dh	delicious	لَذيذ	seeds	بُذور	fly	ذُبابَة	ذ
r	prince	أَمير	dirt	تُراب	spring	رَبيع	ر
z	dear	عَزيز	auction	مَزاد	lily	زَنْبَق	ز
s	sun	شَمْس	muslim	مُسْلِم	fish	سَمَك	س
sh	grass	حَشيش	apricot	مِشْمِش	hair	شَعْر	ش
• S	robber	لِصّ	juice	عَصير	hunting	صَيْد	ص
• D	sick	مَريض	harmful	مُضِّر	molar/tooth	ضِرْس	ض
• T	ducks	بَطّ	airport	مَطار	bird	طَيْر	ط
• TH	pronunci-ation	لَفْظ	dim	مُظْلِم	noon	ظُهْر	ظ
• A'	spring water	نَبع	taste	طَعْم	knowled-ge	عِلْم	ع
• GH	dye	صَبْغ	adven-ture	مُغامَرَة	strange	غَريب	غ
f	Wrapped up	مَلَفوف	key	مُفْتاح	movie	فِلْم	ف

English	End		Middle		Beginning		Alone
C	compan-ion	رَفيق	Poor	فَقير	pencil/pen	قَلَم	ق
k	king	مَلِك	letter	مَكْتوب	treasure	كَنْز	ك
l	evidence	دَليل	milk	حَليب	almonds	لَوْز	ل
m	poison	سَمّ	sesame	سُمْسُم	salt	مِلْح	م
n	art	فَنّ	Treasure	كَنْز	glow	نور	ن
h	queen	مَلِكَه	river	نَهْر	cat	هِرَّة	هـ
w	bucket	دَلو	strong	قَوِيّ	boy	وَلَد	و
y	neighbor-hood	حَيّ	stream	سَيْل	day	يَوْم	ي

- Keep in mind that while practicing reading Arabic, it is important to remember that Arabic is a cursive script and is read and written from right to left.

- The examples provided in the tables for this lesson are all in spoken Modern Standard Arabic, which means that the words do not have vowels marked at the end of each word.

- Please be aware that the pronunciation system used in this book is explained on page six for your reference.

Lesson Three
The Long Vowels

The letters 'a' ا, 'w' و, and 'y' ي are all part of the 28 Arabic alphabets. They are unique letters because they have three different functions. They can be used as long vowel signs, regular consonants, and seats for the 'hamza' ء symbol.

When these three letters come after other consonants, they are used as lengthening vowels, extending the sounds of the preceding letters. Specifically, the letter 'a' ا has the sound of (aa), the letter 'w' و has the sound of (oo), and the letter 'y' ي has the sound of (ee). It's worth noting that the length of the sound of long vowels in Arabic is twice as long as the sound of English vowels.

- As mentioned previously, in Arabic, all letters require vowels to produce their full sounds. These vowels can be in the form of short vowel symbols placed above or below the letters, or as long vowels represented by specific letters that follow other letters.

- In the spoken Modern Standard Arabic language, it is not customary to pronounce the vowels on the last letter of a word. Arabic speakers generally do not find it necessary to vocalize the vowels at the end on every word, as they rely on the context to understand the intended meaning.

- If we consider fully vocalized Classical Arabic, there are specific rules regarding the default vowel for the last letter of independent nouns and adjectives. For words that begin with the definite article 'al' ال meaning "the," the default vowel for the last letter is 'dammah' , which sounds like 'o' at the end. On the other hand, for independent nouns and adjectives that do not start with 'al' ال, the default vowel for the last letter is a doubling of 'dammah' indicated by the symbol . This doubled 'dammah' sounds like 'on' at the end of the word.

- When practicing reading Arabic, remember that it is a cursive script read and written from right to left. Writing words with disconnected letters, as shown in the first column of some lessons, is incorrect.

- The examples provided in the tables for this lesson are all in spoken Modern Standard Arabic, which means that the words do not have vowels marked at the end.

The following are examples of the long vowels ي و ا after the alphabet 'b' ب

and 't' ت

'b' ب as in 'bag' and 'beach'. 't' ت as in 'tank' and 'tip'.

Meaning	Modern Standard Arabic	Disconnected
Door	باب baab	ب ا ب baa b
Owl	بوم boom	ب و م boo m
Big	كَبير kabeer	كَ ب ي ر ka bee r
Crown	تاج taaj	ت ا ج taa j
Raspberry	توت toot	ت و ت too t
Fig	تين teen	ت ي ن tee n

The letter 't' in Arabic has another form known as the 'closed t.' This form is exclusively used at the end of a feminine noun or adjective and serves as a common indicator of feminine gender. It appears as ة when preceded by a one-way connector letter, and

as ﺔ when preceded by a two-way connector letter.

In spoken Modern Standard Arabic, this letter is written but is not commonly pronounced. However, the 'fatHah' vowel, which has the sound of 'a,' always appears just before the 'closed t' and is consistently pronounced in spoken Modern Standard Arabic. Hearing the sound of the 'fatHah' at the end of a noun or adjective is typically an indication of a feminine word. It's worth noting that the closed 't' ة is only pronounced in fully vocalized and old classical Arabic. Examples:

Meaning	Modern Standard Arabic	Disconnected
Fatima **Female name**	فاطِمَة faTima	ف ا ط مَ ة faa Ti ma
Female leader	رائِدة ra ,i da	ر ا ئِ د ة raa ,i da
Female scientist	عالِمَة A'alima	ع ا ل مَ ة A'a li ma
Female leader	قائِدَة Caa,ida	ق ا ئِ دَ ة Caa ,I da
Successful fe-male	ناجِحَة naajiHa	ن ا ج حَ ة naa ji Ha
Noble / Generous female	كَريمَة kareema	كَ ر ي مَ ة ka ree ma
Female teacher	أُسْتاذَة ostaadha	أُ سْ ت ا ذَ ة os taa dha

Meaning	Modern Standard Arabic	Disconnected
Polite (for female)	لَطيفَة laTeefa	لَ ط ي فَ ة la Tee fa
Wise (for female)	حَكيمَة Hakeema	حَ ك ي مَ ة Ha kee ma

Examples of the long vowels ي و ا after the alphabet 'th' ث and 'j' ج.

'th' ث as in 'think' and 'throw'. 'j' ج as in 'jacket' and 'June'.

Meaning	Modern Standard Arabic	Disconnected
Example	مِثال mithaal	مِ ث ا ل mi thaa l
Garlic	ثوم thoom	ث و م thoo m
Acting	تَمْثيل tamtheel	تَ مْ ث ي ل tam thee l
Neighbor	جار jaar	ج ا ر jaa r
Present / Existent	مَوْجود mawjood	مَ وْ ج و د maw joo d
Generation	جيل jeel	ج ي ل jee l

42

Examples of the long vowels ي و ا after the alphabet 'H' ح and 'KH' خ.

Letter 'H' ح and 'KH' خ do not exist in the English language. Therefore, their pronunciation is more difficult than the other letters. When pronouncing these two letters, the sound originates from the depth of the throat, almost as if the person is clearing the bottom of the throat when pronouncing ح and cleaning the top of the throat when pronouncing خ.

Meaning	Modern Standard Arabic	Disconnected
Situation / Condition	حال Haal	ح ا ل Haa l
Whale	حوت Hoot	ح و ت Hoo t
Alone / Lonely	وَحيد waHeed	وَ ح ي د wa Hee d
Uncle (mother's side)	خال KHaal	خ ا ل KHaa l
Entering	دُخول doKHool	دُ خ و ل do KHoo l
Stingy	بَخيل baKHeel	بَ خ ي ل ba KHee l

Examples of the long vowels ي و ا after the alphabet 'd' د and 'dh' ذ:

The 'd' د as in 'dance' and 'deer'. Letter 'dh' ذ as in 'the' and 'that'. Both of these letters belong to the group of six one-way connector letters. We must also distinguish letter 'dh' ذ from letter 'th' ث as in 'think' and 'throw'.

Meaning	Modern Standard Arabic	Disconnected
House / Home	دار daar	د ا ر daa r
Ants / Worms	دود dood	د و د doo d
Religion	دين deen	د ي ن dee n
Drizzle	رَذاذ radhaadh	رَ ذ ا ذ ra dhaa dh
Roots	جُذور jodhoor	جُ ذ و ر jo dhoo r
Delicious	لَذيذ ladheedh	لَ ذ ي ذ la dhee dh

Examples of the long vowels ي و ا after the alphabets 'r' ر and 'z' ز:

'r' ر as in 'room' and 'ring'. 'z' ز as in 'zebra' and 'zoo'. Both of these letters belong to the group of six one-way connector letters.

Meaning	Modern Standard Arabic	Disconnected
Satisfied	راضي raaDee	ر ا ض ي raa Dee
Bride	عَروس A'aroos	ع َ ر و س A'a roo s
Groom	عَريس A'arees	ع َ ر ي س A'a ree s
Shrine	مَزار mazaar	مَ ز ا ر ma zaa r
False	زور zoor	ز و ر zoo r
Dear / Darling	عَزيز A'azeez	ع َ ز ي ز A'a zee z

Examples of the long vowels ا و ي after the alphabets 's' س and 'sh' ش:

's' س as in 'sand' and 'soon'. 'sh' ش as in 'shark' and 'should'.

Meaning	Modern Standard Arabic	Disconnected
Toxic	سام saam	س ا م saa m
Marketplace	سوق sooC	س و ق soo C

Meaning	Modern Standard Arabic	Disconnected
Coordination	تَنْسِيق tanseeC	ت َ نْ س ي ق tan see C
Hard	شاق shaaC	ش ا ق shaa C
Stuck	مَحْشور maHshoor	مَ حْ ش و ر maH shoo r
Grass / Hay	حَشيش Hasheesh	ح َ ش ي ش Ha shee sh

Examples of the long vowels ا و ي after the alphabets 'S' ص and 'D' ض:

'S' ص as in 'sun' and 'subway', with more emphasis of the tongue on the 'S' ص.

'D' ض as in 'done' and 'double', with more emphasis of the tongue on the 'D' ض.

Meaning	Modern Standard Arabic	Disconnected
Patient	صابِر Saabir	ص ا بِ ر Saa bir
Trapped	مَحْصور maHSoor	مَ حْ ص و ر maH Soo r
Fate	نَصيب naSeeb	نَ ص ي ب na See b
Harmful	ضار Daar	ض ا ر Daa r

Meaning	Modern Standard Arabic	Disconnected
Curiosity	فُضول foDool	ف ُ ض و ل fo Doo l
Hardship	ضيق DeeC	ض ي ق Dee C

Examples of the long vowels ي و ا after the alphabets 'T' ط and 'DH' ظ:

'T' ط as in 'but' and 'cut', with more emphasis of the tongue on the 'T' ط.

'DH' ظ as in 'thus' and 'mother', with more emphasis of the tongue on the 'DH' ظ.

Meaning	Modern Standard Arabic	Disconnected
Airport	مَطار maTaar	مَ ط ا ر ma Taa r
Length	طول Tool	ط و ل Too l
Mud	طين Teen	ط ي ن Tee n
Unjust/Unfair	ظالِم DHaalim	ظ ا لِ م DHaa lim
Restricted	مَحْظور maDTHoor	مَ حْ ظ و ر maH DHoo r
Clean	نَظيف naDHeef	نَ ظ ي ف na DHee f

47

Examples of the long vowels ي و ا after the alphabet 'A' ع and 'GH' غ:

The letter ع in Arabic represents a deep "A" sound that originates from the back and bottom of the throat. It doesn't have an equivalent sound in English and can be challenging to pronounce. With practice and guidance, learners can improve their pronunciation.

Similarly, the letter غ, often represented as 'GH' in English, is also difficult to pronounce. It comes from the deep upper throat and sounds like a mixture of a gargle and a french "R" sound. With practice and guidance, learners can develop the ability to pronounce it correctly.

Meaning	Modern Standard Arabic	Disconnected
Disabled	مُعاق moA'aC	مُ ع ا ق mo A'a C
Stick	عود A'ood	ع و د A'oo d
Holiday	عيد A'eed	ع ي د A'ee d
Angry / Furious	غاضِب GHaaDib	غ ا ضِ ب GHaa Dib
Monster	غول GHool	غ و ل GHoo l
Loaf	رَغيف raGHeef	رَ غ ي ف ra GHee f

Examples of the long vowels ي و ا after the alphabet 'f' ف and 'C' ق.

'f' ف as in 'fat' and 'food'. 'C' ق , the nearest sound is 'C' as in 'come' and 'column' with the emphasis in the throat on the 'C' ق .

Meaning	Modern Standard Arabic	Disconnected
Fatin (Female Name) Charming/Enchanting	فَاتِن fatin	ف ا تِ ن faa ti n
Bean	فول fool	ف و ل foo l
Elephant	فيل feel	ف ي ل fee l
Shrine / Status	مَقام maCaam	مَ ق ا م ma Caa m
Substance	قوت Coot	ق و ت Coo t
Certainty	يَقين yaCeen	يَ ق ي ن ya Cee n

Examples of the long vowels ي و ا after the alphabet 'k' ك and 'l' ل :

'k' ك as in 'keep' and 'kitten'. When the 'k' ك comes at the beginning or in the middle of the word, it has a distinguished different shape that looks like a zig-zag coming from top to bottom, ك as in the Arabic word كلب (dog) and the word فِكرَة (idea).

'l' ل as in 'land' and 'lesson'.

• When the 'a' ا follows 'l' ل they are written as 'laa' لا and it means 'No' in English.

Meaning	Modern Standard Arabic	Disconnected
Place / Position	مَكان makaan	مَ ك ا ن ma kaan
Cottage / Hut	كوخ kooKH	ك و خ koo KH
Bag	كيس kees	ك ي س kee s
Talk / Words	كَلام kalaam	كَ ل ا م ka laa m
Solutions	حُلول Holool	حُ ل و ل Ho loo l
Healthy / Good condition	سَليم saleem	سَ ل ي م sa lee m

Examples of the long vowels ي و ا after the alphabet 'm' م and 'n' ن:

'm' م as in 'mad' and 'miss'. 'n' ن as in 'nap' and 'neck':

Meaning	Modern Standard Arabic	Disconnected
Money	مال maal	م ا ل maa l
Worries	هُموم homoom	هُ م و م ho moo m

Meaning	Modern Standard Arabic	Disconnected
Beautiful	جَميل jameel	جَ م ي ل ja mee l
Fire	نار naar	ن ا ر naa r
Glow / Gleam / Light	نور noor	ن و ر noo r
Lightsome	مُنير moneer	مُ ن ي ر mo nee r

The long vowels ي و ا after the alphabet 'h' ـه , 'w' و , and 'y' ي .

Examples:

Meaning	Modern Standard Arabic	Disconnected
Calm / Guide	هادي hadee	هـ ا د ي haa dee
Important	هام haam	هـ ا م haa m
Inspiration	إلْهام ,ilhaam	إ لْ هـ ا م ,il haa m
Prophet Hood	هود hood	هـ و د hoo d

Meaning	Modern Standard Arabic	Disconnected
Efforts	جُهود johood	جُـهـود jo hoo d
Understanding	فَهيم faheem	فَـهـيـم fa hee m
One	واحِد waaHid	واحِد waa Hi d
Dawud (Male name)	داوود daawood	داوود daa woo d
Tall	طَويل Taweel	طَـويـل Ta wee l
hey! (To grab attention)	يا yaa	يا yaa
Limitations / Re- strictions	قُيود Coyood	قُـيـود Co yoo d
Evaluation	تَقْييم taCyeem	تَـقْـيـيـم taC yee m

'h' هـ as in 'hand' and 'hint'.

'w' و as in 'was' and 'when'; it is a one-way connector letter.

'y' ي as in 'yes' and 'you'.

Lesson Four
Short Vowel Signs

In Arabic, short vowels are not typically written in the standard script. However, to aid learners in pronunciation and reading, diacritical marks called short vowel signs or "harakat" (meaning movements) are used. These marks are placed above or below the consonants to indicate the short vowels.

Short vowels in Arabic are important for proper pronunciation and can provide information about the role of a word in a sentence. However, in everyday writing, reading, and speaking, Arabic speakers often rely on context to understand the intended meaning.

Short vowels in Arabic are often left out in everyday writing, except for formal contexts like reciting poetry or studying religious texts. Beginners find short vowels helpful for pronunciation, but as they become more skilled, they rely more on the surrounding words for clues.

The short vowel signs are two kinds: Basic Vowel Signs and Derived Vowel Signs.

Short Basic Vowel Signs

sukoon	kasra	Dammeh	fatHa

Short Derived Vowel Signs

sheddeh	tanween kasra	tanween Dammeh	tanween fatHa

The Short Basic Vowel Signs: They are the foundation of the writing and reading rules. They go above and below the Arabic alphabet and they function as short vowels:

1. Fatha ( ): The fatha sign is a small slanted line placed above a letter. It represents the short "a" sound.

2. Damma ( ): The damma sign is a small curl-like shape placed above a letter, resembling a mini letter "w". It represents the short "o" sound.

3. Kasra ( ): The kasra sign is a small slanted line placed below a letter. It represents the short "i" sound,

4. The sukoon (⎯) in Arabic is a small circle placed above a letter. It signifies silence or no movement and indicates that the letter should be pronounced without any accompanying vowel sound.

• **The examples in the tables for this lesson are in spoken Modern Standard Arabic, where vowels at the end of words are not marked.**

Examples of words that have 'fatHa' ( ) at the beginning and in the middle:

Meaning	Modern Standard Arabic	Disconnected
Generosity	كَرَم karam	كَ رَ م ka ra m
Honey	عَسَل A'asal	عَ سَ ل A'a sa l
Camel	جَمَل jamal	جَ مَ ل ja ma l

Meaning	Modern Standard Arabic	Disconnected
Work	عَمَل A'amal	ع مَ ل A'a ma l
Happiness	فَرَح faraH	ف رَ ح fa ra H
Hope	أَمَل ,amal	أ مَ ل ,a ma l
Moon	قَمَر Camar	ق مَ ر Ca ma r
Fate	قَدَر Cadar	ق دَ ر Ca da r
Danger	خَطَر KHaTar	خَ طَ ر KHa Ta r

Examples of words that have 'Dammeh' at the beginning (ُ) :

Meaning	Modern Standard Arabic	Disconnected
Reconciliation	صُلْح SolH	صُ لْ ح So l H
Opportunities	فُرَص foraS	فُ رَ ص fo ra S
Science	عُلوم A'oloom	عُ ل و م A'o loo m

Meaning	Modern Standard Arabic	Disconnected
Souvenirs / Antiques	تُحَف toHaf	تُ حَ ف to Ha f
Sesame seed	سُمْسُم somsom	سُ مْ سُ م som som
Pepper	فُلْفُل folfol	فُ لْ فُ ل fol fol
Wound	جُرْح jorH	جُ رْ ح jo r H
Seeds	بُذور bodhoor	بُ ذ و ر bo dhoor
Clouds	غُيوم GHoyoom	غُ ي و م GHo yoom

Examples of words that have 'kasra' at the beginning (   ):

Meaning	Modern Standard Arabic	Disconnected
Grapes	عِنَب A'inab	عِ نَ ب A'i nab
Race	عِرْق A'irC	عِ رْ ق A'i r C
Honesty	صِدْق SidC	صِ دْ ق Si d C

Meaning	Modern Standard Arabic	Disconnected
Salt	مِلْح milH	مِ لْ ح mi l H
Enchantment / Magic	سِحْر siHr	سِ حْ ر si H r
Class / Kind	صِنْف Sinf	صِ نْ ف Si n f
Monkey	قِرْد Cird	قِ رْ د Ci r d
Pieces	قِطَع CiTaA'	قِ طَ ع Ci Ta A'
Cat	هِرَّة hirrah	هِ رْ رَ ة hir rah

The fourth short vowel sign: 'sukoon' ( ):

The sukoon ( ) is the fourth short vowel sign in Arabic. It is represented by a small circle and can be placed above any letter in a word, except the first letter. When a letter has the sukoon, it indicates that there is no vowel sound associated with that letter. If the sukoon appears at the end of a word, it causes a pause at the last letter without adding a vowel sign. This pause, resembling silence or no movement, helps to avoid errors in using incorrect vowel signs.

While pausing at the end of any word helps to prevent such errors, it is important to note that in most cases, marking vowels on the last letter is not essential for understanding conversations in Modern Standard Arabic. The context of the conversation usually provides enough information to comprehend the meaning without requiring vowel markings on every word's last letter.

Examples of words that have 'sukoon' ( ) in the middle like the first

eight examples and words that have 'sukoon' in the middle and at the end like the rest
of the examples of command verbs:

Translation	Modern Standard Arabic	Disconnected
Heart	قَلْب Calb	قَ لْ ب Ca l b
Magic	سِحْر siHr	سِ حْ ر si H r
Dog	كَلْب kalb	كَ لْ ب ka l b
Wound	جُرْح jorH	جُ رْ ح jo r H
Salt	مِلْح milH	مِ لْ ح mi l H
Reconciliation	صُلْح SolH	صُ لْ ح So l H
Cold	بَرْد bard	بَ رْ د ba r d
Molar	ضِرْس Dirs	ضِ رْ س Di r s
Study! **(You, masculine)**	أُدْرُسْ odros	أُ دْ رُ سْ od ros

58

Translation	Modern Standard Arabic	Disconnected
Write! (You, masculine)	أُكْتُبْ oktob	أ كْ تُ بْ ok tob
Look! (You, masculine)	أُنْظُرْ onDHor	أ نْ ظُ رْ on DHor
Sit! (You, masculine)	إِجْلِسْ ijlis	إِجْ لِ سْ ij lis
Work! (You, masculine)	إِعْمَلْ iA'mal	إِ عْ مَ لْ iA' mal
Open! (You, masculine)	إِفْتَحْ iftaH	إِ فْ تَ حْ if taH
Explain! (You, masculine)	إِشْرَحْ ishraH	إِ شْ رَ حْ ish raH
Plant! (You, masculine)	إِزْرَعْ izraA'	إِ زْ رَ عْ Iz raA'
Read! (You, masculine)	إِقْرَأْ iCra,	إِ قْ رَ أْ iC ra,
Understand! (You, masculine)	إِفْهَمْ ifham	إِ فْ هَـ مْ if ham

Here are summary of the 6 important points you need to know about the Arabic alphabets and vowels:

1. Letters and Vowels: All Arabic letters are consonants, which means they have a still sound that require vowels to move it to achieve a complete sound.

2. Vowel Types: Arabic has three short vowels and three long vowels.

3. Short Vowel Sounds: Short vowels have the same sounds as their corresponding long vowels but shorter. For example, "fatHa" sounds like "alif," "Dammeh" sounds like "waw," and "kasrah" sounds like "yaa.

4. Duration of Long Vowels: Pronunciation of long vowels lasts twice as long as short vowels.

5. Function of Long Vowels: Long vowels are part of the 28 Arabic alphabets. They can function as regular consonants and also they can function as long vowels that elongate the pronunciation of the letters that they follow, making those letters sound longer.

6. Short Vowel Markings: Short vowels are marks or symbols placed above or below the consonants.

The alphabets with Long vowels			The alphabets with short vowels			
"yaa" (ee)	"waw" (oo)	"alif" (aa)	"kasrah" (i)	"Dammeh" (o)	"fatHa" (a)	Names of the letters
إِي	أو	آ	إِ	أُ	أَ	alif
ee	oo	aa	i	o	a	
بِي	بو	با	بِ	بُ	بَ	baa
bee	boo	baa	bi	bo	ba	
تِي	تو	تا	تِ	تُ	تَ	taa
tee	too	taa	ti	to	ta	
ثِي	ثو	ثا	ثِ	ثُ	ثَ	thaa
thee	thoo	thaa	thi	tho	tha	
جِي	جو	جا	جِ	جُ	جَ	jeem
jee	joo	jaa	ji	jo	ja	

The alphabets with Long vowels			The alphabets with short vowels			
"yaa" (ee)	"waw" (oo)	"alif" (aa)	"kasrah" (i)	"Dammeh" (o)	"fatHa" (a)	Names of the letters
حي Hee	حو Hoo	حا Haa	حِ Hi	حُ Ho	حَ Ha	Haa
خي KHee	خو KHoo	خا KHaa	خِ KHi	خُ KHo	خَ KHa	KHaa
دي dee	دو doo	دا daa	دِ di	دُ do	دَ da	daal
ذي dhee	ذو dhoo	ذا dhaa	ذِ dhi	ذُ dho	ذَ dha	dhaal
ري ree	رو roo	را raa	رِ ri	رُ ro	رَ ra	raa
زي zee	زو zoo	زا zaa	زِ zi	زُ zo	زَ za	zay
سي see	سو soo	سا saa	سِ si	سُ so	سَ sa	seen
شي shee	شو shoo	شا shaa	شِ shi	شُ sho	شَ sha	sheen
صي See	صو Soo	صا Saa	صِ Si	صُ So	صَ Sa	SaaD

The alphabets with Long vowels			The alphabets with short vowels			
"yaa" (ee)	"waw" (oo)	"alif" (aa)	"kasrah" (i)	"Dammeh" (o)	"fatHa" (a)	Names of the letters
ضي Dee	ضو Doo	ضا Daa	ضِ Di	ضُ Do	ضَ Da	DaaD
طي Tee	طو Too	طا Taa	طِ Ti	طُ To	طَ Ta	Taa
ظي DHee	ظو DHoo	ظا DHaa	ظِ DHi	ظُ DHo	ظَ DHa	DHaa
عي A'ee	عو A'oo	عا A'aa	عِ A'i	عُ A'o	عَ A'a	A'ayn
غي GHee	غو GHoo	غا Ghaa	غِ GHi	غُ GHo	غَ GHa	GHayn
في fee	فو foo	فا faa	فِ fi	فُ fo	فَ fa	faa
قي Cee	قو Coo	قا Caa	قِ Ci	قُ Co	قَ Ca	Qaaf
كي kee	كو koo	كا kaa	كِ ki	كُ ko	كَ ka	kaaf
لي lee	لو loo	لا laa	لِ li	لُ lo	لَ la	laam

The alphabets with Long vowels			The alphabets with short vowels			
"yaa" (ee)	"waw" (oo)	"alif" (aa)	"kasrah" (i)	"Dammeh" (o)	"fatHa" (a)	Names of the letters
مـي mee	مـو moo	مـا maa	مِ mi	مُ mo	مَ ma	meem
نـي nee	نـو noo	نـا naa	نِ ni	نُ no	نَ na	noon
هـي hee	هـو hoo	هـا haa	هِـ hi	هُـ ho	هَـ ha	haa
وي wee	وو woo	وا waa	وِ wi	وُ wo	وَ wa	waw
يـي yee	يـو yoo	يـا yaa	يِ yi	يُ yo	يَ ya	yaa

- Note: The use of capitalized letters in the English pronunciation represents the 9 deep letters that are pronounced deep in the throat.

- Keep in mind that while practicing reading Arabic, it is important to remember that Arabic is a cursive script and is read and written from right to left.

- Please be aware that the pronunciation system used in this book is explained on page six for your reference.

Lesson Five
The Derived Vowel Signs

The derived vowel signs in Arabic include tanween and shaddah. Tanween signs are formed from the three short vowels: fatḥah, ḍammah, and kasrah. However, tanween signs are mostly used in classical Arabic writing, reading, or formal conversation.

Tanween signs appear only at the end of a noun or adjective and represent the doubling of the final vowel sound. They indicate that the noun or adjective is indefinite.

Here are the tanween signs and their corresponding short vowels:

1. If the duplicated vowel symbol is a 'fatHa'   , it gives the sound of "an" at the end.

2. If the duplicated vowel symbol is a 'Dammeh'   , it gives the sound "on" at the end.

3. If the duplicated vowel symbol is a 'kasra'   , it gives the sound of "in" at the end.

Note: When a word has a tanween sign at the end, it does not have the definite article "the" (al-الْ) at the beginning. As a result, it is considered an indefinite or unspecified word. In this sense, the tanween sign is equivalent to the indefinite articles "a" or "an" in English. It indicates that the word refers to a non-specific item or entity. The tanween sign helps in distinguishing between definite and indefinite nouns in Arabic grammar and contributes to the overall meaning and clarity of the sentence.

If the word is feminine and has a closed 't' (ة) at the end, marked with a tanween sign, it will give the sound of an unwritten letter as follows:

4. If the duplicated vowel symbol is a 'fatHa'   , it gives the sound of "tan" at the end.

5. If the duplicated vowel symbol is a 'Dammeh'   , it gives the sound "ton" at the end.

6. If the duplicated vowel symbol is a 'kasra'   , it gives the sound of "tin" at the end.

In spoken Modern Standard Arabic, the doubling of vowels at the end of a word is not commonly pronounced. This is different from Classical Arabic, where the doubling of vowels is more prevalent.

Regarding the letter "ta marbuta" (ة), also known as the closed "t," it is usually not pronounced as a distinct sound at the end of words in spoken Modern Standard Arabic. Instead, it is often pronounced as an "h" sound or omitted altogether, however, the short vowel that precedes the closed "t," such as "fatHa" (   ), is typically pronounced in spoken Modern Standard Arabic. It is a short "a" sound and is consistently pronounced.

- **The next three tables in this lesson follows the classic Arabic style, where the words are voweled at the end.**

Examples of doubling the 'fatHa'   vowel at the end. In this case, the ending sound is 'an', which is pronounced but not written:

- Note: The letter 'a' ا in the table below is not pronounced; it serves as a placeholder to carry the double 'fatHa'.

Meaning	Classical Arabic	Disconnected
House	دارًا daaran	ا د ا ر ا daa ran
Home	بَيْتًا baytan	بَ يْ ت ا bay tan
Dog	كَلْبًا kalban	كَ لْ ب ا kal ban

Meaning	Classical Arabic	Disconnected
River	نَهْرا nahran	ا ر هْ نَ nah ran
Sea	بَحْرا baHran	ا ر حْ بَ baH ran
Book	كِتابا kitaaban	ا ب ا ت كِ ki taa ban
Pen	قَلَما Calaman	ا م لَ قَ Ca la man
In summer	صَيْفا Sayfan	ا ف يْ صَ Say fan
In winter	شِتاءً shita,an	ءً ا ت شِ shi ta an
Girl	بِنْتا bintan	ا ت نْ بِ bin tan
Boy	وَلَدا waladan	ا د لَ وَ wa la dan
Baby boy	طِفْلا Tiflan	ا ل فْ طِ Tif lan
Baby girl	طِفْلَة Tiflatan	ة لَ فْ طِ Tif la tan
School	مَدْرَسَة madrasatan	ة سَ رَ دْ مَ mad ra sa tan

66

Examples of the doubling of 'Dammeh' ُّ vowel at the end. In this case, the ending sound is 'on', which is pronounced but not written.

Meaning	Classical Arabic	Disconnected
House	دارٌ daaron	د ا رٌ daa ron
Home / House	بَيْتٌ bayton	بَ يْ تٌ bay ton
Dog	كَلْبٌ kalbon	كَ لْ بٌ kal bon
River	نَهْرٌ nahron	نَ هـ رٌ nah ron
Sea	بَحْرٌ baHron	بَ حْ رٌ baH ron
Book	كِتابٌ kitaabon	كِ ت ا بٌ ki taa bon
In summer	صَيْفٌ Sayfon	صَ يْ فٌ Say fon
In winter	شِتاءٌ shita,on	شِ ت ا ءٌ shi ta on
Girl	بِنْتٌ binton	بِ نْ تٌ bin ton
School	مَدْرَسَةٌ madrasaton	مَ دْ رَ سَ ةٌ mad ra sa ton

Examples of doubling 'kasra' $\underset{}{\text{/}}$ vowel at the end. In this case, the ending sound is 'in', which is pronounced but not written.

Meaning	Classic Arabic	Disconnected
House	دارٍ daarin	د ا رٍ daa rin
Home	بَيْتٍ baytin	بَ يْ تٍ bay tin
Dog	كَلْبٍ kalbin	كَ لْ بٍ kal bin
River	نَهْرٍ nahrin	نَ هْ رٍ nah rin
Sea	بَحْرٍ baHrin	بَ حْ رٍ baH rin
Book	كِتابٍ kitaabin	كِ ت ا بٍ ki taa bin
In summer	صَيْفٍ Sayfin	صَ يْ فٍ Say fin
In winter	شِتاءٍ shita,in	شِ ت ا ءٍ shi ta in
Girl	بِنْتٍ bintin	بِ نْ تٍ bin tin
School	مَدْرَسَةٍ madrasatin	مَ دْ رَ سَ ةٍ mad ra sa tin

The shaddah sign ّ in Arabic is used to indicate the doubling of a letter. The

'shaddeh' can accrue on top of any letter in a word, except the first letter. It is placed on top of the letter that is doubled instead of writing the letter twice. The shaddah can also be accompanied by other vowel marks like fatḥah, ḍammah, or kasrah.

Examples of words that have a 'shaddeh' sign marked with a 'fatHa' ّ vowel in the

middle:

Meaning	Modern Standard Arabic	Disconnected
Mohammad (Male name)	مُحَمَّد moHammad	مُ حَ مْ مَ د mo Ham med
Honored	مُكَرَّم mokarram	مُ كَ رْ رَ م mo kar ram
Polite	مُهَذَّب mohadhdhab	مُ هَ ذْ ذَ ب mo hadh dhab
Comet	مُذَنَّب modhannab	مُ ذَ نْ نَ ب mo dhan nab
Manufactured	مُصَنَّع moSannaA'	مُ صَ نْ نَ ع mo San naA'
Amphitheater	مُدَرَّج modarraj	مُ دَ رْ رَ ج mo dar raj
Square	مُرَبَّع morabbaA'	مُ رَ بْ بَ ع mo rab baA'
Stripe	مُقَلَّم moCallam	مُ قَ لْ لَ م mo Cal lam

Meaning	Modern Standard Arabic	Disconnected
Colorfull	مُلَوَّن molawwan	مُ لَ وْ وَ ن mo law wan
Business complex	مُجَمَّع mojammaA'	مُ جَ مْ مَ ع mo jam maA'
Employee	مُوَظَّف mowaDHDHaf	مُ وَ ظْ ظَ ف mo waDH DHaf
Rate	مُعَدَّل moA'addal	مُ عَ دْ دَ ل mo A'ad dal

Example of words that have a 'shaddeh' sign ّ marked with a 'Dammeh' ُّ vowel in the middle:

Meaning	Modern Standard Arabic	Disconnected
Tolerance	تَحَمُّل taHammol	تَ حَ مْ مُ ل ta Ham mol
Avoiding	تَجَنُّب tajannob	تَ جَ نْ نُ ب ta Jan nob
Changing	تَغَيُّر taGHayyor	تَ غَ يْ يُ ر ta GHay yor
Arrogance	تَكَبُّر takabbor	تَ كَ بْ بُ ر ta kab bor
Confusion	تَحَيُّر taHayyor	تَ حَ يْ يُ ر ta Hay yor

Meaning	Modern Standard Arabic	Disconnected
Progress	تَقَدُّم taCaddom	تَ قَ دْ دُ م ta Cad dom
Development	تَطَوُّر taTawwor	تَ طَ وْ وُ ر ta Taw wor
Volunteering	تَطَوُّع taTawwoA'	تَ طَ وْ وُ ع ta Taw woA'
Contemplating	تَأَمُّل ta,ammol	تَ أَ مْ مُ ل ta ,am mol
Imagining	تَخَيُّل taKHayyol	تَ خَ يْ يُ ل ta KHay yol

Examples of words that have a 'shaddeh' sign ّ marked with a 'kasra' ِّ vowel in the middle. Note that, the 'kasra' vowel comes below the 'shaddeh' sign :

Meaning	Modern Standard Arabic	Disconnected
Teacher	مُدَرِّس modarris	مُ دَ رْ رِ س mo dar ris
Sanitizer	مُعَقِّم moA'aCCim	مُ عَ قْ قِ م mo A'aC Cim
Cleanser	مُنَظِّف monaDHDHif	مُ نَ ظْ ظِ ف mo naDH DHif

Meaning	Modern Standard Arabic	Disconnected
Arrogant	مُتَكَبِّر motakabbir	مُ تَ كَ بْ بِ ر mo ta kab bir
Beggar	مُتَسَوِّل motasawwil	مُ تَ سَ وْ وِ ل mo ta saw wil
Understanding	مُتَفَهِّم motafahhim	مُ تَ فَ هْ هِ م mo ta fah him
Educated	مُتَعَلِّم motaA'allim	مُ تَ عَ لْ لِ م mo ta A'al lim
One-sided	مُتَحَيِّز motaHayyiz	مُ تَ حَ يْ يِ ز mo ta Hay yiz
Hasty / Rush	مُتَسَرِّع motasarriA'	مُ تَ سَ رْ رِ ع mo ta sar riA'
Volunteer	مُتَطَوِّع motaTawwiA'	مُ تَ طَ وْ وِ ع mo ta Taw wiA'
Photographer	مُصَوِّر moSawwir	مُ صَ وْ وِ ر mo Saw wir
Composer	مُلَحِّن molaHHin	مُ لَ حْ حِ ن mo laH Hin
Organizer	مُنَظِّم monaTHTHim	مُ نَ ظْ ظِ م mo naTH THim

Lesson Six
Specific and Non-Specific

Part One

The definite article "the" in the English language is equivalent to the definite sign "al" (ال) in Arabic. The "al" (ال) always comes attached at the beginning of a word and changes indefinite non-specific nouns or adjectives to definite specific words.

In Classical Arabic, when a noun or adjective starts with the definite sign "al" (ال), the default vowel sign at the end is the "ḍammah" sign. This means that the last letter of the word will typically have a "ḍammah" as its default vowel.

In Classical Arabic, for independent nouns and adjectives that do not have the "al" (ال) at the beginning, the default vowel at the end is the doubling of the "ḍammah" sign. This means that the last letter of the word will have a doubled "ḍammah" as its default vowel. However, in spoken Modern Standard Arabic, you have the flexibility to pause at the last letter of all words and not indicate a specific vowel ending.

Examples of non-specific and specific nouns in the Classical Arabic:

	Specific Nouns Classical Arabic		Non-Specific Nouns Classical Arabic
The book	الكِتابُ al-kitaabo	A book	كِتابٌ kitaabon
The school	المَدْرَسَةُ al-madrasato	A school	مَدْرَسَةٌ madrasaton

Specific Nouns Classical Arabic		Non-Specific Nouns Classical Arabic	
The teacher	الأُسْتاذُ al-,ostaadho	A teacher	أُسْتاذٌ ,ostaadhon
The student	الطّالِبُ al-Taalibo	A student	طالِبٌ Taalibon

The absence of the definite sign "the" or "al" (ال) in Arabic can be considered equivalent to the indefinite articles "a" and "an" in English. When a noun or adjective in Arabic does not have the definite article attached to it, it indicates an indefinite or non-specific meaning, similar to how "a" or "an" is used in English. Examples:

Taalibon
A student

madrasaton
A school

kitaabon
A book

Proper nouns in Arabic are indeed specific without the presence of the definite sign "al" (ال). Proper nouns are names of specific people, places, or things and are inherently specific in Arabic without the need for the definite article "al" (ال). Examples:

Mariam
(Female name)

Mohammad
(Male name)

Fatima
(Female name)

eeTalia
Italy

breeTania
Britain

Abstract or absolute nouns in Arabic often take the definite sign "al" (ال) to indicate their specificity. Abstract nouns refer to concepts, qualities, or states that are not tangible or concrete. When using abstract nouns in Arabic, it is common to include the definite article "al" (ال) at the beginning of the noun to make it specific. Examples:

الطِّبُّ	الهَنْدَسَةُ	العَرَبِيَّةُ	الأَدَبُ	الحِسابُ
al-Tibbo	**al-handasato**	**al-A'arabiyyato**	**al-,adabo**	**al-Hisaabo**
Medicine	**Engineering**	**Arabic Language**	**Literature**	**Mathematics**

Some names in Arabic include the definite sign "al" (الـ) as an integral part of the word.

These names can be the names of individuals or family names, and the "al" (الـ) is not used as a separate definite article but rather as an essential component of the name itself. Examples:

القُبْرُصِيُّ	الهاشِمِيُّ	الْحُسَيْنُ	الحَسَنُ	القاسِمُ
al-CobroSiyyo	**al-hashimiyyo**	**al-Hosayno**	**al-Hasano**	**al-Casimo**
Family name	**Family name**	**Male name**	**Male name**	**Male name**

Some Arab countries, cities, and other geographic locations have the definite sign "al" (الـ) as an integral part of the word. These names are exceptions and do not follow the usual rules of definite or indefinite marking in Arabic. In the case of such geographic names, the presence of "al" (الـ) is primarily a matter of memorization. It is not used as a separate definite article but rather as an inherent part of the name itself. Examples:

الكُويْتُ	المَغْرِبُ	الإماراتُ	الجَزائِرُ	الأُرْدُنُ
al-kowayto	**al-maGHribo**	**al-imarato**	**al-jazaa,iro**	**al-,ordonno**
Kuwait	**Morocco**	**United Arab Emirates**	**Algeria**	**Jordan**

75

THE DEFINITE SIGN 'THE' ال

Part Two

The "tanween" represents the doubling of the final vowel sign in an unspecific noun or adjective in Classical Arabic. The "tanween" has a similar function to the English indefinite articles "a" and "an." It adds an unspecific or indefinite meaning to the word.

However, when a word starts with the definite article "al" (ال), the noun or adjective

loses the "tanween" and becomes a specific word. In this case, "al" (ال) is equivalent

to the definite article "the" in English. It signifies that the noun or adjective is specific and refers to a particular entity.

- Regarding the default ending vowel signs for isolated words in Classical Arabic, the "ḍammah" and the doubling of "ḍammah" are indeed commonly used. These vowel signs provide a default pronunciation for the final letter of the word.

- In a sentence, however, the choice of ending vowel marks depends on the role of the word within the sentence. For example, if the word functions as the **object of the**

sentence or an adverb, it may take a "fatḥah"　as the ending vowel.

Examples of words losing the doubling of 'fatHa'　and changing from unspecific to

specific words:

Specific Words Classic Arabic		Non-Specific Words Classic Arabic	
The girl	البِنْتَ al-binta	A girl	بِنْتًا bintan
The boy	الوَلَدَ al-walada	A boy	وَلَدًا waladan
The egg	البَيْضَةَ al-bayData	An egg	بَيْضَةً bayDatan

76

Specific Words Classic Arabic		Non-Specific Words Classic Arabic	
The chicken	الدَجاجَةَ al-dajajata	A chicken	دَجاجَةً dajaajatan
The tree	الشِجَرَةَ al-shajarata	A tree	شَجَرَةً shajaratan
The student	الطالِبَ al-Taaliba	A student	طالِباً Taaliban
The spring	الرَبيعَ al-rabeeA'a	A spring	رَبيعاً rabee-A'an
The summer	الصيْفَ al-Sayfa	A summer	صيْفاً Sayfan
The fall	الخَريفَ al-KHareefa	A fall	خَريفاً KHareefan
The winter	الشِتاءَ al-shitaa,a	A winter	شِتاءاً shitaa,an
The sun	الشَمْسَ al-shamsa	A sun	شَمْساً shamsan
The moon	القَمَرَ al-Camara	A moon	قَمَراً Camaran
The night	اللّيْلَ al-layla	A night	لَيْلاً laylan
The daytime	النَهارَ al-nahaara	A daytime	نَهاراً nahaaran

Good sentence examples of cases in Classic Arabic that require a 'fatHa' ́ vowel at

the end of the noun is when the noun serves as **the object of the sentence,** like the

last word in the three sentences below:

Meaning	Pronunciation	Classic Arabic
The boy heard the voice.	samiA'a al-walado al-SawTa	سَمِعَ اَلوَلَدُ اَلصَوْتَ.
The student read the book.	Cara,a al-Talibo al-kitaba	قَرَأَ اَلطالِبُ اَلكِتابَ.
Ahmad drank the water.	shariba aHmado al-maa,a	شَرِبَ أَحْمَدُ اَلماءَ.

Here are examples of words losing the doubling of 'dammeh' ́ and changing from un-

specific to specific words. In Classic Arabic, the default vowel ending for isolated

nouns and adjectives is 'dammeh' ́ :

Specific Words Classic Arabic		Non-Specific Words Classic Arabic	
The girl	البِنْتُ al-binto	A girl	بِنْتُ binton
The boy	الوَلَدُ al-walado	A boy	وَلَدُ waladon
The egg	البَيْضَةُ al-bayDato	An egg	بَيْضَةُ bayDaton

Specific Words Classic Arabic		Non-Specific Words Classic Arabic	
The chicken	الدَّجَاجَةُ al-dajaajato	A chicken	دَجَاجَةٌ dajaajaton
The tree	الشَّجَرَةُ al-shajarato	A tree	شَجَرَةٌ shajaraton
The student	الطَّالِبُ al-Taalibo	A student	طَالِبٌ Taalibon
The spring	الرَبِيعُ al-rabeeA'o	A spring	رَبِيعٌ rabeeA'on
The summer	الصيْفُ al-Sayfo	A summer	صيْفٌ Sayfon
The fall	الخَرِيفُ al-KHareefo	A fall	خَرِيفٌ KHareefon
The winter	الشِتَاءُ al-shitaa,o	A winter	شِتَاءٌ shitaa,on
The night	اللَيْلُ al-laylo	A night	لَيْلٌ laylon
The daytime	النَّهَارُ al-nahaaro	A daytime	نَهَارٌ nahaaron

Good sentence examples of cases in Classic Arabic that require a 'dammeh'

vowel at the end of the noun is when the noun serves as **the subject of the sentence,** like the second word in the three sentences below:

Meaning	Pronunciation	Classic Arabic
The boy heard the voice.	samiA'a al-walado al-SawTa	سَمِعَ ٱلوَلَدُ ٱلصَوْتَ.
The student read the book.	Cara,a al-Talibo al-kitaba	قَرَأَ ٱلطّالِبُ ٱلكِتابَ.
Ahmad drank the water.	shariba aHmado al-maa,a	شَرِبَ أَحْمَدُ ٱلْماءَ.

Here are examples of words when they lose the doubling of 'kasra'　and change from

unspecific to specific words. In Classic Arabic, 'kasra'　is not the default vowel for the

end of isolated nouns or adjectives, but 'dammeh'　and the doubling of 'dammeh'

signs are:

Specific Words Classic Arabic		Non-Specific Words Classic Arabic	
The girl	البِنْتِ al-binti	A girl	بِنْتٍ bintin
The boy	الوَلَدِ al-waladi	A boy	وَلَدٍ waladin
The egg	البَيْضَة al-bayDati	An egg	بَيْضَة bayDatin

Specific Words Classic Arabic		Non-Specific Words Classic Arabic	
The chicken	الدَّجَاجَةِ al-dajaajati	A chicken	دَجاجَةٍ dajajatin
The tree	الشَّجَرَةِ al-shajarati	A tree	شَجَرَةٍ shajaratin
The student	الطَّالِبِ al-Taalibi	A student	طَالِبٍ Taalibin
The spring	الرَبِيعِ al-rabeeA'i	A spring	رَبِيعٍ rabeeA'in
The Summer	الصيْفِ al-Sayfi	A summer	صيْفٍ Sayfin
The fall	الخَرِيفِ al-KHareefi	A fall	خَرِيفٍ KHareefin
The winter	الشِتاءِ al-shitaa,i	A winter	شِتاءٍ shitaa,in
The night	اللَيْلِ al-layli	A night	لَيْلٍ laylin
The daytime	النَّهارِ al-nahaari	A daytime	نَهارٍ nahaarin

A good sentence example of cases that require a 'kasra' vowel at the end of the

noun in Classic Arabic is when **the noun is preceded by a preposition**, like the last word in the three sentences as shown in the following examples:

Meaning	Pronunciation	Classic Arabic
The bird is on the tree.	al-A'oSfooro A'ala al-shajarati	العُصْفورُ عَلى ٱلشَجَرَةِ.
I go to work.	adhhabo ilaa al-A'amali	أَذْهَبُ إلى ٱلعَمَلِ.
The girl is in the house.	al-binto fee al-bayti	البِنْتُ في ٱلبَيْتِ.

The main role of the ending markers in Arabic is to indicate the grammatical function of a word in a sentence, such as whether it functions as a subject, object, or part of a prepositional phrase. However, in both writing and speech, these markers are often unnecessary because we can deduce the function of words based on the overall meaning of the sentence or the word order.

In spoken Modern Standard Arabic, vowel endings or the doubling of vowels are not commonly used. However, in classical Arabic writing, such as religious texts, poetry, formal speeches, and certain educational materials, they play an important role. They contribute to the beauty and rhythm of poetry and help convey precise meaning in formal written Arabic. Although they are not commonly used in everyday speech, they are still taught and studied for understanding classical texts and formal language proficiency.

In spoken Modern Standard Arabic, it is not necessary to include any of the short vowels (fatHa, Dammah, kasrah) at the end of words. This is because Arabic speakers are accustomed to the reduced vocalization in spoken Modern Standard Arabic. However, in classical Arabic, the use of vowel markings is important for precise pronunciation and understanding, particularly in formal written texts like religious books and poetry.

When a noun or adjective starts with the definite article 'al' ٱل in Arabic, it is already considered specific and definite. In such cases, there is no need to add any of the three short vowels at the end of the word. The presence of 'al' ٱل itself indicates definiteness.

If the noun or the adjective does not have the definite sign 'al' ٱل 'the', it means that they are indefinite words or unspecific words, and they do not accept any of the three ending vowels (fatHa َ , Dammeh ُ or kasra ِ) unless these vowels are doubled.

In other words, the presence of a doubled vowel at the end of a word in Arabic serves as a marker of indefiniteness or non-specificity, as it replaces the definite sign 'al' ال.

The doubling of the 'fatHa' vowel at the end of some common adverbs and a few words and expressions is an exception in spoken modern standard Arabic.

مَساءً	صَباحاً	أهْلاً وَسَهْلاً	عَفْواً	شُكْراً
masaa,an	**SabaaHan**	**ahlan wa-sahlan**	**A'afwan**	**shokran**
In the evening.	**In the morning.**	**Welcome.**	**You are welcome.**	**Thank you.**

Note:

- If the last letter of a noun or adjective in Arabic is 'alif' ا and it is marked with a doubled 'fatHa' the 'alif' اً functions as a seat for the 'tanween' only and not as a long vowel. In this case, the 'alif' does not have its own sound because Arabic words usually do not end with a long vowel 'alif' ا. Instead, they typically end with a 'broken' 'alif' or what is known as 'alif maksura' ى. Therefore, the 'alif' ا serves as a seat for the 'tanween' اً even if the 'tanween' marker is not explicitly written.
- If a noun or adjective in Arabic ends with a closed 't' ة and is marked with 'tanween', the closed 't' ة is pronounced as a regular 't' ت. To summarize:

- Closed 't' ة + doubled 'fatHa' = 'tan' sound at the end.

- Closed 't' ة + doubled 'Dammah' = 'ton' sound at the end.

- Closed 't' ة + doubled 'kasrah' = 'tin' sound at the end. Examples:

Meaning	Pronunciation	Classic Arabic
A school	madrasatan	مَدْرَسَةً
A school	madrasaton	مَدْرَسَةٌ
A school	madrasatin	مَدْرَسَةٍ
A library	maktabatan	مَكْتَبَةً
A library	maktabaton	مَكْتَبَةٌ
A library	maktabatin	مَكْتَبَةٍ
A nice	laTeefatan	لَطيفةً
A nice	laTeefaton	لَطيفةٌ
A nice	laTeefatin	لَطيفةٍ
A dear	A'azeezatan	عَزيزةً
A dear	A'azeezaton	عَزيزةٌ
A dear	A'azeezatin	عَزيزةٍ

In classical Arabic, doubling the 'fatHa' ً is commonly used in two cases. Firstly, it is used in **adverbs** to add emphasis, like in the first four example. Secondly, it is used with verbs to mark the direct **object**, like in the rest of the examples below. Therefore, the doubling of the 'fatHa' helps in indicating the role of the word in the sentence.

Meaning	Pronunciation	Classic Arabic
He traveled at night.	saafara laylan	سافَرَ لَيْلاً.
He came back in the morning.	rajaA'a SabaaHan	رجَعَ صَباحاً.
He studies daily.	yadroso yawmiyan	يَدْرُسُ يوميًا.
He sings beautifully.	yoGHannee jameelan	يُغنّي جَميلاً.
I saw Mohammad.	ra,ayto moHammadan	رأَيْتُ مُحَمّداً.
I saw a movie.	shaahadto filman	شاهَدْتُ فِلْماً.
I read a book.	Cara,to kitaaban	قرأْتُ كِتابا.
I wrote a letter.	katabto risaalatan	كَتَبْتُ رِسالةً.

- Keep in mind that while practicing reading Arabic, it is important to remember that Arabic is a cursive script and is read and written from right to left.

- The examples provided in the tables for this lesson are all in spoken Modern Standard Arabic, which means that the words do not have vowels marked at the end of each word.

- Please be aware that the pronunciation system used in this book is explained on page six for your reference.

Lesson Seven
The Pronouns

In the Arabic language, nouns are either masculine or feminine. There is no equivalent to the English pronoun 'it' in Arabic. Instead, pronouns, adjectives, and verbs in Arabic typically agree with the gender of their corresponding noun. There are three types of pronouns in Arabic:

Subject Pronouns	**Possessive Pronouns**	**Object Pronouns**
They are the subject of the sentence, indicating who or what performs the action.	They indicate a relationship to the nouns they are attached to, showing ownership or possession	They are used as the object of a sentence, receiving the action of the verb.

Singular subject pronouns and singular possessive pronouns that correspond are:

Singular Possessive Pronouns for Masculine and Feminine			Singular Subject Pronouns for Masculine and Feminine		
My	ee	ي	I	anaa	أنَا
Your (masculine)	ka	كَ	**You (masculine)**	anta	أنتَ
Your (feminine)	ki	كِ	**You (feminine)**	anti	أنتِ
His	ho	هُ	he	howa	هُوَ
Her	haa	ها	**She**	hiya	هِي

86

Dual subject pronouns and dual possessive pronouns that corresponds are:

Dual Possessive Pronouns for Masculine and Feminine			Dual Subject Pronouns for Masculine and Feminine		
Your	komaa	كُما	You	antomaa	أَنْتُما
Their	homaa	هُما	They	homaa	هُما

- In spoken modern standard Arabic, the plural masculine form is used instead of the dual and plural feminine forms, as well as the dual masculine form. The dual and plural feminine forms are mainly used in formal or classical Arabic, such as in poetry.

Plural subject pronouns and Plural possessive pronouns that correspond are:

Plural Possessive Pronouns for Masculine and Feminine			Plural Subject Pronouns for Masculine and Feminine		
Our	naa	نا	We	naHno	نَحْنُ
Your (M. plural)	kom	كُم	You (masculine)	antom	أَنْتُم
Your (F. plural)	konna	كُنَّ	You (feminine)	antonna	أَنْتُنَّ
Their (masculine)	hom	هُم	They (masculine)	hom	هُم
Their (feminine)	honna	هُنَّ	They (feminine)	honna	هُنَّ

In the Arabic language, the possessive pronoun follows the noun and it is attached to it. In the example below, the noun 'book' كِتَاب is connected with all possessive pronouns.

Singular possessive pronouns for (masculine and feminine):

Meaning	Possessive pronouns attached to the noun	Singular possessive pronouns	Singular Subject Pronouns
My book	كِتَابِي kitaabee	ي ee	أَنَا anaa
Your book (masculine)	كِتَابكَ kitaaboka	كَ ka	أَنتَ anta
Your book (feminine)	كِتَابكِ kitaaboki	كِ ki	أَنتِ anti
His book	كِتَابهُ kitaaboho	هُ ho	هُوَ howa
Her book	كِتَابهَا kitaabohaa	هَا haa	هِيَ hiya

Dual possessive pronouns for (masculine and feminine):

Meaning	Possessive pronouns attached to the noun	Dual possessive pronouns	Dual Subject pronouns
Your book (for two people)	كِتابُكُما kitaabokomaa	كُما komaa	أَنْتُما antomaa
Their book (for two people)	كِتابُهُما kitaabohomaa	هُما homaa	هُما homaa

Plural possessive pronouns for (masculine and feminine):

Meaning	Possessive pronouns attached to the noun	Plural possessive pronouns	Plural Subject pronouns
Our book	كِتابُنا kitaabonaa	نا naa	نَحنُ naHno
Your book (M. plural)	كِتابُكُم kitaabokom	كُم kom	أَنْتُم antom
Your book (F. plural)	كِتابُكُنَّ kitaabokonna	كُنَّ konna	أَنْتُنَّ antonna
Their book (masculine)	كِتابُهُم kitaabohom	هُم hom	هُم hom
Their book (feminine)	كِتابُهُنَّ kitaabohonna	هُنَّ honna	هُنَّ honna

• Note that when the possessive pronoun "their" هُم and the possessive pronoun "his" هُ are attached to a noun ending with a "kasrah" vowel or a long vowel ي, their pronunciation shifts to هِم for the plural possessive pronoun and هِ for the singular masculine possessive pronoun "his." Examples:

نادِيهِم	نادِيهِ	كِتابِهِم	كِتابِهِ
naadeehim	naadeehi	kitaabihim	kitaabihi
Their club	His club	Their book	His book
قَرارِهِم	قَرارِهِ	بَيْتِهِم	بَيْتِهِ
Cararihim	Cararihi	baytihim	baytihi
Their decision	His decision	Their home	His home

Keep in mind that the noun must ends with a 'kasrah' vowel if it was preceded by a preposition in the classic Arabic. Sentence examples:

أَلْعَبُ في نادِيهِ.	قَرَأتُ مِن كِتابِهِ.
alA'abo fee naadeehi	Cara,to min kitaabihi
I play at his club.	I read from his book.
أَلْعَبُ في نادِيهِم.	قَرَأتُ مِن كِتابِهِم.
alA'abo fee naadeehim	Cara,to min kitaabihim
I play at their club.	I read from their book.

In the Arabic language, if the noun gender is feminine and ends with a closed 't' ة, a regular 't' ت will replace the closed 't' ة before adding the possessive pronoun. Example the noun 'School' مَدْرَسَة:

Singular possessive pronouns for (masculine and feminine):

Meaning	Possessive pronouns attached to the noun	Singular possessive pronouns	Singular Subject Pronouns
My school	مَدْرَسَتي madrasatee	ي ee	أنا anaa
Your school (masculine)	مَدْرَسَتُكَ madrasatoka	كَ ka	أنتَ anta
Your school (feminine)	مَدْرَسَتُكِ madrasatoki	كِ ki	أنتِ anti
His school	مَدْرَسَتُهُ madrasatoho	هُ ho	هُوَ howa
Her school	مَدْرَسَتُها madrasatohaa	ها haa	هِيَ hiya

Dual possessive pronouns for (masculine and feminine):

Meaning	Possessive pronouns attached to the noun	Dual possessive pronouns (M&F)	Dual Subject pronouns(M&F)
Your school (masculine and feminine)	مَدْرَسَتُكُما madrasatokomaa	كُما komaa	أَنْتُما antomaa
Their school (masculine and feminine)	مَدْرَسَتُهُما madrasatohomaa	هُما homaa	هُما homaa

Plural possessive pronouns for (masculine and feminine):

Meaning	Possessive pronouns attached to the noun	Plural possessive pronouns	Plural Subject pronouns
Our school	مَدْرَسَتُنا madrasatonaa	نا naa	نَحْنُ naHno
Your school (M. plural)	مَدْرَسَتُكُم madrasatokom	كُم kom	أَنْتُم antom
Your school (F. plural)	مَدْرَسَتُكُنّ madrasatokonna	كُنّ konna	أَنْتُنّ antonna
Their school (M. plural)	مَدْرَسَتُهُم madrasatohom	هُم hom	هُم hom
Their school (F. plural)	مَدْرَسَتُهُنّ madrasatohonna	هُنّ honna	هُنّ honna

Lesson Eight
Words and Gender

The Arabic noun is either masculine or feminine, regardless of whether it refers to a person, an animal, or an object. In Arabic, there is no equivalent of the pronoun 'it' for non-human nouns. Instead, we use 'he' or 'she' to refer to them. Masculine nouns do not have any gender signs, while feminine nouns have specific gender indicators.

Examples of masculine words:

طارِق	أَسَد	يوسِف	قَمَر	مُحَمَّد
Tariq	**asad**	**Yousef**	**Camar**	**Mohammad**
Male name	Lion	Male name	Moon	Male name

عَدْنان	نَجْم	وَقْت	حِصان	بُسْتان
A'adnan	**najm**	**waCt**	**HiSaan**	**bostaan**
Male name	Star	Time	Horse	Garden

مَسْرَح	بَيْت	مَكْتَب	كَلْب	عُصْفور
masraH	**bayt**	**maktab**	**kalb**	**A'osfoor**
Theater	House	Office	Dog	Little bird

مُحيط	بَحْر	طَريق	شِتاء	صَيْف
moHeeT	**baHr**	**TareeC**	**shitaa,**	**Sayf**
Ocean	Sea	Road	Winter	Summer

Feminine nouns and adjectives in Arabic are marked with specific signs indicating their feminine gender. There are three main signs used for this purpose.

a.   The first sign is the closed 'ta' (ة), which is derived from the regular 'ta' (ت). It is

      written as a small loop and placed at the end of a feminine word. The closed 'ta' is the most common feminine sign in Arabic. Here are some examples of feminine nouns and adjectives marked with the first sign:

مائِدَة	فاطِمَة	مَدْرَسَة	مَركَبَة	رائِدَة
maa,ida	**Fatima**	**madrasa**	**markaba**	**Ra,ida**
Dining-table	(female name)	School	Vehicle	Female leader

بَقَرَة	حَقيبَة	قِطَّة	أُسْتاذَة	سارَة
baCara	**HaCeeba**	**CiTTa**	**ostaadha**	**Sara**
Cow	Bag	Cat	Teacher	(female name)

b.   The second feminine sign in Arabic is the letter 'alif' followed by a 'hamza' sitting on the line (ءا). This combination represents a glottal stop. When used as a feminine sign, it is typically placed at the end of a word. Examples of feminine nouns and adjectives marked with the second sign:

خَضْراء	رَجاء	كَهْرُباء	هَيْفاء	صَفاء
KHaDraa,	**rajaa,**	**kahrobaa,**	**hayfaa,**	**Safaa,**
Green	(female name)	Electricity	(female name)	Purity

صَحْراء	هَناء	سَوْداء	بَيْضاء	سَماء
SaHraa,	**hanaa,**	**sawdaa,**	**bayDaa,**	**samaa,**
Desert	(female name)	Black	White	Sky

c. The third sign used to indicate feminine gender in Arabic is the broken 'alif,' which resembles a 'ya' without the two dots (ى). It is primarily used as a feminine marker in certain dialects and specific contexts. Here are some examples of feminine nouns and adjectives marked with the third sign:

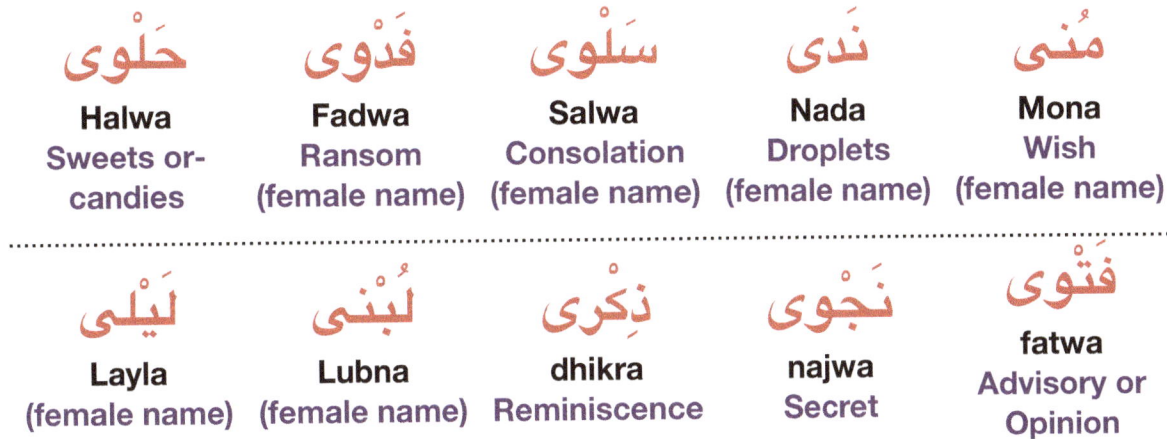

حَلْوى	فَدْوى	سَلْوى	نَدى	مُنى
Halwa	**Fadwa**	**Salwa**	**Nada**	**Mona**
Sweets or-candies	Ransom (female name)	Consolation (female name)	Droplets (female name)	Wish (female name)

لَيْلى	لُبْنى	ذِكْرى	نَجْوى	فَتْوى
Layla	**Lubna**	**dhikra**	**najwa**	**fatwa**
(female name)	(female name)	Reminiscence	Secret	Advisory or Opinion

In Arabic, some feminine nouns do not have a specific feminine sign but are recognized as feminine based on tradition and usage. These nouns are understood to be feminine without the need for a specific marker, relying on cultural understanding in the Arabic language. Examples:

سَحَر	فاتِن	مَيْس	لينا	أَرْض
SaHar	**Fatin**	**Mais**	**Leena**	**arD**
Dawn (female name)	Glamorous (female name)	To walk proud (female name)	Mellow (female name)	Earth

نورجان	دار	نِسْرين	شَمْس	مَرْيَم
Nurjan	**daar**	**Nisreen**	**shams**	**Mariam**
Radiant light (female name)	House	White rose (female name)	Sun	Mariam (female name)

In Arabic, the gender of adjectives, verbs, and pronouns usually agrees with the gender of their corresponding nouns. However, there is one exception: when a noun refers to something non-human and is in the plural form, the associated adjective, verb, and pronoun are treated as singular feminine. This grammatical rule applies to nouns that represent objects, animals, or abstract concepts. When these nouns are plural, the grammar treats them as if they were singular feminine.

In Arabic, you can change the gender of many masculine nouns and adjectives to feminine by adding a feminine sign at the end of the word. Examples:

Meaning	Feminine Words	Masculine Words
Star	نَجْمَة naJma	نَجم naJm
Scientist	عالِمَة A'alima	عالِم A'alim
Housekeeper	خادِمَة KHaadima	خادِم KHaadim
Guest	ضَيْفَة Dayfa	ضَيْف Dayf
Generous / Honorable	كَريمَة kareema	كَريم kareem
Great	عَظيمَة A'aDHeema	عَظيم A'aDHeem
Teacher	أُستاذَة ostaadha	أُستاذ ostaadh
White	بَيْضاء bayDaa,	أبْيَض abyaD
Black	سَوْداء sawdaa,	أسْوَد aswad
Green	خَضْراء KHaDraa,	أخْضَر aKHDar
Red	حَمْراء Hamraa,	أحْمَر aHmar

Lesson Nine
Singular and Dual

Arabic has a dual form that is used specifically when referring to two people, two animals, or two things. The dual form is created by adding ان or ين to the end of singular nouns or singular adjectives. The use of ين is more common in spoken Modern Standard Arabic as well as in different Arabic dialects.

In this lesson, we will focus on the signs and rules of the dual form. To simplify the learning process, we will remove the default vowel ending for all singular words, which is 'Dammeh'   , and the doubling of the 'Dammeh'   . By doing so, we can pay more attention to the specific signs and rules associated with the dual form.

- **In spoken Modern Standard Arabic, the dual forms (both masculine and feminine) are not commonly used. Instead, the plural masculine form is often used as a substitute for the dual form. The dual forms are mainly found in formal or classical contexts, such as poetry or formal religious texts.**

The examples in the tables for this lesson are all in spoken Modern Standard Arabic, which means that the words are presented without vowels at the end.

Meaning	Dual Masculine Words	Meaning	Singular Masculine Words
Two boys	وَلَدان waladaan	Boy	وَلَد walad
Two seasons / Two semesters	فَصْلان faSlaan	Season / Semester	فَصْل faSl
Two offers	عَرْضان A'arDaan	Offer	عَرْض A'arD
Two days	يَوْمان yawmaan	Day	يَوْم yawm

Meaning	Dual Masculine Words	Meaning	Singular Masculine Words
Two lessons	دَرْسان darsaan	Lesson	دَرْس dars
Two houses	بَيْتان baytaan	House	بَيْت bayt
Two offices	مَكْتَبان maktabaan	Office	مَكْتَب maktab
Two books	كِتابان kitaabaan	Book	كِتاب kitaab
Two roads	طَريقان TareeCaan	Road	طَريق TareeC
Two male workers	عامِلان A'amilan	Male worker	عامِل A'amil
Two male assistants	مُساعِدان mosaaA'idaan	Male assistant	مُساعِد mosaaA'id
Two male house-keepers	خادِمان KHaadimaan	Male housekeeper	خادِم KHaadim
Two male guests	ضَيْفان Dayfaan	Male guest	ضَيْف Dayf
Two honorable men / Two generous men	كَريمان kareemaan	Honorable man / Generous man	كَريم kareem

Meaning	Dual Masculine Words	Meaning	Singular Masculine Words
Two handsome men	وَسيمان waseemaan	Handsome man	وَسيم waseem
Two nice men	لَطيفان laTeefaan	Nice man	لَطيف laTeef
Two male teachers	أُسْتاذان ostaadhaan	Male teacher	أُسْتاذ ostaadh

If the singular noun or adjective is feminine and ends with the feminine sign ة 't', the closed 't' ة should be replaced with a regular 't' ت before adding ان or ين to the end of the singular word.

Examples of dual feminine nouns and adjectives in spoken Modern Standard Arabic:

Meaning	Dual Feminine Words	Meaning	Singular Feminine Words
Two girls	بِنْتان bintaan	Girl	بِنْت bint
Two nice females	لَطيفَتان laTeefataan	Nice (female)	لَطيفة laTeefa
Two schools	مَدْرَسَتان madrasataan	School	مَدْرَسة madrasa
Two girl classmates	زَميلَتان zameelataan	Girl classmate	زَميلة zameela

Meaning	Dual Feminine Words	Meaning	Singular Feminine Words
Two girl friends	صَديقَتان SadeeCataan	Girl friend	صَديقَة SadeeCa
Two gardens	حَديقَتان HadeeCataan	Garden	حَديقَة HadeeCa
Two libraries	مَكْتَبَتان maktabataan	Library	مَكْتَبَة maktaba
Two letters	رِسالَتان risaalataan	Letter	رِسالَة risaala
Two ways	طَريقَتان TareeCataan	Way	طَريقَة TareeCa
Two ideas	فِكْرَتان fikrataan	Idea	فِكْرَة fikra
Two female as-sistants	مُساعِدَتان mosaA'idataan	Female as-sistant	مُساعِدة mosaA'ida
Two female housekeepers	خَادِمَتان KHaadimataan	Female house-keeper	خَادِمة KHaadima
Two female guests	ضَيْفَتان Dayfataan	Female guest	ضَيْفة Dayfa

• Note, refer to page six for a refresher on the pronunciation system used in this book.

Lesson Ten
Singular and Plural

The plural in Arabic expresses three or more persons, animals, or things. There are three-forms of plurals in Arabic:

1. **Regular masculine plural:** This form is created by adding ون to the end of the singular masculine word when it functions as the subject in the sentence. However, if the singular word functions as the object in a passive sentence, ين is added to form the plural in more formal or classical Arabic. In spoken Modern Standard Arabic, the use of ين is more common than ون in both situations, regardless of whether the singular word is an active or passive participial.

- **Note: The majority of masculine words in Arabic have irregular plurals, with the exception of words related to professions, nationalities, and many adjectives.**

Examples in the spoken Modern Standard Arabic:

Meaning	Plural Masculine Words		Singular Masculine Words
Close	قَرِيبِين Careebeen	قَرِيبُون Careeboon	قَرِيب Careeb
Far	بَعِيدِين baA'eedeen	بَعِيدُون baA'eedoon	بَعِيد baA'eed
Happy / Delighted	مَسْرُورِين masrooreen	مَسْرُورُون masrooroon	مَسْرُور masroor
Carpenters	نَجَّارِين najjareen	نَجَّارُون najjaroon	نَجَّار najjaar

Meaning	Plural Masculine Words		Singular Masculine Words
Cooks / Chefs	طَبّاخين TabbaaKHeen	طَبّاخون TabbaKHoon	طَبّاخ TabbaaKH
Syrians	سوريِّين sooriyyeen	سوريّون sooriyyoon	سوريّ sooriy
Egyptians	مِصريِّين miSriyyeen	مِصريّون miSriyyoon	مِصْريّ miSriy
Workers	عامِلين A'amileen	عامِلون A'amiloon	عامِل A'amil
Winners	فائِزين faa,izeen	فائِزون faa,izoon	فائِز faa,iz
Successful	ناجِحين naajiHeen	ناجِحون naajiHoon	ناجِح naajiH
Supporters	ناصِرين naaSireen	ناصِرون naaSiroon	ناصِر naaSir
Conquerors	فاتِحين faatiHeen	فاتِحون faatiHoon	فاتِح faatiH

2. **Regular feminine plural:** To form the plural of a singular feminine noun or adjective, you add ات to the end of the word. However, if the singular word ends with the closed 't' ة, you need to remove the closed 't' ة before adding ات. It's important to note that the majority of feminine nouns and adjectives have regular plurals.

Examples in the spoken Modern Standard Arabic:

Meaning	Plural Feminine Words	Meaning	Singular Feminine Words
Girlfriends	صاحِبات SaaHibaat	Girlfriend	صاحِبَة SaaHiba
Female class-mates	زَميلات zameelaat	Female class-mate	زَميلَة zameela
Nice (plural feminine)	لَطيفات laTeefaat	Nice (singular feminine)	لَطيفَة laTeefa
Beautiful (plural feminine)	جَميلات jameelat	Beautiful (singular feminine)	جَميلَة jameela
Wives	زَوْجات zawjaat	Wife	زَوْجَة zawja
Mothers	والِدات walidaat	Mother	والِدَة walida
Pages	صَفْحات SafHaat	Page	صَفْحَة SafHa
Assistants (plural feminine)	مُساعِدات mosaaA'idaat	Assistant (singular feminine)	مُساعِدَة mosaaA'ida
Trips	رِحْلات riHlaat	Trip	رِحْلَة riHla

Meaning	Plural Feminine Words	Meaning	Singular Feminine Words
Dining tables	مائِدات maa,idaat	Dining table	مائِدَة maa,ida
Married (plural feminine)	مُتَزَوِّجات motazawwijaat	Married (singular feminine)	مُتَزَوِّجَة motazawwija
Libraries	مَكْتَبات maktabaat	Library	مَكْتَبَة maktaba
Sages	حَكيمات Hakeemaat	Wise	حَكيمَة Hakeema
Scholars or knowledgeable (plural feminine)	عالِمات A'alimaat	Scholar or-knowledgeable	عالِمَة A'alima

3. **Irregular plural:** Similar to the English language, Arabic also has irregular plurals that require memorization. These plurals involve changing the structure of the singular word in a specific way.

Examples in the spoken Modern Standard Arabic:

Meaning	Plural Words	Meaning	Singular Words
Classes	صُفوف Sofoof	Class	صَفّ Saff
Lessons	دُروس doroos	Lesson	دَرْس dars
Eyes	عُيون A'oyoon	Eye	عَيْن A'ayn

Meaning	Plural Words	Meaning	Singular Words
Pens or pencils	أقْلام aClaam	Pen or pencil	قَلَم Calam
Men	رِجال rijaal	Man	رَجُل rajol
Spouses	أزْواج azwaaj	Spouse	زَوْج zawj
Sciences	عُلوم A'oloom	Science	عِلْم A'ilm
Gardens	حَدائِق Hadaa,iC	Garden	حَديقة HadeeCa
Schools	مَدارِس madaaris	School	مَدْرَسَة madrasa
Girls	بَنات banaat	Girl	بِنْت bint
Moons	أقْمار aCmaar	Moon	قَمَر Camar
Suns	شُموس shomoos	Sun	شَمْس shams
Lights	أضْواء aDwaa,	Light	ضَوْء Daw,
Candles	شُموع shomooA'	Candle	شَمْعَة shamA'a

Meaning	Plural Words	Meaning	Singular Words
Seas	بُحور boHoor	Sea	بَحْر baHr
Hearts	قُلوب Coloob	Heart	قَلْب Calb
Seasons	فُصول foSool	Season	فَصْل faSl
News	أخْبار aKHbaar	News	خَبَر KHabar
Days	أيّام ayyaam	Day	يَوم yawm
Weeks	أَسابيع asaabeeA'	Week	أُسْبوع osbooA'
Years	سَنَوات sanawaat	Year	سَنَة sanah
Numbers	أرْقام arCam	Number	رَقِم raCam
Laws	قَوانين Cawaaneen	Law	قانون Canoon
Restrictions	قُيود Coyood	Restriction	قَيْد Cayd
Sins	ذُنوب dhonoob	Sin	ذَنْب dhanb

Lesson Eleven
The Arabic Sentence

There are two basic types of sentences in Arabic: nominal sentences and verbal sentences.

1. **The nominal sentence** is a sentence type in Arabic that starts with a noun, pronoun, or preposition. It conveys a complete thought or idea and can function as an independent sentence.

Here are some examples of nominal sentences:

A. Noun and Adjective in a sentence or phrases: This type of sentence consists of a noun followed by an adjective that describes the noun. For example: "The sky is blue."

B. (I have), (There is), and (There are) sentences or phrases: These sentences indicate possession or existence. For example: "(I have) a cat." "(There is) a park nearby." "(There are) many books on the shelf."

C. Prepositional phrases: These sentences start with a preposition followed by a noun phrase. For example: "In the garden, (there are) flowers."

D. Comparative and Superlative phrases: These sentences compare two or more nouns using comparative or superlative forms of adjectives. For example: "She is (taller) than him." "This is (the biggest) building in the city."

E. Adverb phrases: These sentences consist of a subject followed by an adverb that modifies the verb or the adjective. For example: "He sings (beautifully)." "She speaks (fluently)."

F. Two or more nouns related in a sentence (The Construct Phrase): This type of sentence involves two or more nouns that are connected to express a relationship or possession. For example: "The (book) of my (friend)."These are just a few examples of the different types of nominal sentences.

2. **The verbal sentence** in Arabic is a sentence that starts with a verb. It helps us talk about actions, states, or conditions. The subject tells us who or what is doing the action, and the verb shows the action itself. By using different verb forms and tenses, we can say different things.

Here are the different tenses in Arabic:

A. Present Tense: This tense is used to describe actions happening in the present time.
المضارع

B. Past Tense: This tense is used to describe actions that have already occurred in the past. الماضي

C. Future Tense: This tense is used to describe actions that will happen in the future.
المستقبل

D. Imperative or Command Verb: This form is used to give commands or instructions to someone. الأمر

In Arabic, sentences can be expressed using either the nominal sentence or the verbal sentence form. The structure and order of these sentences differ. Let's begin with the nominal sentence and later on, we will explain the verbal sentence in more detail in this book.

In Arabic, the nominal sentence consists of a subject and a predicate. The subject is the main noun or pronoun in the sentence, while the predicate provides information about the subject. The predicate can take the form of an adjective, a verb, a noun, or even a prepositional phrase.

It is important to note that Arabic does not have a direct equivalent of the verb "to be" (am, is, are) like in English. Instead, the presence or absence of the verb is understood from the context of the sentence. The point between the subject and the predicate is where the meaning of "to be" is implied and comprehended.

Examples of nominal sentences in spoken Modern Standard Arabic where the **adjective** functions as the predicate. In these sentences, the adjective comes after the subject and describes or provides information about it. The verb "to be" is not directly mentioned in Arabic, but understood based on the context of the sentence:

"He" is the subject and "rich" is the predicate.	هُوَ غَنِيّ. **howa GHaniyy** **He is rich.**
"The place" is the subject and "beautiful" is the predicate.	المَكان جَميل. **al-makaan jameel** **The place is beautiful.**

"The car" is the subject and "new" is the predicate.	السَّيَّارَة جَديدَة. al-sayyara jadeeda The car is new.
"The sky" is the subject and "clear" is the predicate.	السَّماء صافِيَة. al-samaa' Saafiya The sky is clear.

In spoken Modern Standard Arabic, we can find sentences where the predicate is a **prepositional phrase**. These sentences use a prepositional phrase to give more information about the subject. The prepositional phrase comes after the subject and helps us understand the relationship or location of the subject. In Arabic, the verb "to be" is not explicitly used, but it is understood from the context of the sentence. Here are some simple examples:

"the book" is the subject and "on the table" is the predicate.	الكِتاب عَلى ٱلطّاولَة. al-kitaab A'ala al-Tawila The book is on the table.
"the student" is the subject and "in the school" is the predicate.	الطّالِب في ٱلمَدرَسَة. al-Taalib fee al-madrasa The student is in the school.
"Abdo Allah" is the subject and "in school" is the predicate.	عَبْدُ ٱلله في ٱلمَدْرَسَة. A'abdo allah fee al-madrasa Abdo Allah is in school.
"The bird" is the subject and "on the tree" is the predicate.	العُصفور عَلى ٱلشَّجَرَة. al-A'osfoor A'ala al-shajara The bird is on the tree.

In spoken Modern Standard Arabic, we can find sentences where the predicate is a **verb**. These sentences use a verb as the main action or description of the subject. The verb comes after the subject and provides information about what the subject is doing or being. Here are some simple examples:

109

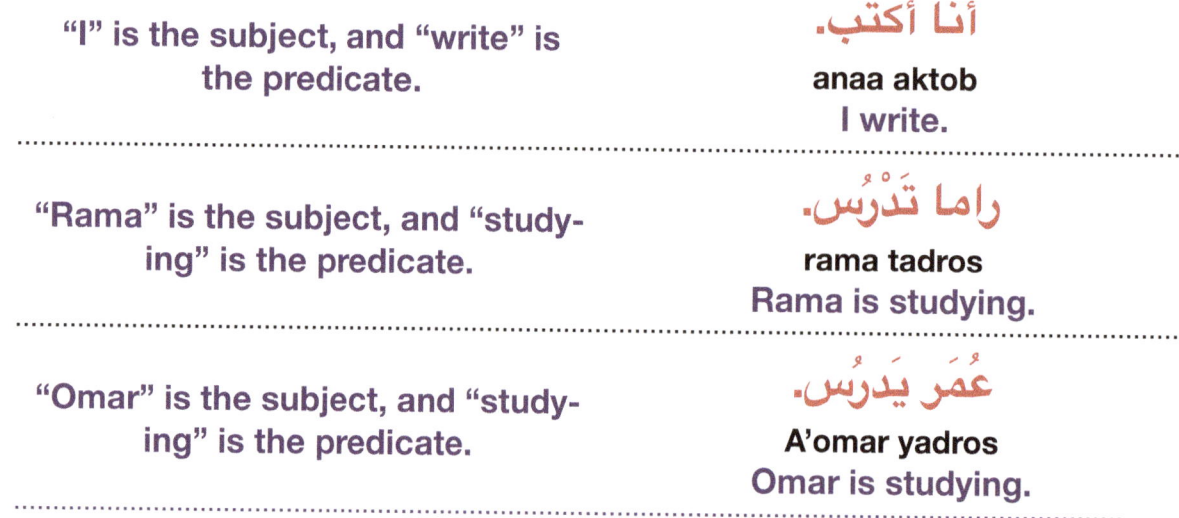

"I" is the subject, and "write" is the predicate.	أَنَا أَكْتب. **anaa aktob** I write.
"Rama" is the subject, and "study-ing" is the predicate.	رَامَا تَدْرُس. **rama tadros** Rama is studying.
"Omar" is the subject, and "study-ing" is the predicate.	عُمَر يَدرُس. **A'omar yadros** Omar is studying.

In spoken Modern Standard Arabic, we can also find sentences where the predicate is **a noun**. In these cases, the noun serves as the main description or identifier of the subject. Here are some simple examples:

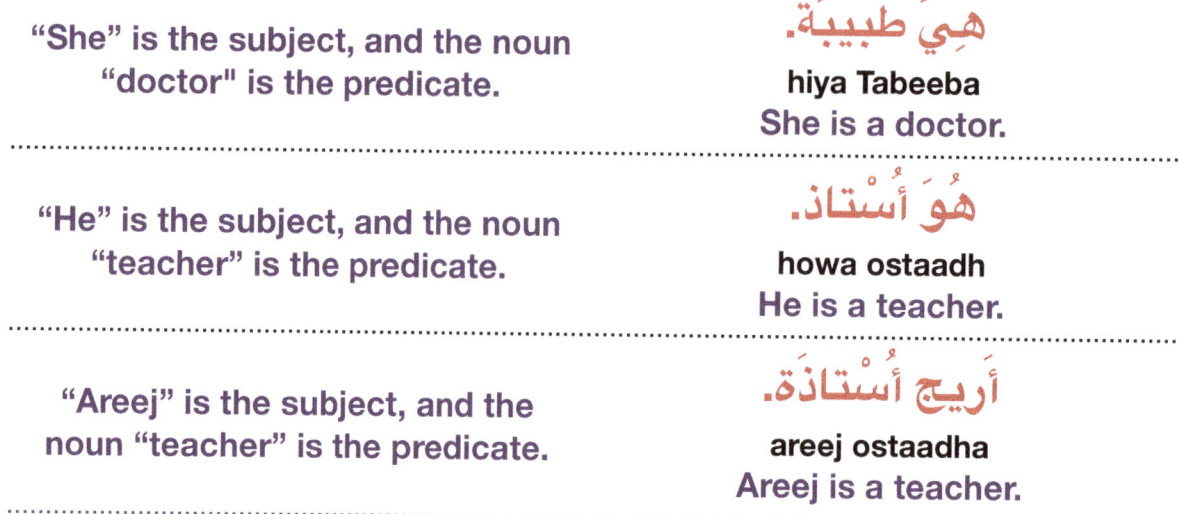

"She" is the subject, and the noun "doctor" is the predicate.	هِيَ طَبِيبَة. **hiya Tabeeba** She is a doctor.
"He" is the subject, and the noun "teacher" is the predicate.	هُوَ أُسْتاذ. **howa ostaadh** He is a teacher.
"Areej" is the subject, and the noun "teacher" is the predicate.	أَرِيج أُسْتاذَة. **areej ostaadha** Areej is a teacher.

In nominal sentences, it is important for the predicate to agree with the subject in terms of gender and number. This means that the predicate should match the gender and number of the subject it is referring to. We will explore the concept of agreement between the subject and the predicate in more detail when we discuss the different types of nominal and verbal sentences. However, it's worth noting that there are exceptions to this agreement when dealing with non-person plural nouns.

In Arabic, nominal sentences and phrases can be negated using the words "laysa" لَيْسَ for masculine nouns and pronouns, and "laysat" لَيْسَتْ for feminine nouns and pronouns. These words are used to indicate the negation of the nominal sentences. Examples:

Negating Modern Standard Arabic	Medern Standard Arabic
البَيْت لَيْسَ كَبير. al-bayt laysa kabeer The house is not big.	البَيْت كَبير. al-bayt kabeer The house is big.
الحَديقَة لَيْسَتْ كَبيرَة. al-HadeeCa laysat kabeera The garden is not big.	الحَديقَة كَبيرَة. al-HadeeCa kabeera The garden is big.
المَكان لَيْسَ بَعيد. al-makaan laysa baA'eed The place is not far.	المَكان بَعيد. al-makaan baA'eed The place is far.
الصّورَة لَيْسَتْ جَميلَة. al-Soora laysat jameela The picture is not beautiful.	الصّورَة جَميلَة. al-Soora jameela The picture is beautiful.
أحْمَد لَيْسَ في ٱلمَدْرَسَة. aHmad laysa fee al-madrasa Ahmad is not at school.	أحْمَد في ٱلمَدْرَسَة. aHmad fee al-madrasa Ahmad is at school.
فاطِمَة لَيْسَتْ في ٱلمَدْرَسَة. faaTima laysat fee al-madrasa Fatima is not at school.	فاطِمَة في ٱلمَدْرَسَة. faaTima fee al-madrasa Fatima is at school.
هُوَ لَيْسَ أسْتاذ. howa laysa ostaadh He is not a teacher.	هُوَ أسْتاذ. howa ostaadh He is a teacher.
هِيَ لَيْسَتْ أسْتاذة. hiya laysat ostaadha She is not a teacher.	هِيَ أسْتاذة. hiya ostaadha She is a teacher.

هُوَ لَيْسَ صادِقٍ.	هُوَ صادِقٍ.
howa laysa saadiC	howa saadiC
He is not honest.	He is honest.
هِيَ لَيْسَتْ صادِقَة.	هِيَ صادِقَة.
hiya laysat saadiCa	hiya saadiCa
She is not honest.	She is honest.
البِنْت لَيْسَتْ طَويلَة.	البِنْت طَويلَة.
al-bint laysat Taweela	al-bint Taweela
The girl is not tall.	The girl is tall.
البِنْت لَيْسَت قَصيرَة.	البِنْت قَصيرَة.
al-bint laysat CaSeera	al-bint CaSeera
The girl is not short.	The girl is short.
لَيْسَ عِنْدي كَلْب.	عِنْدي كَلْب.
laysa A'indee kalb	A'indee kalb
I do not have a dog.	I have a dog.
لَيْسَ عِنْدي قِطَّة.	عِنْدي قِطَّة.
laysa A'indee CiTTa	A'indee CiTTa
I do not have a cat.	I have a cat.
الطَّقْس لَيْسَ حار.	الطَّقْس حار.
al-TaCs laysa Haar	al-TaCs Haar
The weather is not hot.	The weather is hot.
الطَّقْس لَيْسَ بارِد.	الطَّقْس بارِد.
al-TaCs laysa baarid	al-TaCs baarid
The weather is not cold.	The weather is cold.

In dialectal Arabic (Arabic slang), there are various ways to negate nominal sentences using different negation particles. Some commonly used particles include "مِش" (mesh), "مَافي" (mafi), and "مَا" (ma) which can be used for both genders.

Here are some examples:

Negating in the dialect Arabic	Dialect and standard Arabic
البيت مِش كبير. al-bait mish kbeer The house is not big.	البَيْت كَبير. al-bait kabeer The house is big.
أحْمَد مِش في ٱلْمَدْرَسَة. aHmad mish fee al-madrasa Ahmad is not at school.	أحْمَد في ٱلْمَدْرَسَة. aHmad fee al-madrasa Ahmad is at school.
هُوَ مِش أُسْتاذ. howa mish ostaadh He is not a teacher.	هُوَ أُسْتاذ. howa ostaadh He is a teacher.
الطَقْس مِش حار. al-TaCs mish Haar The weather is not hot.	الطَقْس حار. al-TaCs Haar The weather is hot.
الأَكِل مِش زاكي. al-akil mish zaakee The food is not good.	الأَكِل زاكي. al-akil zaakee The food is good.
الْمَطْعَم مِش نَظيف. al-maTA'am mish naDHeef The restaurant is not clean.	الْمَطْعَم نَظيف. al-maTA'am naDHeef The restaurant is clean.
ما عِنْدي كَلْب. maa A'indee kalb I do not have a dog.	عِنْدي كَلْب. A'indee kalb I have a dog.

Negating in the dialect Arabic	Dialect and standard Arabic
ما عِنْدي إِقْتِراح.	عِنْدي إِقْتِراح.
maa A'indee iCtiraaH	A'indee iCtiraaH
I do not have a suggestion.	I have a suggestion.
ما عِنْدي حِلْم.	عِنْدي حِلْم.
maa A'indee Hilm	A'indee Hilm
I do not have a dream.	I have a dream.
مافي مِشْكِلة.	في مِشْكِلة.
mafee mishkileh	fee mishkileh
There is no problem.	There is a problem.
ما في هُناك وَقْت كافي.	هُناك وَقْت كافي.
maa fee honaak waCt kaafee	honaak waCt kaafee
There isn't plenty of time.	There is plenty of time.
مافي هُناك تَطَوُّر.	هُناك تَطَوُّر.
maa fee honaak taTawwor	honaak taTawwor
There is no progress.	There is progress.
ما عِنْدي فِكْرَه.	عِنْدي فِكْرَه.
maa A'indee fikra	A'indee fikra
I do not have any idea.	I have an idea.
ما عِنْدي طُموح.	عِنْدي طُموح.
maa A'indee TomooH	A'indee TomooH
I do not have any ambitions.	I have ambition.

- Keep in mind that while practicing reading Arabic, it is important to remember that Arabic is a cursive script and is read and written from right to left.

- The examples provided in the tables for this lesson are all in spoken Modern Standard Arabic, which means that the words do not have vowels marked at the end of each word.

- Please be aware that the pronunciation system used in this book is explained on page six for your reference.

Lesson Twelve
'I Have'

In Arabic, the expression 'I have' is translated as a prepositional phrase within the nominal sentence structure. Unlike in English, where 'I have' is a verb, in Arabic it is constructed using a preposition followed by a noun phrase. It is important to note that in these constructions, the prepositional phrase typically appears before the subject in the sentence. The noun in the prepositional phrase is usually indefinite, meaning it does not have the definite article 'the' (ال) at the beginning. There are four different ways to express 'I have' in Arabic, by using different prepositions and attaching the appropriate possessive pronouns to them.

مَعي	لَدَيَّ	لي	عِنْدي
maA'ee	ladayya	lee	A'indee
I have	I have	I have	I have

In formal classic Arabic, لَدَيَّ And the preposition لي is usually used in the relations between people or in people possessions. However, in spoken Modern Standard Arabic and in the Informal Arabic, it is more common to use عِنْدي with people relations and in possessing things.

It's important to note that the choice of expression may vary depending on the region and dialect.

Examples in the spoken Modern Standard Arabic:

Meaning	Pronunciation	I have
I have a house.	A'indee bayt	عِنْدي بَيْت.
I have a house.	lee bayt	لي بَيْت.
I have a house.	ladayya bayt	لَدَيَّ بَيْت.
I have a brother.	A'indee akh	عِنْدي أخ.

115

Meaning	Pronunciation	I have
I have a brother.	lee akh	لي أخ.
I have a brother.	ladayya akh	لَدَيَّ أخ.
I have a job.	A'indee A'amal	عِنْدي عَمَل.
I have a job.	lee A'amal	لي عَمَل.
I have a job.	ladayya A'amal	لَدَيَّ عَمَل.
I have a vacation time.	A'indee ijaaza	عِنْدي إجازَة.
I have a vacation time.	lee ijaaza	لي إجازَة
I have a vacation time.	ladayya ijaaza	لَدَيَّ إجازَة.
I have a right.	A'indee HaC	عِنْدي حَقّ.
I have a right.	lee HaC	لي حَقّ.
I have a right.	ladayya HaC	لَدَيَّ حَقّ.
I have a note.	A'indee molaaHaDHa	عِنْدي مُلاحَظَة.
I have a note.	lee molaaHaDHa	لي مُلاحَظَة.
I have a note.	ladayya molaHaDHa	لَدَيَّ مُلاحَظَة.

The expression 'I have' can be negated using 'لَيْسَ**'** in formal classical Arabic, which follows the same pattern as negating any nominal sentence. However, in spoken modern standard Arabic and informal Arabic, it is more common to use 'ما' for negation.

In the last four examples in the table below, the expression 'مَعِي' is used to indicate physical possession of something at the time of speaking, in spoken modern standard Arabic and informal Arabic. For instance, it can denote having something with you at the moment, like saying 'I have with me now,' or it can refer to being accompanied by someone at the time of speaking, such as saying 'I have my friend with me now.'

Negating with ما	Negating with لَيْسَ	Nominal Phrases In Standard Arabic
ما عِنْدي بَيْت.	لَيْسَ عِنْدي بَيْت.	عِنْدي بَيْت.
maa A'indee bayt	laysa A'indee bayt	A'indee bayt
I don't have a house.	I don't have a house.	I have a house.
ما لي بَيْت.	لَيْسَ لي بَيْت.	لي بَيْت.
maa lee bayt	laysa lee bayt	lee bayt
I don't have a house.	I don't have a house.	I have a house.
ما لَدَيَّ بَيْت.	لَيْسَ لَدَيَّ بَيْت.	لَدَيَّ بَيْت.
maa ladayya bayt	laysa ladayya bayt	ladayya bayt
I don't have a house.	I don't have a house.	I have a house.
ما عِنْدي عَمَل.	لَيْسَ عِنْدي عَمَل.	عِنْدي عَمَل.
maa A'indee A'amal	laysa A'indee A'amal	A'indee A'amal
I don't have a job.	I don't have a job.	I have a job.
ما لي عَمَل.	لَيْسَ لي عَمَل.	لي عَمَل.
maa lee A'amal	laysa lee A'amal	lee A'amal
I don't have a job.	I don't have a job.	I have a job.
ما لَدَيَّ عَمَل.	لَيْسَ لَدَيَّ عَمَل.	لَدَيَّ عَمَل.
maa ladayya A'amal	laysa ladayya A'amal	ladayya A'amal
I don't have a job.	I don't have a job.	I have a job.

Negating with ما	Negating with لَيْسَ	Nominal Phrases In Standard Arabic
ما عِنْدي أخ. maa A'indee akh I don't have a brother.	لَيْسَ عِنْدي أخ. laysa A'indee akh I don't have a brother.	عِنْدي أخ. A'indee akh I have a brother.
ما لي أخ. maa lee aKH I don't have a brother.	لَيْسَ لي أخ. laysa lee aKH I don't have a brother.	لي أخ. lee aKH I have a brother.
ما لَدَيَّ أخ. maa ladayya aKH I don't have a brother.	لَيْسَ لَدَيَّ أخ. laysa ladayya aKH I don't have a brother.	لَدَيَّ أخ. ladayya aKH I have a brother.
ما مَعي قَلَم. maa maA'ee Calam I don't have a pen.	لَيْسَ مَعي قَلَم. laysa maA'ee Calam I don't have a pen.	مَعي قَلَم. maA'ee Calam I have a pen.
ما مَعي مال. maa maA'ee maal I don't have money.	لَيْسَ مَعي مال. laysa maA'ee maal I don't have money.	مَعي مال. maA'ee maal I have money.
ما مَعي حَقّ. maa maA'ee Haqq I don't have a right.	لَيْسَ مَعي حَقّ. laysa maA'ee Haqq I don't have a right.	مَعي حَقّ. maA'ee Haqq I have a right.
صَديقي مِش مَعي. SadeeCee mish maA'ee My friend is not with me. (Common slang for "not")	صَديقي لَيْسَ مَعي. SadeeCee laysa maA'ee My friend is not with me.	مَعي صَديقي. maA'ee SadeeCee My friend is with me.

'I have' sentences in Arabic can be transformed into the past tense by using the verbs "كانَ" (kana) or "كانَتْ" (kanat) at the beginning of the sentence. These verbs carry meanings such as "was," "were," "had," and "used to." It's worth noting that the feminine form "كانَتْ" (kanat) is typically used with singular feminine nouns or non-human plurals. However, in spoken Arabic, it is common to use both forms, "كانَ" (kana) and "كانَتْ" (kanat), with non-human plurals as well. This allows for flexibility and variation in everyday conversation. Examples:

In The Past Tense Modern Standard Arabic	Nominal Phrases Modern Standard Arabic
كانَ عِنْدي بَيْت كَبير.	عِنْدي بَيْت كَبير.
kaana A'indee bayt kabeer	A'indee bayt kabeer
I used to have a big house.	I have a big house.
كانَ لي بَيْت كَبير.	لي بَيْت كَبير.
kaana lee bayt kabeer	lee bayt kabeer
I used to have a big house.	I have a big house.
كانَ لَدَيَّ بَيْت كَبير.	لَدَيَّ بَيْت كَبير.
kaana ladayya bayt kabeer	ladayya bayt kabeer
I used to have a big house.	I have a big house.
كانَ عِنْدي صَديق طَبيب.	عِنْدي صَديق طَبيب.
kaana A'indee SadeeC Tabeeb	A'indee SadeeC Tabeeb
I had a friend who is a doctor.	I have a friend who is a doctor.
كانَ لي صَديق طَبيب.	لي صَديق طَبيب.
kaana lee SadeeC Tabeeb	lee SadeeC Tabeeb
I had a friend who is a doctor.	I have a friend who is a doctor.
كانَ لَدَيَّ صَديق طَبيب.	لَدَيَّ صَديق طَبيب.
kaana ladayya SadeeC Tabeeb	ladayya SadeeC Tabeeb
I had a friend who is a doctor.	I have a friend who is a doctor.

In The Past Tense Modern Standard Arabic	Nominal Phrases Modern Standard Arabic
كانَ مَعي قَلَم. kaana maA'ee Calam I had a pen.	مَعي قَلَم. maA'ee Calam I have a pen.
كانَتْ مَعي صَديقَة قَديمَة. Kaanat maA'ee SadeeCa Cadeema I had an old friend with me.	مَعي صَديقَة قَديمَة. maA'ee SadeeCa Cadeema I have an old friend with me.
كانَتْ عِنْدي فِكْرَة. Kanat A'indee fikra I had an idea.	عِنْدي فِكْرَة. A'indee fikra I have an idea.
كانَتْ لَدَيَّ فِكْرَة. Kanat ladayya fikra I had an idea.	لَدَيَّ فِكْرَة . ladayya fikra I have an idea.
كانَتْ عِنْدي أخْبار جَديدَة. Kanat A'indee akhbaar jadeeda I had new news.	عِنْدي أخْبار جَديدَة. A'indee akhbaar jadeeda I have new news.
كانَتْ لَدَيَّ أخْبار جَديدَة. Kanat ladayya akhbaar jadeeda I had new news.	لَدَيَّ أخْبار جَديدَة . ladayya akhbaar jadeeda I have new news.
كانَ عِنْدي طُموح. kana A'indee TomooH I had ambition.	عِنْدي طُموح. A'indee TomooH I have ambition.
كانَ لَدَيَّ طُموح. kaana ladayya TomooH I had ambition.	لَدَيَّ طُموح. ladayya TomooH I have ambition.

In The Past Tense Modern Standard Arabic	Nominal Phrases Modern Standard Arabic
 كَانَتْ عِنْدي مُلاحَظَة. Kanat A'indee molaaHaDHa I had a note.	 عِنْدي مُلاحَظَة. A'indee molaaHaDHa I have a note.
 كَانَتْ لي مُلاحَظَة. Kanat lee molaaHaDHa I had a note.	 لي مُلاحَظَة. lee molaaHaDHa I have a note.
 كَانَتْ لَدَيَّ مُلاحَظَة. Kanat ladayya molaaHaDHa I had a note.	 لَدَيَّ مُلاحَظَة. ladayya molaaHaDHa I have a note.

Sentences that start with 'kana' كانَ are negated by using 'maa' ما at the beginning, just like negating the past tense, because 'kana' كانَ is in the past tense.

Negating The Nominal Phrases in The Past Tense Modern Standard Arabic	Nominal Phrases in The Past Tense Modern Standard Arabic
 ما كانَ عِنْدي بَيْت كَبير. maa kaana A'indee bayt kabeer I never had a big house.	 كانَ عِنْدي بَيْت كَبير. kaana A'indee bayt kabeer I used to have a big house.
 ما كانَ لي بَيْت كَبير. maa kaana lee bayt kabeer I never had a big house.	 كانَ لي بَيْت كَبير. kaana lee bayt kabeer I used to have a big house.
 ما كانَ لَدَيَّ بَيْت كَبير. maa kaana ladayya bayt kabeer I never had a big house.	 كانَ لَدَيَّ بَيْت كَبير. kaana ladayya bayt kabeer I used to have a big house.

Negating The Nominal Phrases in The Past Tense Modern Standard Arabic	Nominal Phrases in The Past Tense Modern Standard Arabic
ما كانَ عِنْدي صَديق طَبيب. maa kaana A'indee SadeeC Tabeeb I never had a friend who is a doctor.	كانَ عِنْدي صَديق طَبيب. kaana A'indee SadeeC Tabeeb I had a friend who is a doctor.
ما كانَ لي صَديق طَبيب. maa kaana lee SadeeC Tabeeb I never had a friend who is a doctor.	كانَ لي صَديق طَبيب. kaana lee SadeeC Tabeeb I had a friend who is a doctor.
ما كانَ لَدَيَّ صَديق طَبيب. maa kaana ladayya SadeeC Tabeeb I never had a friend who is a doctor.	كانَ لَدَيَّ صَديق طَبيب. kaana ladayya SadeeC Tabeeb I had a friend who is a doctor.
ما كانَ مَعي قَلَم. maa kaana maA'ee Calam I did not have a pen.	كانَ مَعي قَلَم. kaana maA'ee Calam I had a pen.
ما كانَتْ مَعي صَديقَة قَديمَة maa kaanat maA'ee SadeeCa Cadeema I did not have an old friend with me	كانَتْ مَعي صَديقَة قَديمَة. kaanat maA'ee SadeeCa Cadeema I had an old friend with me.
ما كانَ عِنْدي فِكْرَة. maa kaana A'indee fikra I did not have any idea.	كانَ عِنْدي فِكْرَة. kana A'indee fikra I had an idea.
ما كانَ لَدَيَّ فِكْرَة. maa kana ladayya fikra I had no idea.	كانَ لَدَيَّ فِكْرَة. kana ladayya fikra I had an idea.
ما كانَتْ عِنْدي أخْبار جَديدَة. maa kaanat A'indee akhbaar jadeeda I did not have any new news.	كانَتْ عِنْدي أخْبار جَديدَة. kanat A'indee akhbaar jadeeda I had new news.

The phrase "I have" can be conjugated using possessive pronouns in Modern Standard Arabic to refer to different people. Here are some examples in spoken Modern Standard Arabic:

Meaning	I have (at the time of) speaking	I have (more formal)	I have (more formal)	I have (less formal)
I have	مَعي maA'ee	لَدَيَّ ladayya	لي lee	عِنْدي A'indee
You have (masculine)	مَعك maA'ka	لَدَيْك ladayka	لَك laka	عِنْدَك A'indaka
You have (feminine)	مَعك maA'ki	لَدَيْك ladayki	لَك laki	عِنْدَك A'indaki
You have (dual feminine and masculine)	مَعكُما maA'koma	لَدَيْكُما ladaykoma	لَكُما lakoma	عِنْدكُما A'indakoma
You have (plural feminine and masculine)	مَعكُم maA'kom	لَدَيكُم ladaykom	لَكُم lakom	عِنْدَكُم A'indakom
You have (plural feminine)	مَعْكُنَّ maA'konna	لَدَيْكُنَّ ladaykona	لَكُنَّ lakonna	عِنْدَكُنَّ A'indakonna
We have	مَعْنا maA'naa	لَدَيْنا ladaynaa	لَنا lanaa	عِنْدَنا A'indana
He has	مَعهُ maA'ho	لَدَيْه ladayhi	لَهُ laho	عِنْدهُ A'indaho
She has	مَعها maA'haa	لَدَيْها ladayhaa	لَها lahaa	عِنْدَها A'indahaa

Meaning	I have (at the time of) speaking	I have (more formal)	I have (more formal)	I have (less formal)
They have (dual feminine and masculine)	مَعْهُمَا maA'homa	لَدَيْهُمَا ladayhoma	لَهُمَا lahoma	عِنْدَهُمَا A'indahoma
They have (plural feminine)	مَعْهُنَّ maA'honna	لَدَيْهِنَّ ladayhina	لَهُنَّ lahonna	عِنْدَهُنَّ A'indahonna
They have (plural feminine and masculine)	مَعْهُمْ maA'hom	لَدَيْهِمْ ladayhim	لَهُمْ lahom	عِنْدَهُمْ A'indahom

- Keep in mind that while practicing reading Arabic, it is important to remember that Arabic is a cursive script and is read and written from right to left.

- The examples provided in the tables for this lesson are all in spoken Modern Standard Arabic, which means that the words do not have vowels marked at the end of each word.

- Please be aware that the pronunciation system used in this book is explained on page six for your reference.

Lesson Thirteen
"There is" and "There are"

In nominal sentences, the prepositional phrases "There is" and "There are" serve as the predicates and indicate existence or presence. These phrases are positioned before the subject in the sentence.

In spoken Modern Standard Arabic, the terms 'there is' and 'there are' are expressed using the word 'honaaka' هُنَاكَ. When negating these statements, the word 'laysa' لَيْسَ is used. However, in informal or dialect Arabic, 'honaaka' هُنَاكَ is preceded by 'fee' في to indicate the presence, and it can be negated using either 'ma fee' مافي or 'mish honaak' مِش هُنَاك. Compare the two tables below and notice the difference between informal/dialect Arabic and spoken Modern Standard Arabic.

Negating Standard Arabic	Modern Standard Arabic
لَيْسَ هُنَاكَ بَيْت كَبير.	هُنَاكَ بَيْت كَبير.
laysa honaaka bayt kabeer	honaaka bayt kabeer
There isn't a big house there.	There is a big house there.
لَيْسَ هُنَاكَ قِطَّة عَلى ٱلشَجَرَة.	هُنَاكَ قِطَة عَلى ٱلشَجَرَة.
laysa honaaka CiTTa A'ala al-shajara	honaaka CiTTa A'ala al-shajara
There isn't a cat on the tree.	There is a cat on the tree.

Negating Informal / Dialect Arabic	Informal / Dialect Arabic
مافي هُنَاك بَيْت كَبير.	في هُنَاك بَيْت كَبير.
maa fee honaak bait kbeer	fee honaak bait kbeer
There isn't a big house there.	There is a big house there.
مافي هُنَاك قِطَّة عَلى ٱلشَجَرَة.	في هُنَاك قِطَة عَلى ٱلشَجَرَة.
maa fee honaak CiTTa A'ala al-shajara	fee honaak CiTTa A'ala al-shajara
There isn't a cat on the tree.	There is a cat on the tree.

In nominal sentences in spoken Modern Standard Arabic, the prepositional phrase typically comes before the subject. Here are some additional examples:

Negating Modern Standard Arabic	Modern Standard Arabic
لَيْسَ هُناك بَيْت كَبير.	هُناكَ بَيْت كَبير.
laysa honaaka bayt kabeer	honaaka bayt kabeer
There isn't a big house there.	There is a big house there.
لَيْسَ هُناكَ قِطَّة عَلى ٱلشَّجَرَة.	هُناكَ قِطَة على ٱلشَّجَرَة.
laysa honaaka CiTTa A'ala al-shajara	honaaka CiTTa A'ala al-shajara
There isn't a cat on the tree.	There is a cat on the tree.
لَيْسَ هُناكَ إِزْدِحام كَثير.	هُناكَ إزْدِحام كَثير.
laysa honaaka izdiHaam katheer	honaaka izdiHaam katheer
There isn't major traffic congestion.	There is a lot of traffic congestion.
لَيْسَ هُناكَ أَخْبار كَثيرَة.	هُناكَ أخْبار كَثيرَة.
laysa honaaka aKHbaar katheera	honaaka aKHbaar katheera
There isn't much news.	There is a lot of news.
لَيْسَ هُناكَ أفْكار كَثيرَة.	هُناكَ أفْكار كَثيرَة.
laysa honaaka afkaar katheera	honaaka afkaar katheera
There aren't a lot of ideas.	There are lots of ideas.
لَيْسَ هُناك خِطَّة جَديدَة.	هُناكَ خِطَة جَديدَة.
laysa honaaka KHiTTa jadeeda	honaaka KHiTTa jadeeda
There isn't a new plan.	There is a new plan.
لَيْسَ هُناك أيّ مُحاضَرَة مُهِمَّة.	هُناك مُحاضَرَة مُهِمَّة.
laysa honaaka ayy moHaaDara mohimma	honaaka moHaaDara mohimma
There isn't any important lecture.	There is an important lecture.

Negating Modern Standard Arabic	Modern Standard Arabic

لَيْسَ هُناكَ أيّ رِحْلَة مُثيرَة.	هُناكَ رِحْلَة مُثيرَة.
laysa honaaka ayy riHla motheera	honaaka riHla motheera
There isn't any exciting trip.	There is an exciting trip.
لَيْسَ هُناكَ تَسْهيلات كَثيرَة.	هُناكَ تَسْهيلات كَثيرَة.
laysa honaaka tasheelat katheera	honaaka tasheelat katheera
There aren't many arrangements.	There are many arrangements.
لَيْسَ هُناكَ أيّ شُروط جَديدَة.	هُناكَ شُروط جَديدَة.
laysa honaaka ayy shorooT jadeeda	honaaka shorooT jadeeda
There aren't any new conditions.	There are new conditions.
لَيْسَ هُناكَ إحْتِمالات كَثيرَة.	هُناكَ إحْتِمالات كَثيرَة.
laysa honaaka iHtimaalaat katheera	honaaka iHtimaalaat katheera
There aren't many possibilities.	There are many possibilities.

The nominal sentence in Arabic can be transformed into the past tense by using the verbs "كان" (kana) or "كانتْ" (kanat) at the beginning of the sentence. These verbs carry meanings such as "was," "were," "had," and "used to." It's worth noting that the feminine form "كانتْ" (kanat) is typically used with singular feminine nouns or non-human plurals. However, in spoken Arabic, it is common to use both forms, "كان" (kana) and "كانتْ" (kanat), with non-human plurals as well. This allows for flexibility and variation in everyday conversation.

Nominal Phrases in the Past Tense	Modern Standard Arabic

كانَ هُناكَ بَيْت كَبير.	هُناكَ بَيْت كَبير.
kana honaaka bayt kabeer	honaaka bayt kabeer
There was a big house there.	There is a big house there.

كَانَتْ هُنَاكَ قِطَّة عَلَى ٱلشَّجَرَة.	هُنَاكَ قِطَّة عَلَى ٱلشَّجَرَة.
Kanat honaaka CiTTa A'ala al-shajara	honaaka CiTTa A'ala al-shajara
There was a cat on the tree.	There is a cat on the tree.
كَانَ هُنَاكَ إِزْدِحَام كَثير.	هُنَاكَ إِزْدِحَام كَثير.
kana honaaka izdiHaam katheer	honaaka izdiHaam katheer
There was a lot of traffic congestion.	There is a lot of traffic congestion.
كَانَتْ هُنَاكَ أَخْبَار كَثيرَة.	هُنَاكَ أَخْبَار كَثيرَة.
Kanat honaaka aKHbaar katheera	honaaka aKHbaar katheera
There was a lot of news.	There is a lot of news.
كَانَتْ هُنَاكَ أَفْكار كَثيرَة.	هُنَاكَ أَفْكار كَثيرَة.
Kanat honaaka afkaar katheera	honaaka afkaar katheera
There were a lot ideas.	There are a lot of ideas.
كَانَتْ هُنَاكَ خِطَّة جَديدَة.	هُنَاكَ خِطَّة جَديدَة.
kanat honaaka KHiTTa jadeeda	honaaka KHiTTa jadeeda
There was a new plan.	There is a new plan.
كَانَتْ هُنَاكَ تَسْهيلات كَثيرَة.	هُنَاكَ تَسْهيلات كَثيرَة.
Kanat honaaka tasheelat katheera	honaaka tasheelat katheera
There were many arrangements.	There are many arrangements.
كَانَتْ هُنَاكَ شُروط جَديدَة.	هُنَاكَ شُروط جَديدَة.
Kanat honaaka shorooT jadeeda	honaaka shorooT jadeeda
There were new conditions.	There are new conditions.
كَانَتْ هُنَاكَ مُلاحَظات بَسيطَة.	هُنَاكَ مُلاحَظات بَسيطَة.
Kanat honaaka molaaHaDHaat baseeTa	honaaka molaaHaDHaat baseeTa
There were simple notes.	There are simple notes.

Nominal Phrases in the Past Tense	Modern Standard Arabic
كَانَتْ هُنَاكَ إِحْتِمالات كَثِيرَة.	هُنَاكَ إِحْتِمالِات كَثِيرَة.
Kanat honaaka iHtimaalaat katheera There were many possibilities.	honaaka iHtimaalaat katheera There are many possibilities.

Negating the nominal phrases in the past tense in Modern Standard Arabic can be done by using the word "ma"  at the beginning of the sentence. Here are the re-worded examples of the nominal phrases in the past tense with negation:

Negating the Nominal Phrases in Past Tense	Nominal Phrases in Past Tense Modern Standard Arabic
ما كانَ هُنَاكَ بَيْت كبير.	كانَ هُنَاكَ بَيْت كبير.
ma kana honaaka bayt kabeer There wasn't a big house there.	kana honaaka bayt kabeer There was a big house there.
ما كانت هُنَاكَ قِطَّة عَلى ٱلشَجَرَة.	كانَت هُنَاكَ قِطَّة عَلى ٱلشَجَرَة.
ma kanat honaaka CiTTa A'ala al-sha-jara There wasn't a cat on the tree.	Kanat honaaka CiTTa A'ala al-sha-jara There was a cat on the tree.
ما كانَ هُنَاكَ إِزْدِحام كَثير.	كانَ هُنَاكَ إِزْدِحام كَثير.
ma kana honaaka izdiHaam katheer There wasn't much traffic congestion.	kana honaaka izdiHaam katheer There was a lot of traffic congestion.
ما كانت هُنَاكَ أَخْبار كَثِيرَة.	كانَت هُنَاكَ أَخْبار كَثِيرَة.
ma kanat honaaka akhbaar katheera There wasn't much news.	Kanat honaaka akhbaar katheera There were a lot of news.
ما كانَت هُنَاكَ أَفْكار كَثِيرَة.	كانَت هُنَاكَ أَفْكار كَثِيرَة.
ma kanat honaaka afkaar katheera There weren't many ideas.	Kanat honaaka afkaar katheera There were a lot of ideas.

Negating the Nominal Phrases in Past Tense	Nominal Phrases in Past Tense Modern Standard Arabic
ما كانَت هُناكَ خِطَّة جَديدَة.	كانَت هُناكَ خِطَّة جَديدَة.
ma kanat honaka KHiTTa jadeeda	kanat honaaka KHiTTa jadeeda
There wasn't a new a plan.	There was a new plan.
ما كانَت هُناك مُحاضَرَة مُهِمَّة.	كانَت هُناكَ مُحاضَرَة مُهِمَّة.
ma kanat honaaka moHaDara mohimma	Kanat honaaka moHaaDara mohimma
There wasn't an important lecture.	There was an important lecture.
ما كانَت هُناكَ رِحْلَة مُثيرَة.	كانَت هُناكَ رِحْلَة مُثيرَة.
ma kanat honaaka riHla motheera	Kanat honaaka riHla motheera
There wasn't an exciting trip.	There was an exciting trip.
ما كانَت هُناكَ تَسْهيلات كَثيرَة.	كانَت هُناكَ تَسْهيلات كَثيرَة.
ma kanat honaaka tasheelat katheera	Kanat honaaka tasheelat katheera
There weren't many arrangements.	There were many arrangements.
ما كانَتْ هُناكَ فُرْصَة جَديدَة.	كانَتْ هُناكَ فُرْصَة جَديدَة.
maa kanat honaaka forSa jadeeda	kanat honaaka forSa jadeeda
There wasn't a new opportunity.	There was a new opportunity.
ما كانَتْ هُناكَ فِكْرَة مُهِمَّة.	كانَتْ هُناكَ فِكْرَة مُهِمَّة.
maa kanat honaaka fikra mohimma	kanat honaaka fikra mohimma
There wasn't an important idea.	There was an important idea.

- Keep in mind that while practicing reading Arabic, it is important to remember that Arabic is a cursive script and is read and written from right to left.

- The examples provided in the tables for this lesson are all in spoken Modern Standard Arabic, which means that the words do not have vowels marked at the end of each word.

- Please be aware that the pronunciation system used in this book is explained on page six for your reference.

Lesson Fourteen
Connective Words

Connective words in Arabic can be classified into three groups. The first group includes commonly used connecting words that can function as prepositions, conjunctions, or adverbs and are frequently employed. They bridge different parts of a sentence or text, enhancing coherence and logical flow. The second group consists of less common connecting words in comparison to the first group. Finally, the third group comprises common connecting letters that must be directly attached to the word they refer to.

Connective words in Arabic can also be conjugated with different pronouns, which allows for more precise relationships and nuanced meanings within a sentence. This flexibility adds depth and versatility to the language, enabling speakers and writers to express ideas and connections more precisely.

These connective words play a crucial role in establishing relationships between words, contributing to the overall coherence and logical flow of the writing.

In spoken Modern Standard Arabic, it is uncommon to include the final vowels when writing or pronouncing words. This practice applies to the end vowels of each word.

First group of connective words:

Modern Standard Arabic	Connective Words
الكِتاب في اَلْحَقيبَة. al-kitaab fee al-HaCeebat **The book is in the bag.**	في **fee** (In / at) followed by a noun or attached pronoun.
سارَة في اَلمَدْرَسَة. sara fee al-madrasat **Sara is at the school.**	في **fee** (In / at) followed by a noun or attached pronoun.
الكِتاب مَع اَلأُسْتاذ. al-kitaab maA' al-ostaadh **The book is with the teacher.**	مَع **maA'** (with) followed by a noun or attached pronoun.

Modern Standard Arabic	Connective Words
باسِم مِن لُبْنان. baasim min lobnaan Basim is from Lebanon.	مِن min (from / of / than) followed by a noun or attached pronoun.
فيصل مِنَ ٱلأُرْدُن. faySal mina al-ordonn Faisal is from Jordan.	مِنَ mina (from / of / than) followed by a noun or attached pronoun.
أَكَلْتُ قِطعَة مِنَ ٱلبيتزا. akalto CiTA'a mina al-pitza I ate a slice of pizza.	مِنَ mina (from / of / than) followed by a noun or attached pronoun.
الكلام أسْهَل مِنَ العَمَل. al-kalam ashal mina al-A'amal Easier said than done.	مِنَ mina (from / of / than) followed by a noun or attached pronoun.
ذَهَبَ ٱلطّالِب إلى المَدرَسَة. dhahaba aT-Talib ilaa al-madrasat The student went to school.	إلى ila (to) used for places followed by a noun or attached pronoun.
العُصْفور عَلى الشّجَرَة. al-A'osfoor A'ala al-shajarat The bird is on the tree.	عَلى A'ala (on / upon) followed by a noun or attached pronoun.
البَيْت بَعيد عَن السّوق. al-bayt baA'eed A'an al-sooC The house is far from the marketplace.	عَن A'an (from / about) followed by a noun or attached pronoun.

Modern Standard Arabic	Connective Words
 ماذا عَن اليَوم ؟ madhaa A'an al-yawm What about today?	عَن A'an (from / about) followed by a noun or attached pronoun.
أَلْعَب في الخارِج لِأَنَّ ٱلطَقْس جَميل. alA'ab fee al-KHarij li'anna al-TaCs jameel I'm playing outside because the weather is beautiful.	لِأَنَّ li'anna (because) Followed by a noun or attached pronoun.
الجَو لَطيف لِذلِكَ أَنا في الحَديقَة. al-jawo laTeef lidhaalika anaa fee al-HadeeCa The weather is nice, so I am at the park.	لِذلِك lidhaalika (so / thus / for this reason)
 أُحِبّ أَنْ أَسْبَح. oHibb an asbaH I like to swim.	أَنْ an (to) used to express oneself followed by a present verb.
 أَتَمَرَّنْ قَبْلَ أَنْ آكُل. atamarran Cabla an aakol I exercise before I eat.	قَبْلَ Cabla (before) usually followed by أَنْ
 بَعْدَ أَنْ أَدْرُسْ سَوْفَ أَنام. baA'da an adros sawfa anaam I will sleep after I study.	بَعْدَ baA'da (after / next) usually followed by أَنْ
 عِنْدي مِثْلَ هذا القَميص. A'indee mithla haathaa al-CameeS I have a shirt like this.	مِثْلَ mithla (like / as / similar) followed by a noun or attached pronoun

Modern Standard Arabic	Connective Words
سَوْفَ أَلْعَب كُرَةَ القَدَم أَوْ كُرَةَ السَّلَّة. sawfa alA'ab korata al-Cadam aw koraata al-sallat I will play soccer or basketball.	أَوْ aw (or)
أُحِب السَّمَك كَما أُحِب الدَّجاج. oHib al-samak kamaa oHib al-dajaaj I like fish as much as I like chicken.	كَما / بِالإِضافَة إلى ذلِك kamaa / bil iDaafah ilaa dhaalik (also / as / in addition to)
أَنا أَيْضاً فَرْحانَة. anna ayDan farHaana I am happy too.	أَيْضاً ayDan (also / too / as well / and)
أَنا أَيْضاً أَعْرِف. anaa ayDan aA'rif I also know.	أَيْضاً ayDan (also / too / as well / and)

Second group of connective words:

Modern Standard Arabic	Connecting Words
أَذْهَب إلى المَدْرَسَةِ كُلّ يَوْم. adhhab ila al-madrasa koll yawm I go to school every day.	كُلَّ kolla (every / all) followed by a noun or attached pronoun.
عِنْدي أخ واحِد فَقَط. A'indee akh waaHid faCaT I only have one brother.	فَقَط faCat (only / just / merely)
أَزور عائِلَتي أَحْياناً. azoor A'a,ilatee aHyaanan I visit my family sometimes.	أَحْياناً aHyaanan (sometimes)

أَنَّ

an,na
(that) to express opinion
or
information followed by a
noun or attached pronoun.

أَظُنُّ أَنَّ الجَوَّ حار اليَوْم.

aTHon an,na al-jaww Haar al-yawm
I think the weather is hot today.

بِسَبَب

bisabab
(for / because of)
Followed by a noun or at-
tached pronoun.

أَحِبُّ كَليفورنيا بِسَبَب الجَو المُعْتَدِل.

oHibo california bisabab al-jaw al-moA'tadil
I like California because of the moderate
weather.

مُنْذْ

mondho
(since / ago / from)

لَم أَزور عائِلَتي مُنْذْ سَنَتَين.

lam azoor A'a,ilatee mondho sanatayn
I did not visit my family for two years.

عِنْدَما

A'indamaa
(when)
non-interrogative.

سَوْفَ أَزور صَديقي عِنْدَما أعود.

sawfa azoor SadeeCee A'indamaa aA'ood
I will visit my friend when I come back.

بَيْنَما

baynamaa
(while)

بَيْنَما أنا أتَسَوَّق نَزَلَ المَطَر.

baynamaa anaa atasawwaC nazala al-maTar
It rained while I was shopping.

مِن خِلال

min khilaal
(through / during)
followed by a noun or at-
tached pronoun.

مِن خِلال عَمَلي تَعَرَّفْت عَلى زَوْجَتي.

min khilaal A'amalee taA'arraft A'ala zawjatee
I met my wife through work.

حَيْثُ

Haitho
(where) not in question.

كُنْتُ في السوق حَيْثُ رَأَيْتُ مَها.

konto fee al-sooC Haytho ra,ayto maha
I saw Maha while I was at the marketplace.

الجَو دائِماً جَميل هُنا. al-jaww daa,iman jameel honaa The weather is always beautiful here.	دائِماً da,iman (always / constantly / forever)
أنْتَ صَديق مُخْلِص فِعْلاً. anta SadeeC mukhliS fiA'lan You are truly a sincere friend.	فِعْلاً fiA'lan (really / truly / indeed)
في الحَقيقَة أُحِب الشِتاء أكْثَر مِنَ الصيْف fee al-HaCeeCa oHib al-shitaa, akthar mina al-Sayf Actually, I like the winter more than the summer.	في الحَقيقَة fee al-HaCeeCa (actually / in reality / as a matter of fact)
أنا مَشْغول الآن. anaa mashGHool al-aan I am busy now.	ٱلآن alaan (now / at the present / yet)
ٱلآن لا أعْرِف. alaan laa aA'rif At the present, I don't know.	ٱلآن alaan (now / at the present / yet)
سَوْفَ أذْهَب إلى المَكْتَبَة ثُمَّ إلى البَيْت. sawfa adhhab ila al-maktaba thomma ila al-bayt. I will go to the library then to the house.	ثُمَّ thomma (then)
أُحِب أنْ أخْرُج لكِن الجَو بارِد. oHibo an akhroja lakin al-jawa baarid I'd like to go out, but the weather is cold.	لكِن lakin (but / however / only) followed by a noun or attached pronoun.

Third group of connecting letters:

Note that these connecting letters are typically written attached to the following words, except for the last connecting letter, as it is a one-way connector letter.

Modern Standard Arabic	Connecting Letters
أَدْرُس لِأَنْجَح. adros li-anjaH I study to succeed.	لِ / لَ li / la (In order to / for / to)
أَذْهَب إلى العَمَل بالباص. adhhab ila al-A'amal bi al-lbaaS I go to work by bus.	بِ bi (with / by) indicates using an instrument.
مَيْسون جائَت بِسَيّارَة. maysoon jaa,at bi-sayyara Maysoon came by car.	بِ bi (with / by) Indicates using an instrument.
دَرَسْت فَنَجَحْت. darast fanaJaHt I studied and succeeded.	فَ fa (and / so / then / therefore) indicate a sequence of events or actions.
أَكَلْت الدَجاج وَالخُبْز. akalt al-dajaj wa al-khobz I ate the chicken and the bread.	وَ wa (and)
الكتاب أحمر وَالقلم أزرق. al-kitab aHmar wal-qalam azraq The book is red and the pen is blue.	وَ wa (and)

Adding possessive pronouns to the connecting words:

Most of the prepositions and conjunctions we discussed in the lesson can have possessive pronouns attached to them at the end in order to refer to different people.

• When attaching the possessive pronoun 'him/it' (هُ) to the connecting words, there are changes to keep in mind: If the connecting word ends with the letter 'y' (ي) like in the first example, and if the connecting word ends with a 'broken alif' (ى), two dots will be added to the broken alif and it will be changed to the letter 'y' (ي) like in the third example. In these two cases, the 'Dammah' ( ) vowel on the possessive pronoun will be shifted to a 'kasrah'( ) vowel. By following these rules, the possessive pronoun 'him/it' (هُ) can be properly attached to the connecting words:

Modern Standard Arabic	Connecting Words
البَيْت فيهِ غُرَف كَثيرَة. al-bayt feehi GHoraf katheera The house has a lot of rooms in it.	في fee (in / at)
عَلي مَعْهُ صَديقُهُ. A'alee maA'ho SadeeCoho Ali has his friend with him.	مَع maA' (with)
المَكْتَب عَلَيْهِ غُبار. al-maktab A'alayhi GHobaar The disk has dust on it.	عَلى A'ala (on)

138

Modern Standard Arabic	Connecting Words
آكُل السَبانِخ لِأَنَّهُ مُفيد. aakol al-sabanikh li,annaho mofeed I eat spinach because it is healthy.	لِأَنَّ li,anna (Because) followed by a noun.
القَميص جَميل! عِنْدي مِثْلُهُ. al-Camees jameel A'indee mithloho The shirt is beautiful! I have a similar one.	مِثْلُ mithlo (like / as / similar)
البَيْت قَديم! لكِنَّهُ واسِع. al-bayt Cadeem lakinnaho waasiA' The house is old! But it is spacious.	لكِنْ lakin (but / however / only)
اليَوْم كُلُّهُ غَريب. al-yawm kolloho GHareeb! Today is all strange!	كُل kol (all / whole)

Examples of the possessive pronoun (her / it) هَا attached to some of the common connecting words:

Note: If the connecting word ends with a 'broken alif' (ى), two dots will be added to the broken alif and it will be changed to the letter 'y' (ي) like in the third example.

Modern Standard Arabic:	Connecting Words
الحَديقَة فيها أزهار كَثيرَة. al-HadeeCa feehaa azhaar katheera The garden has a lot of flowers in it.	في fee (in / at)

عِنْدي مَلابِس كثيرة مِنْها قَديمَة. A'indee malaabis katheera minhaa Cadeema I have lots of clothes; some of them are old.	مِن min (from / of / than)
الشَّجَرَة عَلَيْها ثِمار لَذيذَة. al-shajara A'alayhaa thimaar ladheedha The tree has a lot of delicious fruits on it.	عَلى A'ala (on)
أَسْكُنْ في كَليفورنيا لِأَنَّها جَميلَة. askon fee california li,annahaa jameela I live in California because it is beautiful.	لِأَنَّ li,anna (because) followed by a pronoun or a noun.
الإسوارَة جَميلَة ! عِنْدي مِثْلُها. al-iswaara jameela! A'indee mithlohaa The bracelet is beautiful! I have a similar one like it.	مِثْلُ mithlo (like / as)
القِصَّة غريبَة لَكِنَّها حَقيقة. al-CiSSa GHareeba lakinnahaa HaCeeCa The story is strange! But it is true.	لَكِن lakin (but / however / only)
الألوانُ كُلّها جَميلَة. al-alwaan kollohaa jameela All the colors are beautiful.	كُل kol (every / all)

Below is the conjunction 'Because' لِأَنَّ followed and attached to the singular possessive pronouns:

- **In spoken Modern Standard Arabic (MSA), the plural masculine form is commonly used instead of the dual and feminine plural forms. The dual and feminine plural forms are more commonly found in Classical Arabic and are used in formal and poetic contexts.**

Meaning	Because (attached to pronouns)	Singular (possessive pronouns)	Meaning	Singular (subject pronouns)
Because I...	لِأَنِّي li,annee	ي ee	I	أَنا anna
Because you... (M)	لِأَنَّكَ li,annaka	كَ ka	You (masculine)	أَنتَ anta
Because you... (F)	لِأَنَّكِ li,annaki	كِ ki	You (feminine)	أَنتِ anti
Because he...	لِأَنَّهُ li,annaho	هُ ho	He	هُوَ howa
Because she...	لِأَنَّها li,annahaa	ها haa	She	هِيَ hiya

'Because' لِأَنَّ attached to the dual possessive pronouns for (masculine and feminine):

Meaning	Because (attached to pronouns)	Dual possessive pronouns (M&F)	Meaning	Dual Subject pronouns (M&F)
Because you both... (dual, for M and F)	لِأَنْكُما li,annakoma	كُما komaa	You both (masculine and feminine)	أَنْتُما antomaa
Because they both... (dual, for M and F)	لِأَنَّهُما li,annahoma	هُما homaa	They both (masculine and feminine)	هُما homaa

'Because' لِأَنَّ attached to the plural possessive pronouns for (masculine and feminine)

Meaning	Because (attached to pronouns)	Plural (possessive pronouns)	Meaning	Plural Subject pronouns
Because we...	لِأَنَّنا li,annanaa	نا naa	We	نَحنُ naHno
Because you... (plural)	لِأَنْكُم li,annakom	كُم kom	You (plural)	أَنْتُم antom
Because they...	لِأَنَّهُم li,annahom	هُم hom	They	هُم hom

Lesson Fifteen
Demonstrative Pronouns

In Arabic, the Demonstrative Pronouns precede the noun or pronoun. There are two types of Demonstrative Pronouns: Near Pronouns, used for people or things that are near, and Far Pronouns, used for people or things that are far. Demonstrative Pronouns have different forms for singular, dual, and plural.

- **In spoken Modern Standard Arabic (MSA), the plural masculine form is commonly used instead of the dual and feminine plural forms. The dual and feminine plural forms are more commonly found in Classical Arabic and are used in formal and poetic contexts.**

It's important to note that the gender of the demonstrative pronoun follows the gender of its noun or pronoun, except in one case: when the noun is a non-person plural. In this case, the noun is treated as a singular feminine noun, and the demonstrative pronoun will be in the singular feminine form. This rule also applies to verbs, adjectives, and other pronouns.

Demonstrative pronouns for a singular person and singular/plural things:

Demonstrative Pronouns (for far nouns)		Demonstrative Pronouns (for near nouns)	
'That is' (masculine)	ذٰلِكَ dhalika	'This is' (masculine)	هٰذا hadhaa
'That is' (feminine and non-person plural nouns)	تِلْكَ tilka	'This is' (feminine and non-person plural nouns)	هٰذِهِ hadhihi

143

Examples in the spoken Modern Standard Arabic:

Demonstrative Pronouns (for far noun)	Demonstrative Pronouns (for near noun)
ذٰلِكَ وَلَد طَويل.	هٰذا وَلَد طَويل.
dhaalika walad Taweel	hadha walad Taweel
That boy is tall.	This is a tall boy.
تِلْكَ بِنت جَميلَة.	هٰذِهِ بِنت جَميلَة.
tilka bint jameela	hadhihi bint jameela
That girl is beautiful.	This is a beautiful girl.
ذٰلِكَ بَيْت كَبير.	هٰذا بَيْت كَبير.
dhalika bayt kabeer	hadha bayt kabeer
That is a big house.	This is a big house.
ذٰلِكَ إِخْتِبار صَعْب.	هٰذا إِخْتِبار صَعْب.
dhalika iKHtibaar SaA'b	hatha iKHtibaar SaA'b
That is a difficult test.	This is a difficult test.
ذٰلِكَ دَرْس صَعْب.	هٰذا دَرْس صَعْب.
dhalika dars SaA'b	hadha dars SaA'b
That is a hard lesson.	This is a hard lesson.
تِلْكَ لَوْحَة ثَمينَة.	هٰذِهِ لَوْحَة ثَمينَة.
tilka lawHa thameena	hadhihi lawHa thameena
That is an expensive painting.	This is an expensive painting.
تِلْكَ بُيوت رَخيصَة.	هٰذِهِ بُيوت رَخيصَة.
tilka boyoot raKHeeSa	hadhihi boyoot raKHeeSa
Those are cheap houses.	These are cheap houses.
تِلْكَ قَرارات سَريعَة.	هٰذِهِ قَرارات سَريعَة.
tilka Cararat sareeAa	hadhihi Cararat sareeAa
Those are fast decisions	These are fast decisions

Demonstrative Pronouns (for far noun)	Demonstrative Pronouns (for near noun)
ذٰلِكَ شَيء رائِع.	هٰذا شَيء رائِع.
dhalika shay raaiA	hadha shay raaiA
That is an amazing thing.	This is an amazing thing.
ذٰلِكَ شَيء مُمْكِن.	هٰذا شَيء مُمْكِن.
dhalika shay momkin	hadha shay momkin
That is a possible thing.	This is a possible thing.
تِلْكَ ذِكْرَياتي.	هٰذِهِ ذِكْرَياتي.
tilka dhikrayatee	hadhihi dhikrayatee
Those are my memories	These are my memories

Demonstrative Pronouns for people or things (plural):

Demonstrative Pronouns (for far people)		Demonstrative Pronouns (for near people)	
'Those are' (masculine and feminine)	أُولٰئِكَ olaa,ika	'These are' (masculine and feminine)	هٰؤُلاء ha,olaa,

Examples in the spoken Modern Standard Arabic:

Plural Demonstrative Pronouns (for far nouns)	Plural Demonstrative Pronouns (for near nouns)
أُولٰئِكَ أوْلاد طِوال.	هٰؤُلاء أولاد طِوال.
,olaa,ika awlaad Tiwaal	ha,olaa, awlaad Tiwaal
Those boys are tall.	These boys are tall.

Plural Demonstrative Pronouns (for far nouns)	Plural Demonstrative Pronouns (for near nouns)

أُولَائِكَ بَنَات جَمِيلَات.	هٰؤُلَاء بَنَات جَمِيلَات.
,olaa,ika banaat jameelaat	ha,olaa, banaat jameelat
Those girls are beautiful.	These girls are beautiful.
أُولَائِكَ رِجَال مُخْلِصُون.	هٰؤُلَاء رِجَال مُخْلِصُون.
,olaa,ika rijaal moKHliSoon	ha,olaa, rijaal moKHliSoon
Those men are loyal.	These men are loyal.
أُولَائِكَ نِسَاء مُخْلِصَات.	هٰؤُلَاء نِسَاء مُخْلِصَات.
,olaa,ika nisaa, moKHliSaat	ha,olaa, nisaa, moKHliSaat
Those women are loyal.	These women are loyal.
أُولَائِكَ شُعُوب مُتَحَضِّرَة.	هٰؤُلَاء شُعُوب مُتَحَضِّرَة.
,olaa,ika shoA'oob motaHaDDira	ha,olaa, shoA'oob motaHaDDira
Those nations are civilized.	These nations are civilized.
أُولَائِكَ شُعُوب وَاعِيَة.	هٰؤُلَاء شُعُوب وَاعِيَة.
,olaa,ika shoA'oob waA'iyah	ha,olaa, shoA'oob waA'iyah
Those nations are conscious.	These nations are conscious.
أُولَائِكَ مُهَنْدِسُون.	هٰؤُلَاء مُهَنْدِسُون.
,olaa,ika mohandisoon	ha,olaa, mohandisoon
Those are engineers.	These are engineers.
أُولَائِكَ قَادَة.	هٰؤُلَاء قَادَة.
,olaa,ika Caadah	ha,olaa, Caadah
Those are leaders.	These are leaders.
أُولَائِكَ مُتَصَوِّفَة.	هٰؤُلَاء مُتَصَوِّفَة.
,olaa,ika motaSawwifa	ha,olaa, motaSawwifa
Those are mystics.	These are mystics.

Lesson Sixteen
Interrogative Pronouns

Interrogative pronouns are used to ask questions in Arabic. They help us inquire about various aspects and seek information. The interrogative pronoun usually comes at the beginning of the sentence in the spoken modern standard Arabic. Here are some common interrogative pronouns:

Meaning	Interrogative Pronouns	Meaning	Interrogative Pronouns
Where?	أَيْنَ ؟ ayna?	What?	ما ؟ ma?
Which?	أَيَّ ؟ ayya?	What? (questions followed by a verb)	ماذا ؟ madha?
When?	مَتى ؟ mataa?	Why? / For what?	لِماذا ؟ limadhaa?
In yes or no questions Do/Does	هَل ؟ hal?	Who?	مَن ؟ man?
In a negative question	ألا؟ alaa?	How?	كَيْفَ ؟ kayfa?
By which/With which/By any means	بِأَيَّ bi-ayya?	How much/many?	كَم؟ kam?

Question Phrases
Spoken Modern Standard Arabic

(speaking to a female)	(speaking to a male)

مَن أنْتِ؟

man anti?

Who are you?

مَن أنْتَ؟

man anta?

Who are you?

ما إسْمُكِ؟

ma ismoki?

What is your name?

ما إسْمُكَ؟

ma ismoka?

What is your name?

مَن هِيَ؟

man hiya?

Who is she?

مَن هُوَ؟

man howa?

Who is he?

أيْنَ تَسْكُنِين؟

ayna taskoneen?

Where do you live?

أيْنَ تَسْكُنْ؟

ayna taskon?

Where do you live?

ما هذِهِ؟

ma hadhihi?

What is this?

ما هذا؟

ma hadha?

What is this?

ماذا تَعْمَلِين؟

madha taA'maleen?

What do you do?

ماذا تَعْمَل؟

madha taA'mal?

What do you do?

ماذا تُحِبّين؟

madha toHibbeen?

What do you like?

ماذا تُحِب؟

madha toHib?

What do you like?

ماذا تَطْبُخِين؟

madha taTboKHeen?

What are you cooking?

ماذا تَطْبُخ؟

madha taTboKH?

What are you cooking?

Question Phrases
Spoken Modern Standard Arabic

لِماذا تَدْرُسينَ ٱلْعَرَبِيَّة؟

limadha tadroseena al-A'arabiyya?
Why do you study Arabic?

لِماذا تَدْرُس العَرَبِيَّةٌ؟

limadha tadros al-A'arabiyyah?
Why do you study Arabic?

لِماذا أَنْتِ سَعيدَة؟

limadha anti saA'eed?
Why are you happy?

لِماذا أَنْتَ سَعيد؟

limadha anta saA'eed?
Why are you happy?

كَيْفَ حالُكِ؟

kayfa Haloki?
How are you?

كَيْفَ حالُكَ؟

kayfa Haloka?
How are you?

كَيْفَ الْوَضْع؟

kayfa alwaDA'?
How is the situation?

كَيْفَ الْوَضْع؟

kayfa alwaDA'?
How is the situation?

أَيْنَ أَنْتِ؟

ayna anti?
Where are you?

أَيْنَ أَنْتَ؟

ayna anta?
Where are you?

أَيَّ يَوْم تُسافِرين؟

ayya yawm tosafireen?
Which day do you travel?

أَيَّ يَوْم تُسافِرٍ؟

ayya yawm tosafir?
Which day do you travel?

أَيَّ لَوْن تُحِبّين؟

ayya lawn toHibbeen?
Which color do you like?

أَيَّ لَوْن تُحِب؟

ayya lawn toHib?
Which color do you like?

مَتى تُسافِرين؟

mataa tosaafireen?
When will you travel?

مَتى تُسافِرٍ؟

mataa tosaafir?
When will you travel?

Question Phrases
Spoken Modern Standard Arabic

مَتى رَجَعْتِ؟

mataa rajaA'ti?
When did you come back?

مَتى رَجَعْتَ؟

mataa rajaA'ta?
When did you come back?

هَل أنْتِ جَوْعانَة؟

hal anti jawA'ana?
Are you hungry?

هَل أنْتَ جَوْعان؟

hal anta jawA'an?
Are you hungry?

هَل أنْتِ نَعْسانَة؟

hal anti naA'sana?
Are you sleepy?

هَل أنْتَ نَعْسان؟

hal anta naA'san?
Are you sleepy?

ألا تَعْمَلينَ اَليَوْم؟

alaa taA'maleena al-yawm?
Don't you work today?

ألا تَعْمَل اليَوْم؟

alaa taA'mal al-yawm?
Don't you work today?

ألا تُساعِديني؟

alaa tosaA'ideenee?
Won't you help me?

ألا تُساعِدني؟

alaa tosaA'idnee?
Won't you help me?

أَيَّ طَعام تُحِبّين؟

ayya TaA'am toHibbeen?
Which food do you like?

أَيَّ طَعام تُحِب؟

ayya TaA'am toHib?
Which food do you like?

كَمْ عُمْرِكِ؟

kam omroka?
How old are you?

كَمْ عُمْرَكَ؟

kam omroka?
How old are you?

بِأَيَّ طَريقَة نُريد حَل.

bi-ayya tareeqa noreed Hal.
By any means, we want a solution.

بِأَيَّ طَريقَة نُريد حَل.

bi-ayya tareeqa noreed Hal.
By any means, we want a solution.

- If the question has a preposition, the preposition will precede the interrogative pronoun.

Examples in the spoken Modern Standard Arabic:

Meaning	Questions starts with Prepositions
Where are you from? (to a male)	مِن أَيْنَ أَنْتَ؟ min ayna anta?
Where are you from? (to a female)	مِن أَيْنَ أَنْتِ؟ min ayna anti?
Which is the way to the airport?	مِن أَيْنَ الطَريق إلى المَطار؟ min ayna al-TareeC ila al-maTaar?
With whom were you? (to a male)	مَع مَنْ كُنْتَ؟ maA' man konta?
With whom were you? (to a female)	مَع مَنْ كُنْتِ؟ maA' man konti?
With whom did you go? (to a male)	مَع مَنْ ذَهَبْتَ؟ maA' man dhahabta?
With whom did you go? (to a female)	مَع مَنْ ذَهَبْتِ؟ maA' man dhahabti?
With whom do you live? (to a male)	مَع مَنْ تَسْكُنْ؟ maA' man taskon?
With whom do you live? (to a female)	مَع مَنْ تَسْكُنِين؟ maA' man taskoneen?

Meaning	Questions starts with Prepositions
To where are you going? (to a male)	إلى أَيْنَ أَنْتَ ذاهِب؟ ilaa ayna anta dhaahib?
To where are you going? (to a female)	إلى أَيْنَ أَنْتِ ذاهِبَة؟ ilaa ayna anti dhaahiba?
In what day are you traveling? (to a male)	في أَيَّ يَوْم تُسافِر؟ fee ayya yawm tosaafir?
In what day are you traveling? (to a female)	في أَيَّ يَوْم تُسافِرين؟ fee ayya yawm tosafireen?
Who are you talking about? (to a male)	عَن مَنْ تَتَحَدَّث؟ A'an man tataHad-dath?
Who are you talking about? (to a female)	عَن مَنْ تَتَحَدَّثين؟ A'an man tataHad-datheen?
Who should I talk to?	إلى مَنْ يَجِب أَنْ أَتَكَلَّم؟ ila man yajib an atakal-lam?
To whom were you speaking? (to a male)	إلى مَنْ كُنْتَ تَتَحَدَّث؟ ila man konta tatahad-dath?
To whom were you speaking? (to a female)	إلى مَنْ كُنْتِ تَتَحَدَّثين؟ ila man konti tatahad-datheen?
With whom were you working? (to a male)	مَع مَنْ كُنْتَ تَعْمَل؟ maA' man konta taA'mal?
With whom were you working? (to a female)	مَع مَنْ كُنْتِ تَعْمَلين؟ maA' man konti taA'maleen?

Lesson Seventeen
Nouns and Adjectives

In spoken Modern Standard Arabic, the noun typically comes before the adjective in word order. Additionally, the gender sign for adjectives is often the same for both masculine and feminine forms, simplifying the agreement between the noun and adjective in terms of gender.

Here are some examples of simple masculine noun-adjective phrases:

Meaning	Singular Masculine Noun-Adjective Phrases
Big house	بَيْت كَبير bayt kabeer
Young boy	وَلَد صَغير walad Sageer
Nice teacher	أُسْتاذ لَطيف ostaadh laTeef
Wonderful orchard	بُسْتان رائِع bostaan ra,iA'
Ugly scene	مَنْظَر قَبيح manDHar CabeeH
Far hope	أَمَل بَعيد amal baA'eed
Glad tidings	فَرَج قَريب faraj Careeb
Beautiful feeling	إحساس جَميل iHsas jameel

Meaning	Singular Masculine Noun-Adjective Phrases
Long hair	شَعر طَويل shaA'r Taweel
Short time	وَقْت قَصير waCt CaSeer
Expensive dress	فُسْتان ثَمين fostan thameen
Cheap house	بَيْت رَخيص bayt raKHeeS
Exciting day	يَوْم مُمْتِع yawm momtiA'
Old office	مَكْتَب قَديم maktab Cadeem

In spoken Modern Standard Arabic, the final letter closed "t" (ـة / ة) is typically not pronounced, and its main purpose is to indicate the feminine form of a noun and adjective. However, the short vowel "fatHa" sound preceding the final "t" is pronounced. Examples in the spoken Modern Standard Arabic:

Meaning	Singular Feminine Noun-Adjective Phrases
Big school	مَدْرَسَة كَبيرَة madrasa kabeera
Little girl	بِنْت صَغيرَة bint SaGeera

Meaning	Singular Feminine Noun-Adjective Phrases
Nice teacher	أُسْتاذَة لَطيفَة ostaadha laTeefa
Beautiful flower	وَرْدَة جَميلَة warda jameela
Ugly picture	صورَة قَبيحَة Soora CabeeHa
Old library	مَكْتَبَة قَديمَة maktaba Cadeema
Happy ending	نِهايَة سَعيدَة nihaaya saA'eeda
Strange habit	عادَة غَريبَة A'ada GHareeba
Tall building	عَمارَة طَويلَة A'amaara Taweela
Talented doctor	طَبيبَة ماهِرَة Tabeeba maahira
Clear sign	عَلامَة واضِحَة A'alaama waDiHa
Maza is truthful	مازا صادِقَة maza SaadiCa

155

Meaning	Singular Feminine Noun-Adjective Phrases
Spiritual connection	عَلاقَة روحِيَّة A'alaCa rooHiyyah
Exciting trip	رِحْلَة مُثيرَة riHla motheera
Beautiful smile	إِبْتِسامَة جَميلَة ibtisaama jameela
Amazing idea	فِكرَة رائِعَة fikra raa,iA'a

In Arabic, the adjective always agrees with the noun in terms of gender and number, except when the noun is non-personal and plural. In such cases, the adjective should be in the singular feminine form. It's important to note that all non-personal plural nouns are treated as singular feminine nouns, which means that pronouns, adjectives, adverbs, and verbs associated with them should also be in the singular feminine form.

Examples of noun-adjective phrases using non-person plural nouns in spoken Modern Standard Arabic:

Meaning	Non-Person Plural Nouns and Adjective Phrases
Big houses	بُيوت كَبيرَة boyoot kabeera
Small schools	مَدارِس صَغيرَة madaaris SaGHeera
Expensive portraits	لَوْحات ثَمينَة lawHaat thameena

Meaning	Non-Person Plural Nouns and Adjective Phrases
Many thoughts	أفْكار كَثيرَة afkaar katheera
Hard exams	إمْتِحانات صَعْبَة imtiHaanat SaA'ba
Great accomplishment	إنْجازات عَظيمَة injaazaat A'aDHeema
Green lands	أراضي خَضْراء araaDee KHaDraa,
New discoveries	إكْتِشافات جَديدَة iktishaafaat jadeeda
Wise decisions	قَرارات حَكيمَة Caraaraat Hakeema
Beautiful poems	أشْعار جَميلَة ashA'ar jameela
Clear signs	عَلامَات واضِحَة A'alaamat waDiHa
Spiritual connections	عَلاقَات روحِيَّة A'alaCaat rooHiyyah
Exciting trips	رِحْلَات مُثيرَة riHlaat motheera

Meaning	Non-Person Plural Nouns and Adjective Phrases
Happy endings	نِهايَات سَعيدَة nihaayaat saA'eeda
Strange habits	عادَات غَريبَة A'adaat GHareeba
Tall buildings	عَمارَات طَويلَة A'amaaraat Taweela
Ugly pictures	صُوَر قَبيحَة Sowar CabeeHa
Old libraries	مَكْتَبات قَديمَة maktabaat Cadeema
Beautiful flowers	أزْهار جَميلَة azhaar jameela
Beautiful memories	ذِكْرَيات جَميلَة dhikrayaat jameela
Heavy rain	أمْطار غَزيرَة amTaar GHazeera

- Keep in mind that while practicing reading Arabic, it is important to remember that Arabic is a cursive script and is read and written from right to left.

- The examples provided in the tables for this lesson are all in spoken Modern Standard Arabic, which means that the words do not have vowels marked at the end of each word.

- Please be aware that the pronunciation system used in this book is explained on page six for your reference.

Lesson Eighteen
Comparatives and Superlatives

Comparative and superlative adjectives describe nouns and are derived from simple adjectives. The same adjective can be used to express the comparative or superlative form. However, they differ in meaning and word order. Comparative adjectives compare two or more persons or things that possess a certain quality, with one being favored over the other. The comparative adjective comes immediately after the preferred noun in a phrase. To indicate a clear comparison between the two nouns, the preposition 'than' is used.

Examples of comparative adjectives in spoken Modern Standard Arabic:

Meaning	Comparative Phrases
The spring is nicer than the summer.	الرَبيـع أَلْطَف مِن الصَيْف. al-rabeeA' alTaf min al-Sayf
Today is colder than yesterday.	اليَوْم أبْرَد مِن الأمْس. al-yawm abrad min al-ams
Rasheed is taller than Khalid.	رَشيد أطْوَل مِنْ خالِد. Rasheed aTwal min KHalid
Hamza is younger than Ashraf.	حَمْزَة أصْغَر مِنْ أشْرَف. Hamza aSGHar min ashraf
Dana is older than Tala.	دانا أكْبَر مِنْ تالا. dana akbar min tala
My house is closer than your house.	بَيْتـي أقْرَب مِنْ بَيْتِك. baytee aCrab min baytik
Omar's idea is better than my idea.	فِكْرَة عُمَر أفْضَل مِنْ فِكْرَتي. fikrat A'omar afDal min fikratee

The superlative form of an adjective gives the meaning of the absolute preferred noun without comparing it to other nouns. In Arabic, the superlative adjective should precede the noun it is referring to. This allows the superlative to emphasize the highest degree of a quality without directly comparing it to other nouns. Examples in the spoken Modern Standard Arabic:

Meaning	Superlative Phrases
The best season is the Spring.	أَحْسَن فَصل هُوَ الرَبيع. aHsan faSl howa al-rabeeA'
The fastest animal is the leopard.	أَسْرَع حَيَوان هُوَ الفَهْد. asraA' Hayawaan howa al-fahd
That is the prettiest painting.	تِلْكَ أَجْمَل لَوْحَة. tilka ajmal lawHa
This is the happiest day of my life.	هٰذا أَسْعَد يَوْم في حَياتي. haadhaa asA'ad yawm fee Hayatee
The farthest house is your house.	أَبْعَد بَيْت هُوَ بَيْتُك. abA'ad bayt howa baytok
This is the strangest story.	هٰذِهِ أَغْرَب قِصَّة. haathihi aGHrab CiSSa
This is the prettiest dream.	هٰذا أَجْمَل حِلْم. haadhaa ajmal Hilm
He is the richest man.	هُوَ أَغْنـى رَجُل. howa aGHnaa rajol
She is the kindest woman.	هِيَ أَطْيَب إِمرَأَة. hiya aTyab imra,a

To say "My idea is the best", we start with the noun and simply add 'the' الـ (al) to the beginning of the superlative adjective. Examples in the spoken Modern Standard Arabic:

Meaning	Superlative Phrases
Spring is the prettiest.	الرَبِيع هُوَ الأجْمَل. al-rabeeA' howa al-ajmal
The leopard is the fastest.	الفَهد هُوَ الأسْرَع. al-fahd howa al-asraA'
The elephant is the heaviest.	الفيل هُوَ الأثْقَل. al-feel howa al-athCal
Today is the coldest.	اليَوم هُوَ الأبْرَد. al-yawm howa al-abrad
My mother is the kindest.	أُمّي هِيَ الأطيَب. ommee hiya al-aTyab
My idea is the best.	فِكْرَتي هِيَ الأحْسَن. fikratee hiya al-aHsan
Your voice is the strongest. (to a male)	صَوْتُكَ هُوَ الأقْوى. sawtoka howa al-aCwaa
Your voice is the prettiest. (to a female)	صَوْتُكِ هُوَ الأجْمَل. sawtoki howa al-ajmal
My plan is the best.	خِطَّتي هِيَ الأفْضَل. KHiTTAtee hiya al-afDal

More examples of comparatives and superlatives that are derived from simple adjectives in the spoken modern standard Arabic:

Meaning	Comparatives or Superlatives	Meaning	Feminine adjectives	Masculine adjectives
Bigger	أَكْبَر akbar	Big	كَبيرَة kabeera	كَبير kabeer
Smaller	أَصْغَر aSGHar	Small	صَغيرَة saGHeera	صَغير saGHeer
Taller	أَطْوَل aTwal	Tall	طَويلة Taweela	طَويل Taweel
Shorter	أَقْصَر aCSar	Short	قَصيرة CaSeera	قَصير CaSeer
Fatter	أَسْمَن asman	Fat	سَمينة sameena	سَمين sameen
Skinnier	أَنْحَل anHal	Thin	نَحيلة naHeela	نَحيل naHeel
Prettier	أَجْمَل ajmal	Beautiful	جَميلة jameela	جَميل jameel
Uglier	أَقْبَح aCbaH	Ugly	قَبيحة CabeeHa	قَبيح CabeeH
More handsome	أَوْسَم awsam	Handsome	used only for male	وَسيم waseem
More generous / More honorable	أَكْرَم akram	Generous / Honorable	كَريمة kareema	كَريم kareem

Meaning	Comparatives or Superlatives	Meaning	Feminine adjectives	Masculine adjectives
Stingier	أَبْخَل abkhal	Stingy	بَخيلة bakheela	بَخيل bakheel
Stranger / Weirder	أغْرَب aGHrab	Strange / Weird	غَريبة GHareeba	غَريب GHareeb
More Incredible / More unbelievable	أعْجَب aA'jab	Incredible / Unbelievable	عَجيبَة A'ajeeba	عَجيب A'ajeeb
Nicer	ألْطَف alTaf	Nice	لَطيفة laTeefa	لَطيف laTeef
Meaner	ألأَم al,am	Mean	لَئيمة la,eema	لَئيم la,eem
More expensive	أثْمَن athman	Expensive	ثَمينة thameena	ثَمين thameen
Cheaper	أرْخَص arKHaS	Cheap	رَخيصة raKHeeSa	رَخيص raKHeeS
Closer	أقْرَب aCrab	Close	قَريبة Careeba	قَريب Careeb
Farther	أبْعَد abA'ad	Far	بَعيدة baA'eeda	بَعيد baA'eed
Older	أقْدَم aCdam	Old / Ancient	قَديمة Cadeema	قَديم Cadeem

Meaning	Compara-tives or Superlatives	Meaning	Feminine adjectives	Masculine adjectives
Newer	أَجْدَد ajdad	New	جَديدة jadeeda	جَديد jadeed
Wiser	أَحْكَم aHkam	Wise	حَكيمة Hakeema	حَكيم Hakeem
More ignorant	أَجْهَل ajhal	Ignorant	جاهِلة jaahila	جاهِل jaahil
More stub-born	أَعْنَد aA'nad	Stubborn	عَنيدة A'aneeda	عَنيد A'aneed
Greater	أَعْظَم aA'DHam	Great	عَظيمة A'aDHeema	عَظيم A'aDHeem
Simpler	أَبْسَط absaT	Simple	بَسيطة baseeTa	بَسيط baseeT
Richer	أَغْنى aGHnaa	Rich	غَنِيّة GHaniyya	غَنِيّ GHaniyy
Poorer	أَفْقَر afCar	Poor	فَقيرة faCeera	فَقير faCeer
Dearest	أَعَزّ aA'az	Dear	عَزيزة A'azeeza	عَزيز A'azeez
Virtuous	أَطْهَر aThar	Virtue	طاهِرة Taahira	طاهِر Taahir

Lesson Nineteen
Adverbs

Adverbs are words that modify or describe parts of a sentence, excluding nouns. Adjectives modify nouns, while adverbs can modify verbs, adjectives, or other adverbs within a phrase or sentence. They provide information about how, when, where, or for how long an action occurred. Most adverbs are derived from masculine nouns or simple adjectives.

To form an adverb in Arabic, the letter "alif" ‏ا‎ with two "fatHas" is added to the end of the noun or adjective, serving as the main indicator for adverbs. In writing, adverbs ending with "alif" can be written with or without "tanween" (the doubling of the fatHa). The "tanween" is always pronounced but not written. Feminine adverbs end with a "closed taa" ‏ة‎, which is the typical feminine indicator but with two "fatHas" above it ‏ة‎.

Adverbs are placed after the verb or adjective they modify in a sentence. They can also come at the end of a sentence, except for the adverb "a lot" ‏جداً‎, which usually follows the word it modifies. If the adverb is derived from a noun or adjective that has the definite article "the" - "al" ‏ال‎, the "al" ‏ال‎ should be dropped before forming the adverb.

Below are examples of adverbs derived from simple adjectives and nouns in the spoken Modern Standard Arabic:

Adverbs		Adjectives	
Gently	‏لَطيفاً‎ laTeefan	Gentle	‏لَطيف‎ laTeef
Smoothly	‏ناعِماً‎ naaA'iman	Smooth	‏ناعِم‎ naaA'im
Further	‏بَعيداً‎ baA'eedan	Far	‏بَعيد‎ baA'eed

Adverbs		Adjectives	
Closely	قَرِيباً Careeban	Close	قَرِيب Careeb
In the morning	صَباحاً SabaHan	Morning	صَباح SabaH
In the evening	مَساءاً masaa,an	Evening	مَساء masaa,
In the summer	صَيْفاً Sayfan	Summer	صَيْف Sayf
In the winter	شِتاءاً shitaa,an	Winter	شِتاء shitaa,
Beautifully	جَميلاً jameelan	Beautiful	جَميل jameel
Quickly	سَريعاً sareeA'an	Quick	سَريع sareeA'
Slowly	بَطيئاً baTee,an	Slow	بَطيء baTee,
Well	جَيِّداً jayyidan	Good	جَيِّد jayyid
Happily	سَعيداً saA'eedan	Happy	سَعيد saA'eed
Sadly	حَزيناً Hazeenan	Sad	حَزين Hazeen

Adverbs		Adjectives	
Patiently	صَبوراً **Sabooran**	Patient	صَبور **Saboor**
Kindly	لَطيفاً **laTeefan**	Kind	لَطيف **laTeef**
Bravely	شُجاعاً **shojaAan**	Brave	شُجاع **shojaA**

In the table below, notice the difference between the adjectives that describe the nouns in the first table, and the adverbs that describe the verbs in the second table.

Examples in the spoken Modern Standard Arabic:

Adverbs Phrases Modern Standard Arabic	Adjective and Noun Phrases Modern Standard Arabic
أَسْكُن بَعيداً مِن هُنا. askon baA'eedan min honaa I live further from here.	أَسْكُن في بَيْت بَعيد مِن هُنا. askon fee bayt baA'eed min honaa I live in a house far from here.
أَعْمَل قَريباً مِن هُنا. aA'mal Careeban min honaa I work closely from here.	أَعْمَل في مَطْعَم قَريب. aA'mal fee maTAam Careeb I work in a close restaurant.
رَشيد يَعْزِف جَميلاً. rasheed yaA'zif jameelan Rasheed plays music beautifully.	رَشيد في عَزْفِهِ جَميل. rasheed fee A'azfihi jameel Rasheed in playing his music is beautiful.
أَلْفَت تُفَكِّر سَريعاً. olfat tofakkir sareeA'an Ulfat thinks quickly.	أَلْفَت سَريعَة في التَفْكير. olfat sareeA'a fee al-tafkeer Ulfat is a quick thinker.

Lesson Twenty
The Construct Phrase

The construct phrase is a way of expressing the relationship between two or more nouns in a sentence, indicating a relationship between them. This relationship can be one of ownership, blood ties, possession, or any other kind of association between the nouns.

In Arabic, the construct phrase is formed differently compared to English. Arabic does not utilize the possessive apostrophe 's' to denote the relationship between the nouns. Instead, the word "of" is employed to convey the same meaning. This translation from Arabic to English accurately reflects the construct phrase in spoken Modern Standard Arabic.

كِتاب الطّالِبة	بَيْت الأمير	صَديق الطالِب
kitaab a-TTaliba	bayt al-ameer	SadeeC a-TTalib
Book of the female student	House of the prince	Friend of the student

In spoken Modern Standard Arabic, the direct translation from Arabic to English in the example sentences below reflects the usage of the construct phrase.

Translation	Word by Word Translation	Modern Standard Arabic
Sara's friend is tall.	The friend of Sara is tall.	صَديقَة سارة طَويلَة. SadeeCat sara Taweela
The research subject is strange.	The subject of the research is strange.	مَوضوع البَحث غَريب. mawDooA' al-baHth GHareeb
This is my home address.	This is the address of my home.	هٰذا عِنْوان بَيْتي. hadha A'inwaan baytee
My friend's home is close.	The home of my friend is close.	بَيْت صاحِبَتي قَريب. bayt SaaHibatee Careeb

168

Translation	Word by Word Translation	Modern Standard Arabic
The teacher's office is big.	The office of the teacher is big.	مَكْتَب الأسْتاذ كَبير. maktab al-ostaadh kabeer
Today's weather is nice.	The weather of today is nice.	طَقس اليَوم لَطيف. TaCs al-yawm lateef
The lemon taste is sour.	The taste of the lemon is sour.	طَعم اليَّمون حامِض. TaA'm al-laymoon HaamiD
The lemon color is yellow.	The color of the lemon is yellow.	لَوْن اليَّمون أصّفَر. lawn al-laymoon aSfar
Autumn season is beautiful.	The season of autumn is beautiful.	فَصْل الْخَريف جَميل. faSl al-KHareef jameel
My family's house is beautiful.	The house of my family is beautiful.	بَيْت عائِلَتي جَميل. bayt A'a,ilatee jameel
Rasheed's promise is truthful.	The promise of Rasheed is truthful.	وَعْد رَشيد صادِق. waA'd rasheed SaadiC

- **Note:** The first word in the relationship does not take the definite sign 'the' 'al' الـ, it is definite by the meaning without 'the' 'al' الـ. However, the second noun in the construct phrase can take 'the' 'al' الـ or any possessive pronoun.

- The pronunciation of the closed "ta" (ة) as a regular "ta" (ت) in construct phrases is an exception to the general rule of not common to pronounce the closed "ta" in spoken Arabic. In spoken Arabic, the closed "ta" is often not pronounced at the end of a feminine word, but when forming construct phrases, it is pronounced as a regular "ta" for the purpose of connecting the words together

Examples in the spoken Modern Standard Arabic:

Translation	Word by Word Translation	Modern Standard Arabic
The bird's garden is amazing.	The garden of the birds is amazing.	حَديقَة الطُيور رائِعَة. HadeeCat al-Toyoor raa,iA'a
My family's tradition is old.	The tradition of my family is old.	عادَة عائِلَتي قَديمَة. A'adat A'a,ilatee Cadeema
Fatima's picture is beautiful.	The picture of Fatima is beautiful.	صورَة فاطِمَة جَميلَة. Soorat faTima jameela
The guest room is spacious.	The room of the guest is spacious.	غُرْفَة الضُّيوف واسِعَة. GHorfat al-Doyoof waasiA'a
My school's playground is not big.	The playground of my school is not big.	ساحَة مَدْرَسَتي لَيْسَت كَبيرَة. saahat madrasatee laysat kabeera
Natalia's idea is new.	The idea of Natalia is new.	فِكرَة نَتاليا جَديدَة. fikrat natalia jadeeda
Noor's plan is good.	The plan of Noor is good.	خِطّة نور جَيِّدَة. KHiTTat noor jayyida
Safa's cat is black.	The cat of Safa is black.	قِطّة صَفا سَوْداء. CiTTat Safa sawdaa,
Sara's dog is white.	The dog of Sara is white.	كَلْبَة سارَة بَيْضاء. kalbat Sara byaDaa,
Youse's job is great.	The job of yousef is great.	مِهْنَة يوسِف عَظيمَة. mihnat yousef A'aDHeema

Translation	Word by Word Translation	Modern Standard Arabic
Rasheed's talent is wonderful.	The talent of Rasheed is wonderful.	مَوْهِبَة رَشيد رائِعَة. mawhibat rasheed raa,iA'a
The fruit's benefit is a lot.	The benefit of the fruits is a lot.	فائِدَة الفاكِهَة كَثيرَة. fa,idat al-fakiha katheera
The story's ending is happy.	The ending of the story is happy.	نِهاية الْقِصَّة سَعيدَة. nihaayet al-CiSSa saA'eeda

If the construct phrase consists of two or more nouns that share a relationship, then only the last noun can take the definite sign 'the' 'al' ال or a possessive pronoun.

Examples in the spoken modern standard Arabic below:

Translation	Word by Word Translation	Modern Standard Arabic
The eye's doctor's report is comforting.	The report of the doctor of the eyes is comforting.	تَقْرير طَبيب العُيون مُريح. taCreer Tabeeb al-A'oyoon moreeH
The Arabic class teacher is new.	The teacher of the class of the Arabic is new.	أُسْتاذ صَفّ العَرَبيَّة جَديد. ostaadh Saff al-A'arabiyyah jadeed
My husband family's tradition is old.	The tradition of the family of my husband is old.	عادَة عائِلَة زَوْجي قَديمَة. A'adat A'a,ilat zawjee Cadeema
My house guest room is spacious.	The room of the guest of my house is spacious.	غُرْفَة ضُيوف بَيْتي واسِعَة. GHorfat Doyoof baytee wasiA'a

Lesson Twenty-One
The Arabic Sentence

In Arabic, a sentence can be expressed in two ways: nominal or verbal.

A nominal sentence is one that begins with a noun or a pronoun, while **a verbal sentence** starts with a verb. Both forms can convey the same meaning in Arabic but with a different word order.

Verbal sentences in Arabic encompass various tenses such as present, past, and future, as well as the imperative or command form of verbs.

In Arabic, the tense of a verb is indicated by specific letters known as "letters of increase." These letters serve the purpose of indicating the time frame of an action, whether it is in the present, past, or future. Additionally, they also represent the subject of the verb.

In Arabic, the subject of a verb is inherently incorporated within the verb itself and cannot be separated from it. However, it is also possible to express the subject of the verb as a separate noun or pronoun in addition to the one already included in the verb. This is done to enhance clarity and emphasize the subject of the verb.

In a nominal sentence, when the subject is a noun or a pronoun that comes before the verb, the verb must agree in its singular, dual, or plural form, as well as in gender, with the noun or pronoun. However, if the subject refers to a plural object or a plural animal, the verb must be in the singular feminine form. This applies to the following four examples:

1. The cats eat. (القِطَط تَأْكُل)
2. The doors close. (الأبواب تُغلَق)
3. The flowers bloom. (الزُهُور تَتَفَتَّح)
4. The birds fly. (الطُيُور تَطِير)

• **In spoken Modern Standard Arabic (MSA), the plural masculine form is commonly used instead of the dual and feminine plural forms. The dual and feminine plural forms are more commonly found in Classical Arabic and are used in formal and poetic contexts.**

• The example sentences provided in the tables for this lesson are all written in Classical Arabic form, which means they are fully vocalized.

Meaning	Nominal Sentence/Classic Arabic
Rashid is playing in the garden.	راشِدٌ يَلْعَبُ فِي أَلْحَدِيقَةِ. Rashidon yalA'abo fee al-HadeeCati
He is playing in the garden.	هُوَ يَلْعَبُ فِي أَلْحَدِيقَةِ. howa yalA'abo fee al-HadeeCati
Ayah is studying at the library.	آيَةَ تَدْرُسُ فِي أَلْمَكْتَبَةِ. aayah tadroso fee al-maktabati
She is studying at the library.	هِيَ تَدْرُسُ فِي أَلْمَكْتَبَةِ. hiya tadroso fee al-maktabati
Mohammad works in a company.	مُحَمَّدٌ يَعْمَلُ فِي شَرِكَةٍ. moHammadon yaA'malo fee sharikatin
He works in a company.	هُوَ يَعْمَلُ فِي شَرِكَةٍ. howa yaA'malo fee sharikatin
The boys like swimming.	الأولادُ يُحِبّونَ أَلسِّباحَةَ. al-awlaado yoHiboona al-sibaaHata
They like swimming.	هُمْ يُحِبّونَ أَلسِّباحَةَ. hom yoHiboona al-sibaaHata
The girls like swimming.	البناتُ يُحْبِبْنَ أَلسِباحَةَ. al-banaato yoHbibna al-sibaaHata
They like swimming.	هُنَّ يُحْبِبْنَ أَلسِباحَةَ. honna yoHbibna al-sibaaHata

Meaning	Nominal Sentence/Classic Arabic
The birds travel far. (non-person plural)	الطُّيورُ تُهاجِرُ بَعيداً. al-Toyooro tohaajiro baA'eedan
She travels far. (non-person plural)	هِيَ تُهاجِرُ بَعيداً. hiya tohaajiro baA'eedan
The giraffes eat the tree leaves. (non-person plural)	الزَّرافاتُ تَأْكُلُ أوْراقَ ٱلشَّجَرِ. al-zaraafaato ta,kolo awraaCa al-shajari
She eats the tree leaves. (non-person plural)	هِيَ تَأْكُلُ أوْراقَ ٱلشَّجَرِ. hiya ta,kolo awraaCa al-shajari

In a verbal sentence, the verb comes before the subject. The verb should be in the singular form regardless of the number of the subject. However, in a verbal sentence, the verb should agree with the subject in terms of gender. Unless the noun is a non-person plural, in which case the verb must be in the singular feminine form. This rule applies to the last eight examples below.

Meaning	Verbal Sentence/Classic Arabic
The boy is playing in the garden.	يَلْعَبُ ٱلْوَلَدُ في ٱلْحَديقَةِ. yalA'abo al-walado fee al-HadeeCati
He is playing in the garden.	يَلْعَبُ هُوَ في ٱلْحَديقَةِ. yalA'abo howa fee al-HadeeCati
The girl is studying at the library.	تَدْرُسُ ٱلْبِنْتُ في ٱلْمَكْتَبَةِ. tadroso al-binto fee al-maktabati
She is studying at the library.	تَدْرُسُ هِيَ في ٱلْمَكْتَبَةِ. tadroso hiya fee al-maktabati

Meaning	Verbal Sentence/Classic Arabic
Mohammad works in a restaurant.	يَعْمَلُ مَحَمَّدٌ في مَطْعَمٍ. yaA'malo moHammadon fee maTA'amin
The boys like swimming.	يُحِبُّ ٱلْأَوْلادُ ٱلسِباحَةَ. yoHibbo al-awlaado al-sibaaHata
The girls like swimming.	تُحِبُّ ٱلْبناتُ ٱلسِباحَةَ. toHibbo al-banaato al-sibaaHata
The fish swim deep in the sea. (non-person plural)	تَسْبَحُ ٱلْأَسْماكُ عَميقاً في ٱلْبَحْرِ. tasbaHo al-asmaako A'ameeCan fee al-baHri
The stars swim in space. (non-person plural)	تَسْبَحُ ٱلنُّجومُ في ٱلْفَضاءِ. tasbaHo al-nojoomo fee al-faDaa,i
The eagles fly high in the sky. (non-person plural)	تَطيرُ ٱلنُّسورُ عالِياً في ٱلسَّماءِ. taTeero al-nosooro A'aliyan fee al-samaa,i
The birds travel far. (non-person plural)	تُهاجِرُ ٱلطُّيورُ بَعيداً. tohaajiro al-Toyooro baA'eedan
She travels far. (non-person plural)	تُهاجِرُ هِيَ بَعيداً. tohaajiro hiya baA'eedan
The giraffes eat the tree leaves. (non-person plural)	تَأْكُلُ ٱلزَّرافاتُ أَوْراقَ ٱلشَّجَرِ. ta,kolo al-zaraafaato awraaCa al-shajari
She eats the tree leaves. (non-person plural)	تَأْكُلُ هِيَ أَوْراقَ ٱلشَّجَرِ. ta,kolo hiya awraaCa al-shajari
The rain falls. (non-person plural)	تَسْقُطُ ٱلْأَمْطارُ. tasCoTo al-amTaaro

Lesson Twenty-Two
The Present Verb

The present verb in Arabic represents an ongoing action or state that has not been completed yet. Both the simple present tense and the present continuous tense are expressed in a similar manner in Arabic.

Arabic is a language that utilizes a root system, where most words are derived from a three-letter root. Each word family in Arabic is based on a specific core of three letters, which can be expanded by adding certain letters known as "letters of increase." These letters contribute to the formation of additional words within the word family.

• The letters of increase in Arabic are a total of nine letters, along with a symbol called 'shaddah'. These letters are:

ش	ة	ت	ن	س	م	ي	و	ا	أ
shaddeh	t	t	n	s	m	ee/y	oo/w	aa	a

From these nine letters, six letters are used to form the present verb in Arabic. These six letters are:

ون	ين	ان	ن	ي	ت	أ
oon	een	aan	n	ee/y	t	a

These letters are indeed added to the core of the word to build the present tense in Arabic. They serve a dual purpose: they are not only modify the verb to indicate the present tense, but they also serve as pronouns attached to the verb itself, representing the subject of the verb. This unique feature of the Arabic language allows the subject of the verb to be incorporated within the verb itself, creating a compact and integrated structure. As a result, the subject and the verb are seamlessly connected in the present verb form, emphasizing the unity between the subject and the action or state expressed by the verb.

To form the present verb and its subject, the three-letter root of the word remains unchanged, maintaining the same order of letters. However, one or more of the nine letters of increase are added to the beginning and the end of the root. These additional letters modify the verb to express the present tense and include the subject within the verb itself. This approach ensures consistency and predictability in constructing present verbs from their root words.

- **In spoken Modern Standard Arabic (MSA), the plural masculine form is commonly used instead of the dual and feminine plural forms. The dual and feminine plural forms are more commonly found in Classical Arabic and are used in formal and poetic contexts.**

The examples provided in the tables below for this lesson are all in spoken Modern Standard Arabic. Consequently, the words are presented without vowel markings at the end.

The present tense conjugations for the verb "to live" with the root ع ي ش:

أ (a)	Is added to the beginning of the root and it represents the subject of the verb 'I', (أعيش / I live).
تَـ (t)	Is added to the beginning of the root and it represents the subject of the verb (you, masculine), (تَعيش / you live).
ين (een)	Is added to the end of the root plus the prefix تَـ at the beginning, to represent the subject of the verb (you, feminine), (تَعيشين / you live).
ان (aan)	Is added to the end of the root and it represents the dual subject of the verb (you) plus the prefix تَـ at the beginning, to represent the subject of the verb (you, dual masculine and feminine) (تَعيشان / you both live).
ون (oon)	Is added to the end of the root and it changes the subject of the verb from singular to plural, plus adding the prefix تَـ at the beginning to represent the subject of the verb (you, plural masculine and feminine), (تَعيشون / you all live).

177

نَ (n)	Is added to the end of the root and it changes the subject of the verb from singular to plural, plus adding the prefix تَ at the beginning to represent the subject of the verb (you, plural feminine), (تَعِشْنَ / you all live).
نَـ (n)	Is added to the beginning of the root and it represents the subject of the verb 'we' (نَعيش / we live).
يَـ (y)	Is added to the beginning of the root and it represents the subject of the verb 'he' (يَعيش / he lives).
تَـ (t)	Is added to the beginning of the root and it represents the subject of the verb 'she' (تَعيش / she lives).
ان (aan)	Is added to the end of the root and it represents the dual subject of the verb (they) plus the prefix يَـ at the beginning, to represent the subject of the verb (they, dual masculine and feminine) يَعيشان / they both live).
ون (oon)	Is added to the end of the root and it changes the subject of the verb from singular to plural, plus adding the prefix يَـ to represent the subject of the verb (they, masculine and feminine), (يَعيشون / they live).
نَ (n)	Is added to the end of the root and it changes the subject of the verb from singular to plural, plus adding the prefix يَـ at the beginning to represent the subject of the verb (they, plural feminine), (يَعِشْنَ / they live).

The present tense conjugations for the verb "to study" with the root د ر س:

Meaning	Present Tense		Subject Pronoun
I study. I am studying.	أنا أَدْرُسُ. anaa adros	I	أنا anaa
You study. You are studying.	أنتَ تَدْرُسُ. anta tadros	You (masculine)	أنتَ anta
You study. You are studying.	أنتِ تَدْرُسين. anti tadroseen	You (feminine)	أنتِ anti
You both study. You are both studying.	أنتُما تَدْرُسان. antomaa tadrosaan	You (dual, masculine and feminine)	أنْتُما antomaa
You all study. You are all studying.	أنتُم تَدْرُسون. antom tadrosoon	You (plural, masculine and feminine)	أنتُم antom
You all study. You are all studying.	أنْتُنَّ تَدْرُسْن. antonna tadrosn	You (plural, feminine)	أنْتُنَّ antonna
We study. We are studying.	نَحْنُ نَدْرُسُ. naHno nadros	We (masculine and feminine)	نَحْنُ naHno
He studies. He is studying.	هُوَ يَدْرُسُ. howa yadros	He/it	هُوَ howa
She studies. She is studying.	هِيَ تَدْرُسُ. hiya tadros	She/it	هِيَ hiya
They both study. They are both studying.	هُما يَدْرُسان. homaa yadrosaan	They (dual, masculine and feminine)	هُما homaa

Meaning	Present Tense	Subject Pronoun	
They study. They are studying.	هُمْ يَدْرُسُون. hom yadrosoon	They (plural, masculine and feminine)	هُمْ hom
They study. They are studying.	هُنَّ يَدْرُسْن. honna yadrosn	They (feminine)	هُنَّ honna

The present tense conjugations for the verb "to write" with the root ك ت ب:

Meaning	Present Tense	Meaning	Subject Pronoun
I write. I am writing.	أَنا أَكْتُب. anaa aktob	I	أَنا anaa
You write. You are writing.	أَنتَ تَكْتُب. anta taktob	You (masculine)	أَنتَ anta
You write. You are writing.	أَنتِ تَكْتُبِين. anti taktobeen	You (feminine)	أَنتِ anti
You both write. You are both writing.	أَنتُمَا تَكْتُبَان. antomaa taktobaan	You (dual, masculine and feminine)	أَنتُمَا antomaa
You all write. You are all writing.	أَنتُم تَكْتُبُون. antom taktoboon	You (plural, masculine and feminine)	أَنتُم antom
You all write. You are all writing.	أَنْتُنَّ تَكْتُبْن. antonna taktobn	You (plural, feminine)	أَنْتُنَّ antonna

Meaning	Present Tense	Meaning	Subject Pronoun
We write. We are writing.	نَحنُ نَكتُب. naHno naktob	We (masculine and feminine)	نَحنُ naHno
He writes. He is writing.	هُوَ يكتُب. howa yaktob	He/it	هُوَ howa
She writes. She is writing.	هِي تَكتُب. hiya taktob	She/it	هِي hiya
They both write. You are both writing.	هُما يَكتُبان. homaa yaktobaan	They (dual, masculine and feminine)	هُما homaa
They write. They are writing.	هُم يكتُبون. hom yaktoboon	They (plural, masculine and feminine)	هُم hom
They write. They are writing.	هُنَّ يكتُبن. honna yaktobn	They (plural, feminine)	هُنَّ honna

The present tense conjugations for the verb "to go" with the root ذ هـ ب:

Meaning	Present Tense	Meaning	Subject Pro-noun
I go. I am going.	أنا أَذْهَب. anaa adh-hab	I	أنا anaa
You go. You are going.	أنتَ تَذْهَب. anta tadh-hab	You (masculine)	أنتَ anta

Meaning	Present Tense	Meaning	Subject Pronoun
You go. You are going.	أَنتِ تَذْهَبين. anti tadh-habeen	You (feminine)	أَنتِ anti
You both go. You are both going.	أَنتُما تَذْهَبانِ. antomaa tadh-habaan	You (dual, masculine and feminine)	أَنتُما antomaa
You all go. You are all going.	أَنتُم تَذْهَبونَ. antom tadh-haboon	You (plural, masculine and feminine)	أَنتُم antom
You all go. You are all going.	أَنْتُنَّ تَذْهَبْنَ. antonna tadh-habna	You (plural, feminine)	أَنْتُنَّ antonna
We go. We are going.	نَحنُ نَذْهَب. naHno nadh-hab	We (masculine and feminine)	نَحنُ naHno
He goes. He is going.	هُوَ يَذْهَب. howa yadh-hab	He/it	هُوَ howa
She goes. She is going.	هِيَ تَذْهَب. hiya tadh-hab	She/it	هِيَ hiya
They both go. You are both going.	هُما يَذْهَبانِ. homaa yadh-habaan	They (dual, masculine and feminine)	هُما homaa
They go. They are going.	هُم يَذْهَبونَ. hom yadh-haboon	They (plural, masculine and feminine)	هُم hom
They go. They are going.	هُنَّ يَذْهَبْنَ. honna yadh-habna	They (plural, feminine)	هُنَّ honna

The present tense conjugations for the verb "to understand" with the root: ف هـ م

Meaning	Present Tense	Meaning	Subject Pronoun
I understand. I am understanding.	أَنَا أَفْهَم. ana afham	I	أَنَا anaa
You understand. You are understanding.	أَنتَ تَفْهَم. anta tafham	You (masculine)	أَنتَ anta
You understand. You are understanding.	أَنتِ تَفْهَمين. anti tafhameen	You (feminine)	أَنتِ anti
You both understand. You are both understanding.	أَنتُما تَفْهَمان. antomaa tafhamaan	You (dual, masculine and feminine)	أَنتُما antomaa
You all understand. You are all understanding.	أَنتُم تَفْهَمون. antom tafhamoon	You (plural, (masculine and feminine)	أَنتُم antom
You all understand. You are all understanding.	أَنْتُنَّ تَفْهَمْنَ. antonna tafhamna	You (plural, feminine)	أَنْتُنَّ antonna
We understand. We are understanding.	نَحنُ نَفْهَم. naHno nafham	We (masculine and feminine)	نَحنُ naHno
He understands. He is understanding.	هُوَ يَفْهَم. howa yafham	He/it	هُوَ howa

Meaning	Present Tense	Meaning	Subject Pronoun
She understands. She is understanding.	هِيَ تَفْهَم. hiya tafham	She/it	هِيَ hiya
They both understand. They are both understanding.	هُمَا يَفْهَمَان. homaa yafhamaan	They (dual, masculine and feminine)	هُمَا homaa
They understand. They are understanding.	هُم يَفْهَمُون. hom yafhamoon	They (plural, masculine and feminine)	هُم hom
They understand. They are understanding.	هُنَّ يَفْهَمْن. honna yafhamn	They (plural, feminine)	هُنَّ honna

- When the subject of the verb is plural and feminine, and the letter 'ي' (ya) is part of the root in the middle of the word, the 'ي' (ya) is replaced with a 'kasrah   vowel.

- The prefixes representing the subject of the present verb for both "you" (masculine) and "she" are the same.

- **Keep in mind that while practicing reading, Arabic is cursive and is read and written from right to left.**

- **Note, refer to page six for a refresher on the pronunciation system used in this book.**

Lesson Twenty-Three
Negating the Present Verb

The present tense is negated by using 'laa' **لا**, which immediately precedes the present verb.

- The examples in the tables for this lesson are all in the spoken Modern Standard Arabic, which means the last letter in each word is not vocalized.

- **In spoken Modern Standard Arabic (MSA), the plural masculine form is commonly used instead of the dual and feminine plural forms. The dual and feminine plural forms are more commonly found in Classical Arabic and are used in formal and poetic contexts.**

Negating the verb "to live" in the present tense. The root for the verb is **ع ي ش**:

Negating the Present Tense Modern Standard Arabic	Present Tense Sentences Modern Standard Arabic
أنا لا أعيش في كَليفورنيا. **anaa laa aA'eesh fee california** I do not live in California. I am not living in California.	أنا أعيش في كَليفورنيا. **anaa aA'eesh fee california** I live in California. I am living in California.
أنْتَ لا تَعيش في كَليفورنيا. **anta laa taA'eesh fee california** You do not live in California. You are not living in California. (singular, masculine)	أنْتَ تَعيش في كَليفورنيا. **anta taA'eesh fee california** You live in California. You are living in California. (singular, masculine)
أنْتِ لا تَعيشي في كَليفورنيا. **anti laa taA'eeshee fee california** You do not live in California. You are not living in California. (singular, feminine)	أنْتِ تَعيشين في كَليفورنيا. **anti taA'eesheen fee california** You live in California. You are living in California. (singular, feminine)

Negating the Present Tense Modern Standard Arabic	Present Tense Sentences Modern Standard Arabic
أَنْتُما لا تَعيشا في كَليفورنيا. antomaa laa taA'eeshaa fee california You both do not live in California. You are both not living in California. (dual, masculine and feminine)	أَنْتُما تَعيشان في كَليفورنيا. antomaa taA'eeshan fee california You both live in a California. You are both living in California. (dual, masculine and feminine)
أَنْتُم لا تَعيشوا في كَليفورنيا. antom laa taA'eeshoo fee california You all do not live in California. You are all not living in California. (plural, masculine and feminine)	أَنْتُم تَعيشون في كَليفورنيا. antom taA'eeshoon fee california You all live in California. You are all living in California. (plural, masculine and feminine)
أَنْتُنَّ لا تَعِشْنَ في كَليفورنيا. antonna laa taA'ishna fee california You all do not live in California. You are all not living in California (plural, feminine)	أَنْتُنَّ تَعِشْنَ في كَليفورنيا. antonna taA'ishna fee california You all live in California. You are all living in California. (plural, feminine)
نَحْنُ لا نَعيش في كَليفورنيا. naHno laa naA'eesh fee california We do not live in California. We are not living in California.	نَحْنُ نَعيش في كَليفورنيا. naHno naA'eesh fee california We live in California. We are living in California.
هُوَ لا يَعيش في كَليفورنيا. howa laa yaA'eesh fee california He does not live in California. He is not living in California.	هُوَ يَعيش في كَليفورنيا. howa yaA'eesh fee california He lives in California. He is living in California.
هِيَ لا تَعيش في كَليفورنيا. hiya laa taA'eesh fee california She does not live in California. She is not living in California.	هِيَ تَعيش في كَليفورنيا. hiya taA'eesh fee california She lives in California. She is living in California.

Negating the Present Tense Modern Standard Arabic	Present Tense Sentences Modern Standard Arabic
هُما لا يَعيشا في كَليفورنيا. homaa laa yaA'eeshaa fee california They both do not live in California. They are both not living in California. (dual, masculine and feminine)	هُما يَعيشان في كَليفورنيا. homaa yaA'eeshan fee california They both live in California. They are both living in California. (dual, masculine and feminine)
هُم لا يَعيشوا في كَليفورنيا. hom laa yaA'eeshoo fee california They do not live in California. They are not living in California. (plural, masculine and feminine)	هُم يَعيشون في كَليفورنيا. hom yaA'eeshoon fee california They live in California. They are living in California. (plural, masculine and feminine)
هُنَّ لا يَعِشْنَ في كَليفورنيا. honna laa yaA'ishna fee california They do not live in California. They are not living in California. (plural, feminine)	هُنَّ يَعِشْنَ في كَليفورنيا. honna yaA'ishna fee california They live in a California. They are living in California. (plural, feminine)

Negating the verb "to study' in the present tense. The root for the verb is د ر س:

Negating the Present Tense Modern Standard Arabic	Present Tense Sentences Modern Standard Arabic
 anaa laa adros fee al-maktaba I do not study at the library. I am not studying at the library.	 anaa adros fee al-maktaba I study at the library. I am studying at the library.
 anta laa tadros fee al-maktaba You do not study at the library. You are not studying at the library. (singular, masculine)	 anta tadros fee al-maktaba You study at the library. You are studying at the library. (singular, masculine)

Negating the Present Tense Modern Standard Arabic	Present Tense Sentences Modern Standard Arabic
أَنْتِ لا تَدْرُسِي فِي ٱلْمَكْتَبَة.	أَنْتِ تَدْرُسِين فِي ٱلْمَكْتَبَة.
anti laa tadrosee fee al-maktaba You do not study at the library. You are not studying at the library. (singular, feminine)	anti tadroseen fee al-maktaba You study at the library. You are studying at the library. (singular, feminine)
أَنْتُمَا لا تَدْرُسا فِي ٱلْمَكْتَبَة.	أَنْتُمَا تَدْرُسان فِي ٱلْمَكْتَبَة.
antomaa laa tadrosaa fee al-maktaba You both do not study at the library. You are both not studying at the library. (dual, masculine and feminine)	antomaa tadrosaan fee al-makta-ba You both study at the library. You are both studying at the li-brary. (dual, masculine and feminine)
أَنْتُم لا تَدْرُسوا فِي ٱلْمَكْتَبَة.	أَنْتُم تَدْرُسون فِي ٱلْمَكْتَبَة.
antom laa tadrosoo fee al-maktaba You all do not study at the library. You are all not studying at the library. (plural, masculine and feminine)	antom tadrosoon fee al-maktaba You all study at the library. You are all studying at the library. (plural, masculine and feminine)
أَنْتُنَّ لا تَدْرُسْنَ فِي ٱلْمَكْتَبَة.	أَنْتُنَّ تَدْرُسْنَ فِي ٱلْمَكْتَبَة.
antonna laa tadrosna fee al-maktaba You all do not study at the library. You are all not studying at the library. (plural, feminine)	antonna tadrosna fee al-maktaba You all study at the library. You are all studying at the library. (plural, feminine)
نَحْنُ لا نَدْرُس فِي ٱلْمَكْتَبَة.	نَحْنُ نَدْرُس فِي ٱلْمَكْتَبَة.
naHno laa nadros fee al-maktaba We do not study at the library. We are not studying at the library.	naHno nadros fee al-maktaba We study at the library. We are studying at the library.
هُوَ لا يَدْرُس فِي ٱلْمَكْتَبَة.	هُوَ يَدْرُس فِي ٱلْمَكْتَبَة.
howa laa yadros fee al-maktaba He does not study at the library. He is not studying at the library.	howa yadros fee al-maktaba He studies at the library. He is studying at the library.
هِيَ لا تَدْرُس فِي ٱلْمَكْتَبَة.	هِيَ تَدْرُس فِي ٱلْمَكْتَبَة.
hiya laa tadros fee al-maktaba She does not study at the library. She is not studying at the library.	hiya tadros fee al-maktaba She studies at the library. She is studying at the library.

Negating the Present Tense Modern Standard Arabic	Present Tense Sentences Modern Standard Arabic
هُمَا لا يَدْرُسا في ٱلْمَكْتَبَة.	هُمَا يَدْرُسان في ٱلْمَكْتَبَة.
homaa laa yadrosaa fee al-maktaba They both do not study at the library. They are both not studying at the library. (dual, masculine and feminine)	homaa yadrosaan fee al-maktaba They both study at the library. They are both studying at the library. (dual, masculine and feminine)
هُمْ لا يَدْرُسوا في ٱلْمَكْتَبَة.	هُمْ يَدْرُسون في ٱلْمَكْتَبَة.
hom laa yadrosoo fee al-maktaba They do not study at the library. They are not studying at the library. (plural, masculine and feminine)	hom yadrosoon fee al-maktaba They study at the library. They are studying at the library. (plural, masculine and feminine)
هُنَّ لا يَدْرُسْنَ في ٱلْمَكْتَبَة.	هُنَّ يَدْرُسْنَ في ٱلْمَكْتَبَة.
honna laa yadrosna fee al-maktaba They do not study at the library. They are not studying at the library. (plural, feminine)	honna yadrosna fee al-maktaba They study at the library. They are studying at the library. (plural, feminine)

Negating the verb "to write' in the present tense. The root for the verb is ك ت ب:

Negating the Present Tense Modern Standard Arabic	Present Tense Sentences Modern Standard Arabic
أنَا لا أكْتُب رِسالَة.	أنَا أكْتُب رِسالَة.
anaa laa aktob risaala I do not write a letter. I am not writing a letter.	anaa aktob risaala I write a letter. I am writing a letter.
أنْتَ لا تَكْتُب رِسالَة.	أنْتَ تَكْتُب رِسالَة.
anta laa taktob risaala You do not write a letter. You are not writing a letter. (singular, masculine)	anta taktob risaala You write a letter. You are writing a letter. (singular, masculine)

أنْتِ لا تَكْتُبي رسالة.

anti laa taktobee risaala
You do not write a letter.
You are not writing a letter.
(singular, feminine)

أنْتِ تَكْتُبين رسالة.

anti taktobeen risaala
You write a letter.
You are writing a letter.
(singular, feminine)

أنْتُما لا تَكْتُبا رِسالة.

antomaa laa taktobaa risaala
You both do not write a letter.
You are both not writing a letter.
(dual, masculine and feminine)

أنْتُما تَكْتُبان رِسالَة.

antomaa taktobaan risaala
You both write a letter.
You are both writing a letter.
(dual, masculine and feminine)

أنْتُم لا تَكْتُبوا رسالة.

antom laa taktoboo risaala
You all do not write a letter.
You are all not writing a letter.
(plural, masculine and feminine)

أنْتُم تَكْتُبون رسالة.

antom taktoboon risaala
You all write a letter.
You are all writing a letter.
(plural, masculine and feminine)

أنْتُنَّ لا تَكْتُبْنَ رسالة.

antonna laa taktobna risaala
You all do not write a letter.
You are all not writing a letter.
(plural, feminine)

أنْتُنَّ تَكْتُبْنَ رسالَة.

antonna taktobna risaala
You all write a letter.
You are all writing a letter.
(plural, feminine)

نَحْنُ لا نَكْتُب رسالة.

naHno laa naktob risaala
We do not write a letter.
We are not writing a letter.

نَحْنُ نَكْتُب رسالَة.

naHno naktob risaala
We write a letter.
We are writing a letter.

هُوَ لا يَكْتُب رسالة.

howa laa yaktob risaala
He does not write a letter.
He is not writing a letter.

هُوَ يَكْتُب رسالة.

howa yaktob risaala
He writes a letter.
He is writing a letter.

هِيَ لا تَكْتُب رسالَة.

hiya laa taktob risaala
She does not write a letter.
She is not writing a letter.

هِيَ تَكْتُب رسالَة.

hiya taktob risaala
She writes a letter.
She is writing a letter.

Negating the Present Tense Modern Standard Arabic	Present Tense Sentences Modern Standard Arabic
هُمَا لَا يَكْتُبَا رِسَالَة. **homaa laa yaktobaa risaala** They both do not write a letter. They are both not writing a letter. (dual, masculine and feminine)	هُمَا يَكْتُبَان رِسَالَة. **homaa yaktobaan risaala** They both write a letter. They are both writing a letter. (dual, masculine and feminine)
هُم لَا يَكْتُبُوا رِسَالَة. **hom laa yaktoboo risaala** They do not write a letter. They are not writing a letter. (plural, masculine and feminine)	هُم يَكْتُبُون رِسَالَة. **hom yaktoboon risaala** They write a letter. They are writing a letter. (plural, masculine and feminine)
هُنَّ لَا يَكْتُبْنَ رِسَالَة. **honna laa yaktobna risaala** They do not write a letter. They are not writing a letter. (plural, feminine)	هُنَّ يَكْتُبْنَ رِسَالَة. **honna yaktobna risaala** They write a letter. They are writing a letter. (plural, feminine)

Negating the verb "to go" in the present tense. The root for the verb is ذ ـ هـ ـ ب:

Negating the Present Tense Modern Standard Arabic	Present Tense Sentences Modern Standard Arabic
أَنَا لَا أَذْهَب إِلَى ٱلْمَدْرَسَة. **anaa laa adh-hab ela al-madrasa** I do not go to school. I am not going to school.	أَنَا أَذْهَب إِلَى ٱلْمَدْرَسَة. **anaa adh-hab ela al-madrasa** I go to school. I am going to school.
أَنْتَ لَا تَذْهَب إِلَى ٱلْمَدْرَسَة. **anta laa tadh-hab ela al-madrasa** You do not go to school. You are not going to school. (singular, masculine)	أَنْتَ تَذْهَب إِلَى ٱلْمَدْرَسَة. **anta tadh-hab ela al-madrasa** You go to school. You are going to school. (singular, masculine)
أَنْتِ لَا تَذْهَبِي إِلَى ٱلْمَدْرَسَة. **anti laa tadh-habee ela al-madrasa** You do not go to school. You are not going to school. (singular, feminine)	أَنْتِ تَذْهَبِينَ إِلَى ٱلْمَدْرَسَة. **anti tadh-habeen ela al-madrasa** You go to school. You are going to school. (singular, feminine)

Negating the Present Tense Modern Standard Arabic	Present Tense Sentences Modern Standard Arabic
أَنتُمَا لا تَذْهَبا إلى ٱلْمَدْرَسَة.	أَنتُمَا تَذْهَبان إلى ٱلْمَدْرَسَة.
antomaa laa tadh-habaa ela al-madrasa You both do not go to school. You are both not going to school. (dual, masculine and feminine)	antomaa tadh-habaan ela al-madrasa You both go to school. You are both going to school. (dual, masculine and feminine)
أَنتُم لا تَذْهَبوا إلى ٱلْمَدْرَسَة.	أَنتُم تَذْهَبون إلى ٱلْمَدْرَسَة.
antom laa tadh-haboo ela al-madrasa You all do not go to school. You are all not going to school. (plural, masculine and feminine)	antom tadh-haboon ela al-madrasa You all go to school. You are all going to school. (plural, masculine and feminine)
أَنْتُنَّ لا تَذْهَبْنَ إلى ٱلْمَدْرَسَة.	أَنْتُنَّ تَذْهَبْنَ إلى ٱلْمَدْرَسَة.
antonna laa tadh-habna ela al-madrasa You all do not go to school. You are all not going to school. (plural, feminine)	antonna tadh-habna ela al-madrasa You all go to school. You are all going to school. (plural, feminine)
نَحنُ لا نَذْهَب إلى ٱلْمَدْرَسَة.	نَحنُ نَذْهَب إلى ٱلْمَدْرَسَة.
naHno laa nadh-hab ela al-madrasa We do not go to school. We are not going to school.	naHno nadh-hab ela al-madrasa We go to school. We are going to school.
هُوَ لا يَذْهَب إلى ٱلْمَدْرَسَة.	هُوَ يَذْهَب إلى ٱلْمَدْرَسَة.
howa laa yadh-hab ela al-madrasa He does not go to school. He is not going to school.	howa yadh-hab ela al-madrasa He goes to school. He is going to school.
هِيَ لا تَذْهَب إلى ٱلْمَدْرَسَة.	هِيَ تَذْهَب إلى ٱلْمَدْرَسَة.
hiya laa tadh-hab ela al-madrasa She does not go to school. She is not going to school.	hiya tadh-hab ela al-madrasa She goes to school. She is going to school.
هُما لا يَذْهَبا إلى ٱلْمَدْرَسَة.	هُما يَذْهَبان إلى ٱلْمَدْرَسَة.
homaa laa yadh-habaa ela al-madrasa They both do not go to school. They are both not going to school. (dual, masculine and feminine)	homaa yadh-habaan ela al-madrasa They both go to school. They are both going to school. (dual, masculine and feminine)

Negating the Present Tense **Modern Standard Arabic**	**Present Tense Sentences** **Modern Standard Arabic**
هُم لا يَذْهَبوا إلَى ٱلْمَدْرَسَة.	هُم يَذْهَبون إلَى ٱلْمَدْرَسَة.
hom laa yadh-haboo ela al-madrasa They do not go to school. They are not going to school. (plural, masculine and feminine)	hom yadh-haboon ela al-madrasa They go to school. They are going to school. (plural, masculine and feminine)
هُنَّ لا يَذْهَبْنَ إلَى ٱلْمَدْرَسَة.	هُنَّ يَذْهَبْنَ إلَى ٱلْمَدْرَسَة.
honna laa yadh-habna ela al-madrasa They do not go to school. They are not going to school. (plural, feminine)	honna yadh-habna ela al-madrasa They go to school. They are going to school. (plural, feminine)

Negating the verb "to understand' in the present tense. The root is :

Negating the Present Tense **Modern Standard Arabic**	**Present Tense Sentences** **Modern Standard Arabic**
أنا لا أفْهَم ٱلدَّرْس.	أنا أفْهَم ٱلدَّرْس.
anaa laa afham al-dars I do not understand the lesson. I am not understanding the lesson.	anaa afham al-dars I understand the lesson. I am understanding the lesson.
أنْتَ لا تَفْهَم ٱلدَّرْس.	أنْتَ تَفْهَم ٱلدَّرْس.
anta laa tafham al-dars You do not understand the lesson. You are not understanding the lesson. (singular, masculine)	anta tafham al-dars You understand the lesson. You are understanding the lesson. (singular, masculine)
أنْتِ لا تَفْهَمي ٱلدَّرْس.	أنْتِ تَفْهَمين ٱلدَّرْس.
anti laa tafhamee al-dars You do not understand the lesson. You are not understanding the lesson. (singular, feminine)	anti tafhameen al-dars You understand the lesson. You are understanding the lesson. (singular, feminine)

Negating the Present Tense Modern Standard Arabic	Present Tense Sentences Modern Standard Arabic
 أَنْتُمَا لَا تَفْهَمَا ٱلدَّرْس. **antomaa laa tafhamaa al-dars** You both do not understand the lesson. You are both not understanding the lesson. (dual, masculine and feminine)	 أَنْتُمَا تَفْهَمَان ٱلدَّرْس. **antomaa tafhamaan al-dars** You both understand the lesson. You are both understanding the lesson. (dual, masculine and feminine)
 أَنْتُم لَا تَفْهَمُوا ٱلدَرْس. **antom laa tafhamoo al-dars** You all do not understand the lesson. You are all not understanding the lesson. (plural, masculine and feminine)	أَنْتُم تَفْهَمُون ٱلدَرْس. **antom tafhamoon al-dars** You all understand the lesson. You are all understanding the lesson. (plural, masculine and feminine)
 أَنْتُنَّ لَا تَفْهَمْنَ ٱلدَرْس. **antonna laa tafhamna al-dars** You all do not understand the lesson. You are all not understanding the lesson. (plural, feminine)	 أَنْتُنَّ تَفْهَمْنَ ٱلدَرْس. **antonna tafhamna al-dars** You all understand the lesson. You are all understanding the lesson. (plural, feminine)
 نَحْنُ لَا نَفْهَم ٱلدَّرْس. **naHno laa nafham al-dars** We do not understand the lesson. We are not understanding the lesson.	 نَحنُ نَفْهَم ٱلدَّرْس. **naHno nafham al-dars** We understand the lesson. We are understanding the lesson.
 هُوَ لَا يَفْهَم ٱلدَّرْس. **howa laa yafham al-dars** He does not understand the lesson. He is not understanding the lesson.	 هُوَ يَفْهَم ٱلدَّرْس. **howa yafham al-dars** He understands the lesson. He is understanding the lesson.
 هِيَ لَا تَفْهَم ٱلدَّرْس. **hiya laa tafham al-dars** She does not understand the lesson. She is not understanding the lesson.	 هِيَ تَفْهَم ٱلدَّرْس. **hiya tafham al-dars** She understands the lesson. She is understanding the lesson.

Negating the Present Tense Modern Standard Arabic	Present Tense Sentences Modern Standard Arabic

هُما لا يَفْهَما ٱلدَّرْس.

homaa laa yafhamaa al-dars

They both do not understand the lesson.
They are both not understanding the lesson.
(dual, masculine and feminine)

هُما يَفْهَمان ٱلدَّرْس.

homaa yafhamaan al-dars

They both understand the lesson.
They are both understanding the lesson.
(dual, masculine and feminine)

هُم لا يَفْهَموا ٱلدَّرْس.

hom laa yafhamoo al-dars

They do not understand the lesson.
They are not understanding the lesson.
(plural, masculine and feminine)

هُم يَفْهَمون ٱلدَّرْس.

hom yafhamoon al-dars

They understand the lesson.
They are understanding the lesson.
(plural, masculine and feminine)

هُنَّ لا يَفْهَمْنَ ٱلدَّرْس.

honna laa yafhamna al-dars

They do not understand the lesson.
The are not understanding the lesson.
(plural, feminine)

هُنَّ يَفْهَمْنَ ٱلدَّرْس.

honna yafhamna al-dars

They understand the lesson.
The are understanding the lesson.
(plural, feminine)

- In spoken Standard Arabic, when the subject of the present verb is 'You' (singular, feminine), the final 'n' ن is typically not pronounced. When the verb is negated, the 'n' ن is dropped in both spoken Standard Arabic and Classical Arabic. In these cases, the present verb ends with the long vowel 'ee' ي sound. Examples:

لا تَفْهَمي	لا تَذْهَبي	لا تَكْتُبي	لا تَدْرُسي	لا تَعيشي
laa tafhamee	laa tadhhabee	laa taktobee	laa tadrosee	laa taA'eeshee
You do not understand.	You do not go.	You do not write.	You do not study.	You do not live.
You are not understanding. (you, singular feminine)	You are not going. (you, singular feminine)	You are not writing. (you, singular feminine)	You are not studying. (you, singular feminine)	you are not living. (you, singular feminine)

- When the subject of the present verb is 'You' (dual or plural, masculine and feminine) and 'They' (dual or plural, masculine and feminine), the final 'n' ن at the end of the present verb is not commonly pronounced in spoken Standard Arabic, but only in Classical Arabic. However, in the negated form of plural and dual verbs, the 'n' ن is dropped from both verbs.

- If the subject of the negated verb is 'You' (plural or they, masculine and feminine) and not dual, the 'n' ن is replaced with a 'silent alif' ا at the end of the plural present verb, serving as a signal of plurality and the present verb will end with pronouncing the long vowel و (waw) as a signal of plurality. Examples:

لا تَفْهَموا	لا تَذْهَبوا	لا تَكْتُبوا	لا تَدْرُسوا	لا تَعيشوا
laa tafhamoo	**laa tadhhaboo**	**laa taktoboo**	**laa tadrosoo**	**laa taA'eeshoo**
You all do not understand.. You are all not understanding. (you, plural masculine and feminine)	You all do not go.. You are all not going. (you, plural masculine and feminine)	You all do not write.. You are all not writing. (you, plural masculine and feminine)	You all do not study.. You are all not studying. (you, plural masculine and feminine)	You all do not live.. you are all not living. (you, plural masculine and feminine)
لا يَفْهَموا	لا يَذْهَبوا	لا يَكْتُبوا	لا يَدْرُسوا	لا يَعيشوا
laa yafhamoo	**laa yadhhaboo**	**laa yaktoboo**	**laa yadrosoo**	**laa yaA'eeshoo**
They do not understand. They are not understanding. (they, masculine and feminine)	They do not go. They are not going. (they, masculine and feminine)	They do not write. They are not writing. (they, masculine and feminine)	They do not study. They are not studying. (they, masculine and feminine)	They do not live. They are not living. (they, masculine and feminine)

Lesson Twenty-Four
The Present Verb With Object Pronouns

The third type of personal pronouns is known as object pronouns. These pronouns are attached to the present verb, past verb, or future verb to indicate the object of the verb.

Object pronouns are similar to possessive pronouns, except for the first possessive pronoun 'my' ـي. In the case of object pronouns, the pronoun is preceded by the letter 'n' ن before it is attached to the verb, resulting in the form ـني.

- **In spoken Modern Standard Arabic (MSA), the plural masculine form is commonly used instead of the dual and feminine plural forms. The dual and feminine plural forms are more commonly found in Classical Arabic and are used in formal and poetic contexts.**

The subject pronouns and their corresponding object pronouns are as follows:

Meaning	Object Pronouns	Meaning	Subject Pronouns
Me	ـني nee	I	أنـا anna
You (masculine)	كَ ka	You (masculine)	أنتَ anta
You (feminine)	كِ ki	You (feminine)	أنتِ anti
You (dual, masculine and feminine)	كُمـا komaa	You (dual, masculine and feminine)	أنْتُمـا antomaa

Meaning	Object Pronouns	Meaning	Subject Pronouns
You (plural, masculine and feminine)	كُم kom	You (plural, masculine and feminine)	أنتُم antom
You (plural, (feminine)	كنَّ konna	You (plural, feminine)	أنتُنَّ antonna
Us (masculine and feminine)	نا naa	We (masculine and feminine)	نَحنُ naHno
Him / it	ه ho	He / it	هُوَ howa
Her / it	ها haa	She / it	هِي hiya
Them (dual, masculine and feminine)	هُما homaa	They (dual, masculine and feminine)	هُما homaa
Them (masculine and feminine)	هُم hom	They (masculine and feminine)	هُم hom
Them (feminine)	هنَّ honna	They (feminine)	هنَّ honna

The tables below demonstrate the common error made by beginners, which involves using subject pronouns instead of object pronouns with present verbs. The first column showcases the improper usage, while the second column presents the correct utilization of object pronouns with present verbs in both classic Arabic and spoken modern standard Arabic.

- The examples provided in the tables for this lesson are all in spoken Modern Standard Arabic. Consequently, the words are presented without vowel markings at the end.

The object pronouns with the present verb "to know" يَعرِف.

Meaning	Proper Sentences	Improper Sentences
Mohammad knows me.	مُحَمَّد يَعرِفُني moHammad yaA'ri-fonee	مُحَمَّد يعرف أَنا moHammad yaA'rif anaa
Mohammad knows you. (singular, masculine)	مُحَمَّد يعرِفُكَ moHammad yaA'rifoka	مُحَمَّد يعرِف أَنتَ moHammad yaA'rif anta
Mohammad knows you. (Singular, feminine)	مُحَمَّد يعرِفُكِ moHammad yaA'rifoki	مُحَمَّد يعرِف أَنتِ moHammad yaA'rif anti
Mohammad knows both of you. (dual, masculine and feminine)	مُحَمَّد يعرِفُكما moHammad yaA'ri-fokoma	مُحَمَّد يعرِف أَنتُما moHammad yaA'rif antoma
Mohammad knows all of you. (plural, masculine and feminine)	مُحَمَّد يَعْرِفُكم moHammad yaA'ri-fokom	مُحَمَّد يعرِف أَنْتُم moHammad yaA'rif antom
Mohammad knows all of you. (plural, feminine)	مُحَمَّد يَعْرِفكنَّ moHammad yaA'ri-fokonna	مُحَمَّد يعرِف أَنتُنَّ moHammad yaA'rif an-tonna
Mohammad knows us. (masculine and feminine)	مُحَمَّد يعرِفُنا moHammad yaA'rifon-aa	مُحَمَّد يعرِف نحنُ moHammad yaA'rif naH-no
Mohammad knows him.	مُحَمَّد يعرِفُه moHammad yaA'rifoho	مُحَمَّد يَعرِف هُوَ moHammad yaA'rif howa

Meaning	Proper Sentences	Improper Sentences
Mohammad knows her.	مُحَمَّد يَعْرِفُها moHammad yaA'rifoha	مُحَمَّد يَعْرِف هِيَ moHammad yaA'rif hiya
Mohammad knows both of them. (dual, masculine and feminine)	مُحَمَّد يعرِفُهُما moHammad yaA'rifo-homa	مُحَمَّد يَعْرِف هُما moHammad yaA'rif homa
Mohammad knows them. (plural, masculine and feminine)	مُحَمَّد يَعْرِفُهُم moHammad yaA'rifo-hom	مُحَمَّد يَعْرِف هُم moHammad yaA'rif hom
Mohammad knows them. (plural, feminine)	مُحَمَّد يَعْرِفُهُنَّ moHammad yaA'rifo-honna	مُحَمَّد يَعْرِف هُنَّ moHammad yaA'rif honna

The object pronouns with the present verb "to talk" يُكَلِّم.

Meaning	Proper Sentences	Improper Sentences
Ahmad is talking to me.	أَحْمَد يُكَلِّمُني aHmad yokallimonee	أَحْمَد يُكَلِّم أَنا aHmad yokallim anaa
Ahmad is talking to you. (singular, masculine)	أَحْمَد يُكَلِّمُكَ aHmad yokallimoka	أَحْمَد يُكَلِّم أَنْتَ aHmad yokallim anta
Ahmad is talking to you. (singular, feminine)	أَحْمَد يُكَلِّمُكِ aHmad yokallimoki	أَحْمَد يُكَلِّم أَنْتِ aHmad yokallim anti
Ahmad is talking to both of you. (dual, masculine and feminine)	أَحْمَد يُكَلِّمُكُما aHmad yokallimokoma	أَحْمَد يُكَلِّم أَنْتُما aHmad yokallim an-tomaa

Meaning	Proper Sentences	Improper Sentences
Ahmad is talking to all of you. (plural, masculine and feminine)	أَحْمَد يُكَلِّمُكم aHmad yokallimokom	أَحْمَد يُكَلِّم أَنْتُم aHmad yokallim antom
Ahmad is talking to all of you. (plural, feminine)	أَحْمَد يُكَلِّمُكُنَّ aHmad yokallimokonna	أَحْمَد يُكَلِّم أَنْتُنَّ aHmad yokallim antonna
Ahmad is talking to us. (masculine and feminine)	أَحْمَد يُكَلِّمُنا aHmad yokallimonaa	أَحْمَد يُكَلِّم نَحْنُ aHmad yokallim naHno
Ahmad is talking to him.	أَحْمَد يُكَلِّمُهُ aHmad yokallimoho	أَحْمَد يُكَلِّم هُوَ aHmad yokallim howa
Ahmad is talking to her.	أَحْمَد يُكَلِّمُها aHmad yokallimohaa	أَحْمَد يُكَلِّم هِيَ aHmad yokallim hiya
Ahmad is talking to both of them. (dual, masculine and feminine)	أَحْمَد يُكَلِّمُهُما aHmad yokallimohoma	أَحْمَد يُكَلِّم هُما aHmad yokallim homa
Ahmad is talking to them. (plural, masculine and feminine)	أَحْمَد يُكَلِّمُهم aHmad yokallimohom	أَحْمَد يُكَلِّم هُم aHmad yokallim hom
Ahmad is talking to them. (plural, feminine)	أَحْمَد يُكَلِّمُهُنَّ aHmad yokallimohonna	أَحْمَد يُكَلِّم هُنَّ aHmad yokallim honna

The object pronouns with the present verb "to teach" يُدَرِّس :

Meaning	Proper Sentences	Improper Sentences
The teacher is teaching me.	الأُسْتاذ يُدَرِّسُني al-ostaadh yodar-risonee	الأُسْتاذ يُدَرِّس أَنا al-ostaadh yodarris anaa

201

Meaning	Proper Sentences	Improper Sentences
The teacher is teaching you. (you, masculine)	الأُسْتاذ يُدَرِّسُكَ al-ostaadh yodarrisoka	الأُسْتاذ يُدَرِّس أَنْتَ al-ostaadh yodarris anta
The teacher is teaching you. (you, feminine)	الأُسْتاذ يُدَرِّسُكِ al-ostaadh yodarrisoki	الأُسْتاذ يُدَرِّس أَنْتِ al-ostaadh yodarris anti
The teacher is teaching both of you. (dual, masculine and feminine)	الأُسْتاذ يُدَرِّسُكُما al-ostaadh yodar-risokomaa	الأُسْتاذ يُدَرِّس أَنْتُما al-ostaadh yodarris antoma
The teacher is teaching all of you. (plural, masculine and feminine)	الأُسْتاذ يُدَرِّسُكُم al-ostaadh yodar-risokom	الأُسْتاذ يُدَرِّس أَنْتُم al-ostaadh yodarris antom
The teacher is teaching all of you. (you, plural feminine)	الأُسْتاذ يُدَرِّسُكُنَّ al-ostaadh yodarris-okonna	الأُسْتاذ يُدَرِّس أَنْتُنَّ al-ostaadh yodarris anton-na
The teacher is teaching us. (masculine and feminine)	الأُسْتاذ يُدَرِّسُنا al-ostaadh yodarrison-aa	الأُسْتاذ يُدَرِّس نَحْنُ al-ostaadh yodarris naHno
The teacher is teaching him.	الأُسْتاذ يُدَرِّسُهُ al-ostaadh yodarrisoho	الأُسْتاذ يُدَرِّس هُوَ al-ostaadh yodarris howa
The teacher is teaching her.	الأُسْتاذ يُدَرِّسُها al-ostaadh yodarriso-haa	الأُسْتاذ يُدَرِّس هِيَ al-ostaadh yodarris hiya
The teacher is teaching both of them. (dual, masculine and feminine)	الأُسْتاذ يُدَرِّسُهُما al-ostaadh yodarriso-homa	الأُسْتاذ يُدَرِّس هُما al-ostaadh yodarris homa

Meaning	Proper Sentences	Improper Sentences
The teacher is teaching them. (plural, masculine and feminine)	الأُسْتاذ يُدَرِّسُهُم al-ostaadh yodarriso-hom	الأُسْتاذ يُدَرِّس هُم al-ostaadh yodarris hom
The teacher is teaching them. (plural, feminine)	الأُسْتاذ يُدَرِّسُهُنَّ al-ostaadh yodarrisohonna	الأُسْتاذ يُدَرِّس هُنَّ al-ostaadh yodarris honna

The object pronouns with the present verb "to ask" يَسْأَل :

Meaning	Proper Sentences	Improper Sentences
The teacher is asking me.	الأُسْتاذَة تَسْأَلُني al-ostaadha tas,alonee	الأُسْتاذَة تَسْأَل أَنا al-ostaadha tas,al anaa
The teacher is asking you. (you, masculine)	الأُسْتاذَة تَسْأَلُكَ al-ostaadha tas,aloka	الأُسْتاذَة تَسْأَل أَنْتَ al-ostaadha tas,al anta
The teacher is asking you. (you, feminine)	الأُسْتاذَة تَسْأَلُكِ al-ostaadha tas,aloki	الأُسْتاذَة تَسْأَل أَنْتِ al-ostaadha tas,al anti
The teacher is asking both of you. (dual, masculine and feminine)	الأُسْتاذَة تَسْأَلُكُما al-ostaadha tas,aloko-maa	الأُسْتاذَة تَسْأَل أَنْتُما al-ostaadha tas,al an-tomaa
The teacher is asking all of you. (plural, masculine and feminine)	الأُسْتاذَة تَسْأَلُكُم al-ostaadha tas,alokom	الأُسْتاذَة تَسْأَل أَنْتُم al-ostaadha tas,al antom
The teacher is asking all of you. (plural, feminine)	الأُسْتاذَة تَسْأَلُكُنَّ al-ostaadha tas,alokon-na	الأُسْتاذَة تَسْأَل أَنْتُنَّ al-ostaadha tas,al anton-na

Meaning	Proper Sentences	Improper Sentences
The teacher is asking us. (masculine and feminine)	الأُسْتاذَة تَسْأَلُنا al-ostaadha tas,alonaa	الأُسْتاذَة تَسْأَل نَحْنُ al-ostaadha tas,al naHno
The teacher is asking him.	الأُسْتاذَة تَسْأَلُهُ al-ostaadha tas,aloho	الأُسْتاذَة تَسْأَل هُوَ al-ostaadha tas,al howa
The teacher is asking her.	الأُسْتاذَة تَسْأَلُها al-ostaadha tas,alohaa	الأُسْتاذَة تَسْأَل هِيَ al-ostaadha tas,al hiya
The teacher is asking both of them. (them, dual masculine and feminine)	الأُسْتاذَة تَسْأَلُهُما al-ostaadha tas,alo-homa	الأُسْتاذَة تَسْأَل هُما al-ostaadha tas,al homa
The teacher is asking them. (plural, masculine and feminine)	الأُسْتاذَة تَسْأَلُهُم al-ostaadha tas,alohom	الأُسْتاذَة تَسْأَل هُم al-ostaadha tas,al hom
The teacher is asking them. (plural, feminine)	الأُسْتاذَة تَسْأَلُهُنَّ al-ostaadha tas,alohon-na	الأُسْتاذَة تَسْأَل هُنَّ al-ostaadha tas,al honna

The object pronouns with the present verb "to understand" يَفْهَم.

Meaning	Proper Sentences	Improper Sentences
He understands me.	هُوَ يَفْهَمُني howa yafhamonee	هُوَ يَفْهَم أَنا howa yafham anaa
He understands you. (you, masculine)	هُوَ يَفْهَمُكَ howa yafhamoka	هُوَ يَفْهَم أَنتَ howa yafham anta

Meaning	Proper Sentences	Improper Sentences
He understands you. (you, feminine)	هُوَ يَفْهَمُكِ howa yafhamoki	هُوَ يَفْهَم أنتِ howa yafham anti
He understands both of you. (you, dual masculine and feminine)	هُوَ يَفْهَمُكُما howa yafhamokoma	هُوَ يَفْهَم أنتُما howa yafham antoma
He understands you all. (you, plural masculine and feminine)	هُوَ يَفْهَمُكُم howa yafhamokom	هُوَ يَفْهَم أنْتُم howa yafham antom
He understands you all. (you, plural feminine)	هُوَ يَفْهَمُكُنَّ howa yafhamokonna	هُوَ يَفْهَم أنتُنَّ howa yafham antonna
He understands us. (masculine and feminine)	هُوَ يَفْهَمُنا howa yafhamonaa	هُوَ يَفْهَم نَحنُ howa yafham naHno
He understands him.	هُوَ يَفْهَمُه howa yafhamoho	هُوَ يَفْهَم هُوَ howa yafham howa
He understands her.	هُوَ يَفْهَمُها howa yafhamoha	هُوَ يَفْهَم هِيَ howa yafham hiya
He understands both of them. (them, dual masculine and feminine)	هُوَ يَفْهَمُهُما howa yafhamohoma	هُوَ يَفْهَم هُما howa yafham homa
He understands them. (them, plural masculine and feminine)	هُوَ يَفْهَمُهُم howa yafhamohom	هُوَ يَفْهَم هُم howa yafham hom
He understands them. (them, plural feminine)	هُوَ يَفْهَمُهُنَّ howa yafhamohonna	هُوَ يَفْهَم هُنَّ howa yafham honna

Lesson Twenty-Five
The Future Tense

In Lesson Twenty Three, we explored the root system upon which the Arabic language is constructed. Typically, each Arabic word is derived from a word family consisting of three letters that share the same root. Within each family, the core of three letters serves as a foundation from which additional words are formed by incorporating specific letters known as "letters of increase."

To expand the word family, a total of nine letters of increase, along with the symbol 'shaddeh,' are added to the core word. These letters of increase facilitate the creation of a wider range of words within the Arabic language. The letters of increase are:

| shaddeh | t | t | n | s | m | ee/y | oo/w | aa | a |

To express the future tense in Arabic, there are two ways to modify the present verb.- Firstly, you can add the letter of increase 's' (سَ) to the beginning of the present verb.

This addition of 's' (سَ) indicates a near future tense. Alternatively, you can incorporate the word 'sawfa' (سَوْفَ) into the sentence just before the present verb to convey a far future tense.

It's important to note that when the subject of the verb is plural and feminine, and the letter 'y' (ي) is one of the root letters located in the middle of the word's core (the three-letter root), the 'y' (ي) is replaced with the vowel 'kasrah'   . An example of this is the verb 'to live' mentioned below.

- **Please note that both the simple present tense and the present continuous tense are expressed in the same manner in Arabic. As a result, the simple future tense and the continuous future tense are also expressed similarly.**

- **In spoken Modern Standard Arabic (MSA), the plural masculine form is commonly used instead of the dual and feminine plural forms. The dual and feminine plural forms are more commonly found in Classical Arabic and are used in formal and poetic contexts.**

The examples provided in the tables for this lesson are all in spoken Modern Standard Arabic. Consequently, the words are presented without vowel markings at the end.

Conjugations of the future tense for the verb "to live" with the root ع ي ش :

سَأَ (sa,a)	Is added to the beginning of the present verb (أَعيش / I live), (سَأَعيش / I will live).
سَتَ (sata)	Is added to the beginning of the present verb (تَعيش / you live), (سَتَعيش / you will live), (you, masculine).
سَتَ (sata)	Is added to the beginning of the present verb (تَعيشين / you live) (سَتَعيشين / you will live), (you, feminine).
سَتَ (sata)	Is added to the beginning of the present verb (تَعيشان / you both live), (سَتَعيشان / you both will live), (you, dual masculine and feminine).
سَتَ (sata)	Is added to the beginning of the present verb (تَعيشون / you all live), (سَتَعيشون / you all will live), (you, plural masculine and feminine).
سَتَ (sata)	Is added to the beginning of the present verb (تَعِشْنَ / you all live), (سَتَعِشْنَ / you all will live), (you, plural feminine).
سَنَ (sana)	Is added to the beginning of the present verb (نَعيش / we live), (سَنَعيش / we will live).
سَيَ (saya)	Is added to the beginning of the present verb (يَعيش / he lives), (سَيَعيش / he will live).
سَتَ (sata)	Is added to the beginning of the present verb (تَعيش / she lives), (سَتَعيش / she will live).

سَيـ (saya)	Is added to the beginning of the present verb (يَعيشانِ / they both live), (سَيَعيشانِ / they both will live), (they, dual masculine and feminine).
سَيـ (saya)	Is added to the beginning of the present verb (يَعيشونَ / they live), (سَيَعيشونَ / they will live), (they, plural masculine and feminine).
سَيـ (saya)	Is added to the beginning of the present verb (يَعِشْنَ / they live), (سَيَعِشْنَ / they will live), (they, plural feminine).

Conjugations of the future tense for the verb "to study" with the root د ر س:

Future Tense	Present Tense	Subject Pronoun
أنا سَأَدْرُس anaa sa,adros I will study. I will be studying.	أنا أَدْرُس anaa adros I study. I am studying.	أنا anaa I
أنتَ سَتَدْرُس anta sa-tadros You will study. You will be studying.	أنتَ تَدْرُس anta tadros You study. You are studying.	أنتَ anta You (masculine)
أنتِ سَتَدْرُسين anti sa-tadroseen You will study. You will be studying.	أنتِ تَدْرُسين anti tadroseen You study. You are studying.	أنتِ anti You (feminine)
أنتُما سَتَدْرُسان antoma sa-tadrosaan You both will study. You both will be studying.	أنتُما تَدْرُسان antoma tadrosaan You both study. You are both studying.	أنْتُما antoma You (dual, masculine and feminine)

Future Tense	Present Tense	Subject Pronoun	
أنتُم سَتَدْرُسون **antom sa-tadrosoon** You all will study. You all will be studying.	أنتُم تَدْرُسون **antom tadrosoon** You all study. You are all studying.	You (plural, masculine and feminine)	أنْتـُم **antom**
أنْتُنَّ سَتَدْرُسْنَ **antonna sa-tadrosna** You all will study. You all will be studying.	أنْتُنَّ تَدْرُسْنَ **antonna tadrosna** You all study. You are all studying.	You (plural, feminine)	أنْتُنَّ **antonna**
نَحنُ سَنَدْرُس **naHno sa-nadros** We will study. We will be studying.	نَحنُ نَدْرُس **naHno nadros** we study. We are studying.	We (masculine and feminine)	نَحنُ **naHno**
هُوَ سَيَدْرُس **howa sa-yadros** He will study. He will be studying.	هُوَ يَدْرُس **howa yadros** He studies. He is studying.	He/it	هُوَ **howa**
هِيَ سَتَدْرُس **hiya sa-tadros** She will study. She will be studying.	هِيَ تَدْرُس **hiya tadros** She studies. She is studying.	She/it	هِيَ **hiya**
هُما سَيَدْرُسان **homaa sa-yadrosan** They both will study. They both will be studying.	هُما يَدْرُسان **homa yadrosan** They both study. They are both studying.	They (dual, masculine and feminine)	هُما **homa**
هُم سَيَدْرُسون **hom sa-yadrosoon** They will study. They will be studying.	هُم يَدْرُسون **hom yadrosoon** They study. They are studying.	They (masculine and feminine)	هُم **hom**

Future Tense	Present Tense	Subject Pronoun	
هُنَّ سَيَدْرُسْنَ honna sa-yadrosna They will study. They will be studying.	هُنَّ يَدْرُسْنَ honna yadrosna They study. They are studying.	They (feminine)	هُنَّ honna

Conjugations of the future tense for the verb "to write" with the root ك ت ب:

Future Tense	Present Tense	Subject Pronoun	
أَنا سَأَكْتُب anaa sa,aktob I will write. I will be writing.	أَنا أَكْتُب anaa aktob I write. I am writing.	I	أَنا anaa
أَنتَ سَتَكْتُب anta sa-taktob You will write. You will be writing.	أَنتَ تَكْتُب anta taktob You write. You are writing.	You (mascu- line)	أَنتَ anta
أَنتِ سَتَكْتُبِين anti sa-taktobeen You will write. You will be writing.	أَنتِ تَكْتُبِين anti taktobeen You write. You are writing.	You (feminine)	أَنتِ anti
أَنتُما سَتَكْتُبان antomaa sa-taktobaan You both will write. You both will be writ- ing.	أَنتُما تَكْتُبان antomaa taktobaan You both write. You are both writing.	You (dual, masculine and femi- nine)	أَنتُما antomaa
أَنتُم سَتَكْتُبون antom sa-taktoboon You all will write. You all will be writing.	أَنتُم تَكْتُبون antom taktoboon You all write. You are all writing.	You (plural, masculine and femi- nine)	أَنتُم antom

Future Tense	Present Tense	Subject Pronoun	
أَنْتُنَّ سَتَكْتُبْنَ **antonna sa-taktobna** You all will write. You all will be writing.	أَنْتُنَّ تَكْتُبْنَ **antonna taktobna** You all write. You are all writing.	You (plural, feminine)	أَنْتُنَّ **antonna**
نَحْنُ سَنَكْتُبُ **naHno sa-naktob** We will write. We will be writing.	نَحْنُ نَكْتُبُ **naHno naktob** We write. We are writing.	We (masculine and femi- nine)	نَحْنُ **naHno**
هُوَ سَيَكْتُبُ **howa sa-yaktob** He will write. He will be writing.	هُوَ يَكْتُبُ **howa yaktob** He writes. He is writing.	He/it	هُوَ **howa**
هِيَ سَتَكْتُبُ **hiya sa-taktob** She will write. She will be writing.	هِيَ تَكْتُبُ **hiya taktob** She writes. She is writing.	She/it	هِيَ **hiya**
هُمَا سَيَكْتُبَان **homaa sa-yaktobaan** They both will write. They both will be writing.	هُمَا يَكْتُبَان **homaa yaktobaan** They both write. They are both writing.	They (dual, masculine and femi- nine)	هُمَا **homaa**
هُمْ سَيَكْتُبُون **hom sa-yaktoboon** They will write. They will be writing.	هُمْ يَكْتُبُون **hom yaktoboon** They write. They are writing.	They (plural, mas- culine and feminine)	هُمْ **hom**
هُنَّ سَيَكْتُبْنَ **honna sa-yaktobna** They will write. They will be writing.	هُنَّ يَكْتُبْنَ **honna yaktobna** They write. They are writing.	They (plural, feminine)	هُنَّ **honna**

Conjugations of the future tense for the verb "to go" with the root ذ ـ هـ ـ ب :

Future Tense	Present Tense	Meaning	Subject Pronoun
أنا سأَذْهَب anaa sa,adh-hab I will go. I will be going.	أنا أَذْهَب anaa adh-hab I go. I am going.	I	أنا anaa
أنتَ ستَذْهب anta sa-tadh-hab You will go. You will be going.	أنتَ تَذْهَب anta tadh-hab You go. You are going.	You (masculine)	أنتَ anta
أنتِ ستَذْهَبين anti sa-tadh-habeen You will go. You will be going.	أنتِ تَذْهَبين anti tadh-habeen You go. You are going.	You (femi- nine)	أنتِ anti
أنتُما ستَذْهَبان antomaa sa-tadh-habaan You both will go. You both will be going.	أنتُما تَذْهَبان antomaa tadh- habaan You both go. You are both going.	You (dual, masculine and feminine)	أنتُما antomaa
أنتُم ستَذْهَبون antom sa-tadh-haboon You all will go. You all will be going.	أنتُم تَذْهَبون antom tadh-haboon You all go. You are all going.	You (plural, masculine and feminine)	أنتُم antom
أنْتُنَّ ستَذْهَبْنَ antonna sa-tadh-habna You all will go. You all will be going.	أنْتُنَّ تَذْهَبْنَ antonna tadh-habna You all go. You are all going.	You (plural, feminine)	أنْتُنَّ antonna

Future Tense	Present Tense	Meaning	Subject Pronoun
نَحنُ سنَذْهَب naHno sa-nadh-hab We will go. We will be going.	نَحنُ نَذْهَب naHno nadh-hab We go. We are going.	We (masculine and feminine)	نَحنُ naHno
هُوَ سيَذْهَب howa sa-yadh-hab He will go. He will be going.	هُوَ يَذْهَب howa yadh-hab He goes. He is going.	He/it	هُوَ howa
هِيَ ستَذْهَب hiya sa-tadh-hab She will go. She will be going.	هِيَ تَذْهَب hiya tadh-hab She goes. She is going.	She/it	هِيَ hiya
هُما سيَذْهَبان homaa sa-yadh-habaan They both will go. They both will be going.	هُما يَذْهَبان homaa yadh-habaan They both go. They are both going.	They (dual, masculine and feminine)	هُما homaa
هُم سيَذْهَبون hom sa-yadh-haboon They will go. They will be going.	هُم يَذْهَبون hom yadh-haboon They go. They are going.	They (plural, masculine and feminine)	هُم hom
هُنَّ سيَذْهَبْنَ honna sa-yadh-habna They will go. They will be going.	هُنَّ يَذْهَبْنَ honna yadh-habna They go. They are going.	They (plural, feminine)	هُنَّ honna

Conjugations of the future tense for the verb "to understand" with the root ف ﻫ م:

Future Tense	Present Tense	Meaning	Subject Pronoun
أَنا سَأَفْهَم anaa sa-afham I will understand. I will be understanding.	أَنا أَفْهَم anaa afham I understand. I am understanding.	I	أَنا anaa
أَنتَ سَتَفْهَم anta sa-tafham You will understand. You will be understanding.	أَنتَ تَفْهَم anta tafham You understand. You are understanding.	You masculine	أَنتَ anta
أَنتِ سَتَفْهَمين anti sa-tafhameen You will understand. You will be understanding.	أَنتِ تَفْهَمين anti tafhameen You understand. You are understanding.	You feminine	أَنتِ anti
أَنتُما سَتَفْهَمان antomaa sa-tafhamaan You both will understand. You both will be understanding.	أَنتُما تَفْهَمان antomaa tafhamaan You both understand. You are both under- standing.	You (dual, masculine and feminine)	أَنتُما antomaa
أَنتُم سَتَفْهَمون antom sa-tafhamoon You all will understand. You all will be understanding.	أَنتُم تَفْهَمون antom tafhamoon You all understand. You are all understanding.	You (plural, (masculine and feminine)	أَنتُم antom
أَنْتُنَّ سَتَفْهَمْنَ antonna sa-tafhamna You all will understand. You all will be understanding.	أَنْتُنَّ تَفْهَمْنَ antonna tafhamna You all understand. You are all understanding.	You (plural, feminine)	أَنْتُنَّ antonna

Future Tense	Present Tense	Meaning	Subject Pronoun
نَحْنُ سَنَفْهَم **naHno sa-nafham** We will understand. We will be understanding.	نَحْنُ نَفْهَم **naHno nafham** We understand. We are understanding.	We (masculine and feminine)	نَحْنُ **naHno**
هُوَ سَيَفْهَم **howa sa-yafham** He will understand. He will be understanding.	هُوَ يَفْهَم **howa yafham** He understands. He is understanding.	He/it	هُوَ **howa**
هِيَ سَتَفْهَم **hiya sa-tafham** She will understand. She will be understanding.	هِيَ تَفْهَم **hiya tafham** She understands. She is understanding.	She/it	هِيَ **hiya**
هُما سَيَفْهَمان **homaa sa-yafhamaan** They both will understand. They both will be understanding.	هُما يَفْهَمان **homaa yafhamaan** They both understand. They are both understanding.	They (dual, masculine and feminine)	هُما **homaa**
هُم سَيَفْهَمون **hom sa-yafhamoon** They will understand. They will be understanding.	هُم يَفْهَمون **hom yafhamoon** They understand. They are understanding.	They (plural, masculine and feminine)	هُم **hom**
هُنَّ سَيَفْهَمْنَ **honna sa-yafhamna** They will understand. They will be understand-ing.	هُنَّ يَفْهَمْنَ **honna yafhamna** They understand. They are understanding.	They (plural feminine)	هُنَّ **honna**

- **Note: The future verb for "you" (masculine) and the future verb for "she" is the same.**

Lesson Twenty-Six
Negating the Future Verb

The future tense is negated by using 'لَنْ' (lan) that precedes the verb immediately.

However, the 'س' (s) or the 'سَوْفَ' (sawfa) is dropped before adding 'لَنْ' (lan) because 'لَنْ' (lan) by itself conveys the meaning of 'negated future' and does not require the letter 'س' (s) or the word 'سَوْفَ' (sawfa) to express the future tense.

- **In spoken Modern Standard Arabic (MSA), the plural masculine form is commonly used instead of the dual and feminine plural forms. The dual and feminine plural forms are more commonly found in Classical Arabic and are used in formal and poetic contexts.**

- The examples in the tables for this lesson are all in spoken Modern Standard Arabic (MSA), which means the words are not vocalized at the end.

Negating the verb 'to live' in the future tense. The root for this verb is  ع ي ش:

Negating the Future Tense Modern Standard Arabic	Future Tense Sentences Modern standard Arabic
أنا لَنْ أعيشُ في كَليفورنيا.	أنا سَوْفَ أعيشُ في كَليفورنيا.
anaa lan aA'eesh fee california I will not live in California. I will not be living in California.	anaa sawfa aA'eesh fee california I will live in California. I will be living in California.
أنتَ لَنْ تَعيشُ في كَليفورنيا.	أنتَ سَوْفَ تَعيشُ في كَليفورنيا.
anta lan taA'eesh fee california You will not live in California. You will not be living in California. (singular, masculine)	anta sawfa taA'eesh fee california You will live in California. You will be living in California. (singular, masculine)

Negating the Future Tense Modern Standard Arabic	Future Tense Sentences Modern standard Arabic
أَنتِ لَنْ تَعيشي في كَليفورنيا. anti lan taA'eeshee fee california You will not live in California. You will not be living in California. (singular, feminine)	أَنتِ سَوْفَ تَعيشين في كَليفورنيا. anti sawfa taA'eesheen fee california You will live in California. You will be living in California. (singular, feminine)
أَنتُما لَنْ تَعيشا في كَليفورنيا. antomaa lan taA'eeshaa fee california You both will not live in California. You both will not be living in California. (dual, masculine and feminine)	أَنتُما سَوْفَ تَعيشان في كَليفورنيا. antomaa sawfa taA'eeshan fee california You both will live in California. You both will be living in California. (dual, masculine and feminine)
أَنتُم لَنْ تَعيشوا في كَليفورنيا. antom lan taA'eeshoo fee california You all will not live in California. You all will not be living in California. (plural, masculine and feminine)	أَنتُم سَوْفَ تَعيشون في كَليفورنيا. antom sawfa taA'eeshoon fee california You all will live in California. You all will be living in California. (plural, masculine and feminine)
أَنتُنَّ لَنْ تَعِشْنَ في كَليفورنيا. antonna lan taA'ishna fee california You all will not live in California. You all will not be living in California. (plural, feminine)	أَنتُنَّ سَوْفَ تَعِشْنَ في كَليفورنيا. antonna sawfa taA'ishna fee california You all will live in California. You all will be living in California. (plural, feminine)
نَحْنُ لَنْ نَعيش في كَليفورنيا. naHno lan naA'eesh fee california We will not live in California. We will not be living in California. (masculine and feminine)	نَحْنُ سَوْفَ نَعيش في كَليفورنيا. naHno sawfa naA'eesh fee california We will live in California. We will be living in California. (masculine and feminine)

Negating the Future Tense Modern Standard Arabic	Future Tense Sentences Modern standard Arabic
هُوَ لَنْ يَعيش في كَليفورنيا.	هُوَ سَوْفَ يَعيش في كَليفورنيا.
howa lan yaA'eesh fee california	howa sawfa yaA'eesh fee california
He will not live in California. He will not be living in California.	He will live in California. He will be living in California.
هِيَ لَنْ تَعيش في كَليفورنيا.	هِيَ سَوْفَ تَعيش في كَليفورنيا.
hiya lan taA'eesh fee california	hiya sawfa taA'eesh fee california
She will not live in California. She will not be living in California.	She will live in California. She will be living in California.
هُما لَنْ يَعيشا في كَليفورنيا.	هُما سَوْفَ يَعيشان في كَليفورنيا.
homaa lan yaA'eeshaa fee california	homaa sawfa yaA'eeshaan fee california
They both will not live in California. They both will not be living in California. (dual, masculine and feminine)	They both will live in California. They both will be living in California. (dual, masculine and feminine)
هُم لَنْ يَعيشوا في كَليفورنيا.	هُم سَوْفَ يَعيشون في كَليفورنيا.
hom lan yaA'eeshoo fee california	hom sawfa yaA'eeshoon fee california
They will not live in California. They will not be living in California. (plural, masculine and feminine)	They will live in California. They will be living in California. (plural, masculine and feminine)
هُنَّ لَنْ يَعِشْنَ في كَليفورنيا.	هُنَّ سَوْفَ يَعِشْنَ في كَليفورنيا.
honna lan yaA'ishna fee california	honna sawfa yaA'ishna fee california
They will not live in California. They will not be living in California. (plural, feminine)	They will live in California. They will be living in California. (plural, feminine)

Negating the verb 'to study' in the future tense. The root for this verb is  **د ر س**:

Negating the Future Tense Modern Standard Arabic	**Future Tense Sentences Modern Standard Arabic**
أَنَا لَنْ أَدْرُس فِي ٱلْمَكْتَبَة. **anaa lan adros fee al-maktaba** I will not study at the library. I will not be studying at the library.	أَنَا سَأَدْرُس فِي ٱلْمَكْتَبَة. **anaa sa,adros fee al-maktaba** I will study at the library. I will be studying at the library.
أَنْتَ لَنْ تَدْرُس فِي ٱلْمَكْتَبَة. **anta lan tadros fee al-maktaba** You will not study at the library. You will not be studying at the library. (singular, masculine)	أَنْتَ سَتَدْرُس فِي ٱلْمَكْتَبَة. **anta satadros fee al-maktaba** You will study at the library. You will be studying at the library. (singular, masculine)
أَنْتِ لَنْ تَدْرُسِي فِي ٱلْمَكْتَبَة. **anti lan tadrosee fee al-maktaba** You will not study at the library. You will not be studying at the library. (singular, feminine)	أَنْتِ سَتَدْرُسِين فِي ٱلْمَكْتَبَة. **anti satadroseen fee al-maktaba** You will study at the library. You will be studying at the library. (singular, feminine)
أَنْتُمَا لَنْ تَدْرُسَا فِي ٱلْمَكْتَبَة. **antoma lan tadrosaa fee al-maktaba** You both will not study at the library. You both will not be studying at the library. (dual, masculine and feminine)	أَنْتُمَا سَتَدْرُسَان فِي ٱلْمَكْتَبَة. **antoma satadrosaan fee al-makta-ba** You both will study at the library. You both will be studying at the library. (dual, masculine and feminine)
أَنْتُم لَنْ تَدْرُسوا فِي ٱلْمَكْتَبَة. **antom lan tadrosoo fee al-maktaba** You all will not study at the library. You all will not be studying at the library. (plural, masculine and feminine)	أَنْتُم سَتَدْرُسون فِي ٱلْمَكْتَبَة. **antom satadrosoon fee al-maktaba** You all will study at the library. You all will be studying at the library. (plural, masculine and feminine)

Negating the Future Tense Modern Standard Arabic	Future Tense Sentences Modern Standard Arabic
أَنْتُنَّ لَنْ تَدْرُسْنَ فِي ٱلْمَكْتَبَة. **antonna lan tadrosna fee al-maktaba** You all will not study at the library. You all will not be studying at the library. (plural, feminine)	أَنْتُنَّ سَتَدْرُسْنَ فِي ٱلْمَكْتَبَة. **antonna satadrosna fee al-maktaba** You all will study at the library. You all will be studying at the library. (plural, feminine)
نَحْنُ لَنْ نَدْرُس فِي ٱلْمَكْتَبَة. **naHno lan nadros fee al-maktaba** We will not study at the library. We will not be studying at the library. (masculine and feminine)	نَحْنُ سَنَدْرُس فِي ٱلْمَكْتَبَة. **naHno sanadros fee al-maktaba** We will study at the library. We will be studying at the library. (masculine and feminine)
هُوَ لَنْ يَدْرُس فِي ٱلْمَكْتَبَة. **howa lan yadros fee al-maktaba** He will not study at the library. He will not be studying at the library.	هُوَ سَيَدْرُس فِي ٱلْمَكْتَبَة. **howa sayadros fee al-maktaba** He will study at the library. He will be studying at the library.
هِيَ لَنْ تَدْرُس فِي ٱلْمَكْتَبَة. **hiya lan tadros fee al-maktaba** She will not study at the library. She will not be studying at the library.	هِيَ سَتَدْرُس فِي ٱلْمَكْتَبَة. **hiya satadros fee al-maktaba** She will study at the library. She will be studying at the library.
هُما لَنْ يَدْرُسا فِي ٱلْمَكْتَبَة. **homaa lan yadrosaa fee al-maktaba** They both will not study at the library. They both will not be studying at the library. (dual, masculine and feminine)	هُما سَيَدْرُسان فِي ٱلْمَكْتَبَة. **homaa sayadrosaan fee al-maktaba** They both will study at the library. They both will be studying at the library. (dual, masculine and feminine)
هُمْ لَنْ يَدْرُسوا فِي ٱلْمَكْتَبَة. **hom lan yadrosoo fee al-maktaba** They will not study at the library. They will not be studying at the library. (plural, masculine and feminine)	هُمْ سَيَدْرُسون فِي ٱلْمَكْتَبَة. **hom sayadrosoon fee al-maktaba** They will study at the library. They will be studying at the library. (plural, masculine and feminine)

Negating the Future Tense **Modern Standard Arabic**	**Future Tense Sentences** **Modern Standard Arabic**
هُنَّ لَنْ يَدْرُسْنَ فِي ٱلْمَكْتَبَة.	هُنَّ سَيَدْرُسْنَ فِي ٱلْمَكْتَبَة.
honna lan yadrosna fee al-maktaba They will not study at the library. They will not be studying at the library. (plural, feminine)	honna sayadrosna fee al-maktaba They will study at the library. They will be studying at the library. (plural, feminine)

Negating the verb 'to write' in the future tense. The root for this verb is :

Negating the Future Tense **Modern Standard Arabic**	**Future Tense Sentences** **Modern Standard Arabic**
أَنا لَنْ أَكْتُب رِسالَة.	أَنا سَأَكْتُب رِسالَة.
anaa lan aktob risaala I will not write a letter. I will not be writing a letter.	anaa sa,aktob risaala I will write a letter. I will be writing a letter.
أَنْتَ لَنْ تَكْتُب رِسالَة.	أَنْتَ سَتَكْتُب رِسالَة.
anta lan taktob risaala You will not write a letter. You will not be writing a letter. (singular, masculine)	anta sa-taktob risaala You will write a letter. You will be writing a letter. (singular, masculine)
أَنْتِ لَنْ تَكْتُبِي رِسالَة.	أَنْتِ سَتَكْتُبِين رِسالَة.
anti lan taktobee risaala You will not write a letter. You will not be writing a letter. (singular, feminine)	anti sa-taktobeen risaala You will write a letter. You will be writing a letter. (singular, feminine)
أَنْتُما لَنْ تَكْتُبا رِسالَة.	أَنْتُما سَتَكْتُبان رِسالَة.
antomaa lan taktobaa risaala You both will not write a letter. You both will not be writing a letter. (dual, masculine and feminine)	antomaa sa-taktobaan risaala You both will write a letter. You both will be writing a letter. (dual, masculine and feminine)

Negating the Future Tense Modern Standard Arabic	Future Tense Sentences Modern Standard Arabic

antom lan taktoboo risaala
You all will not write a letter.
You all will not be writing a letter.
(plural, masculine and feminine)

antom sa-taktoboon risaala
You all will write a letter.
You all will be writing a letter.
(plural, masculine and feminine)

antonna lan taktobna risaala
You all will not write a letter.
You all will not be writing a letter.
(plural, feminine)

antonna sa-taktobna risaala
You all will write a letter.
You all will be writing a letter.
(plural, feminine)

naHno lan naktob risaala
We will not write a letter.
We will not be writing a letter.
(masculine and feminine)

naHno sa-naktob risaala
We will write a letter.
We will be writing a letter.
(masculine and feminine)

howa lan yaktob risaala
He will not write a letter.
He will not be writing a letter.

howa sa-yaktob risaala
He will write a letter.
He will be writing a letter.

hiya lan taktob risaala
She will not write a letter.
She will not be writing a letter.

hiya sa-taktob risaala
She will write a letter.
She will be writing a letter.

homaa lan yaktobaa risaala
They both will not write a letter.
They both will not be writing a letter.
(dual, masculine and feminine)

homaa sa-yaktobaan risaala
They both will write a letter.
They both will be writing a letter.
(dual, masculine and feminine)

Negating the Future Tense Modern Standard Arabic	Future Tense Sentences Modern Standard Arabic
هُمْ لَنْ يَكْتُبوا رسالَة.	هُمْ سَيَكْتُبون رسالَة.
hom lan yaktoboo risaala They will not write a letter. They will not be writing a letter. (plural, masculine and feminine)	hom sa-yaktoboon risaala They will write a letter. They will be writing a letter. (plural, masculine and feminine)
هُنَّ لَنْ يَكْتُبْنَ رسالَة.	هُنَّ سَيَكْتُبْنَ رسالَة.
honna lan yaktobna risaala They will not write a letter. They will not be writing a letter. (plural, feminine)	honna sa-yaktobna risaala They will write a letter. They will be writing a letter. (plural, feminine)

Negating the verb 'to go' in the future tense. The root for this verb is ذ ﻫـ ب:

Negating the Future Tense Modern Standard Arabic	Future Tense Sentences Modern Standard Arabic
أَنا لَنْ أَذْهَب إلى ٱلْمَدْرَسَة.	أَنا سَأَذْهَب إلى ٱلْمَدْرَسَة.
anaa lan adh-hab ela al-madrasa I will not go to school. I will not be going to school.	anaa sa,adh-hab ela al-madrasa I will go to school. I will be going to school.
أَنْتَ لَنْ تَذْهَب إلى ٱلْمَدْرَسَة.	أَنْتَ سَتَذْهَب إلى ٱلْمَدْرَسَة.
anta lan tadh-hab ela al-madrasa You will not go to school. You will not be going to school. (singular, masculine)	anta sa-tadh-hab ela al-madrasa You will go to school. You will be going to school. (singular, masculine)
أَنتِ لَنْ تَذْهَبي إلى ٱلْمَدْرَسَة.	أَنتِ سَتَذْهَبين إلى ٱلْمَدْرَسَة.
anti lan tadh-habee ela al-madrasa You will not go to school. You will not be going to school. (singular, feminine)	anti sa-tadh-habeen ela al-madrasa You will go to school. You will be going to school. (singular, feminine)

Negating the Future Tense Modern Standard Arabic	Future Tense Sentences Modern Standard Arabic

أَنْتُمَا لَنْ تَذْهَبَا إِلَى ٱلْمَدْرَسَةِ.

antomaa lan tadh-habaa ela al-madrasa

You both will not go to school.
You both will not be going to school.
(dual, masculine and feminine)

أَنْتُمَا سَتَذْهَبَانِ إِلَى ٱلْمَدْرَسَةِ.

antomaa sa-tadh-habaan ela al-madrasa

You both will go to school.
You both will be going to school.
(dual, masculine and feminine)

أَنْتُمْ لَنْ تَذْهَبُوا إِلَى ٱلْمَدْرَسَةِ.

antom lan tadh-haboo ela al-madrasa

You all will not go to school.
You all will not be going to school.
(plural, masculine and feminine)

أَنْتُمْ سَتَذْهَبُونَ إِلَى ٱلْمَدْرَسَةِ.

antom sa-tadh-haboon ela al-madrasa

You all will go to school.
You all will be going to school.
(plural, masculine and feminine)

أَنْتُنَّ لَنْ تَذْهَبْنَ إِلَى ٱلْمَدْرَسَةِ.

antonna lan tadh-habna ela al-madrasa

You all will not go to school.
You all will not be going to school.
(plural, feminine)

أَنْتُنَّ سَتَذْهَبْنَ إِلَى ٱلْمَدْرَسَةِ.

antonna sa-tadh-habna ela al-madrasa

You all will go to school.
You all will be going to school.
(plural, feminine)

نَحْنُ لَنْ نَذْهَب إِلَى ٱلْمَدْرَسَةِ.

naHno lan nadh-hab ela al-madrasa

We will not go to school.
We will not be going to school.
(masculine and feminine)

نَحْنُ سَنَذْهَب إِلَى ٱلْمَدْرَسَةِ.

naHno sa-nadh-hab ela al-madrasa

We will go to school.
We will be going to school.
(masculine and feminine)

هُوَ لَنْ يَذْهَب إِلَى ٱلْمَدْرَسَةِ.

howa lan yadh-hab ela al-madrasa

He will not go to school.
He will not be going to school.

هُوَ سَيَذْهَب إِلَى ٱلْمَدْرَسَةِ.

howa sa-yadh-hab ela al-madrasa

He will go to school.
He will be going to school.

هِيَ لَنْ تَذْهَب إِلَى ٱلْمَدْرَسَةِ.

hiya lan tadh-hab ela al-madrasa

She will not go to school.
She will not be going to school.

هِيَ سَتَذْهَب إِلَى ٱلْمَدْرَسَةِ.

hiya sa-tadh-hab ela al-madrasa

She will go to school.
She will be going to school.

Negating the Future Tense Modern Standard Arabic	Future Tense Sentences Modern Standard Arabic
هُما لَنْ يَذْهَبا إلى ٱلْمَدْرَسَة.	هُما سَيَذْهَبان إلى ٱلْمَدْرَسَة.
homaa lan yadh-habaa ela al-madrasa They both will not go to school. They both will not be going to school. (dual, masculine and feminine)	homaa sa-yadh-habaan ela al-madrasa They both will go to school. They both will be going to school. (dual, masculine and feminine)
هُم لَنْ يَذْهَبوا إلى ٱلْمَدْرَسَة.	هُم سَيَذْهَبون إلى ٱلْمَدْرَسَة.
hom lan yadh-haboo ela al-madrasa They will not go to school. They will not be going to school. (plural, masculine and feminine)	hom sa-yadh-haboon ela al-madrasa They will go to school. They will be going to school. (plural, masculine and feminine)
هُنَّ لَنْ يَذْهَبْنَ إلى ٱلْمَدْرَسَة.	هُنَّ سَيَذْهَبْنَ إلى ٱلْمَدْرَسَة.
honna lan yadh-habna ela al-madrasa They will not go to school. They will not be going to school. (plural, feminine)	honna sa-yadh-habna ela al-madrasa They will go to school. They will be going to school. (plural, feminine)

Negating the verb 'to understand' in the future. The root for this verb is :

Negating the Future Tense Modern Spoken Standard Arabic	Future Tense Sentences Modern Spoken Standard Arabic
أنا لَنْ أفْهَم ٱلدَّرْس.	أنا سَأفْهَم ٱلدَّرْس.
anaa lan afham al-dars I will not understand the lesson. I will not be understanding the lesson.	anaa sa,afham al-dars I will understand the lesson. I will be understanding the lesson.
أنْتَ لَنْ تَفْهَم ٱلدَّرْس.	أنْتَ سَتَفْهَم ٱلدَّرْس.
anta lan tafham al-dars You will not understand the lesson. You will not be understanding the lesson. (singular, masculine)	anta sa-tafham al-dars You will understand the lesson. You will be understanding the lesson. (singular, masculine)

Negating the Future Tense Modern Spoken Standard Arabic	Future Tense Sentences Modern Spoken Standard Arabic
أَنْتِ لَنْ تَفْهَمِي ٱلدَّرْس.  anti lan tafhamee al-dars You will not understand the lesson. You will not be understanding the lesson. (singular, feminine)	أَنْتِ سَتَفْهَمِين ٱلدَّرْس.  anti sa-tafhameen al-dars You will understand the lesson. You will be understanding the lesson. (singular, feminine)
أَنْتُما لَنْ تَفْهَما ٱلدَّرْس.  antomaa lan tafhamaa al-dars You both will not understand the lesson. You both will not be understanding the lesson. (dual, masculine and feminine)	أَنْتُما سَتَفْهَمان ٱلدَّرْس. antomaa sa-tafhamaan al-dars You both will understand the lesson. You both will be understanding the lesson. (dual, masculine and feminine)
أَنْتُم لَنْ تَفْهَموا ٱلدَرْس.  antom lan tafhamoo al-dars You all will not understand the lesson. You all will not be understanding the lesson. (plural, masculine and feminine)	أَنْتُم سَتَفْهَمون ٱلدَّرْس. antom sa-tafhamoon al-dars You all will understand the lesson. You all will be understanding the lesson. (plural, masculine and feminine)
أَنْتُنَّ لَنْ تَفْهَمْنَ ٱلدَرْس.  antonna lan tafhamna al-dars You all will not understand the lesson. You all will not be understanding the lesson. (plural, feminine)	أَنْتُنَّ سَتَفْهَمْنَ ٱلدَرْس. antonna sa-tafhamna al-dars You all will understand the lesson. You all will be understanding the lesson. (plural, feminine)
نَحْنُ لَنْ نَفْهَم ٱلدَّرْس.  naHno lan nafham al-dars We will not understand the lesson. We will not be understanding the lesson. (masculine and feminine)	نَحْنُ سَنَفْهَم ٱلدَّرْس.  naHno sa-nafham al-dars We will understand the lesson. We will be understanding the lesson. (masculine and feminine)

Negating the Future Tense Modern Spoken Standard Arabic	Future Tense Sentences Modern Spoken Standard Arabic

هُوَ لَنْ يَفْهَمَ ٱلدَّرْس.

howa lan yafham al-dars

He will not understand the lesson.
He will not be understanding the lesson.

هُوَ سَيَفْهَم ٱلدَّرْس.

howa sa-yafham al-dars

He will understand the lesson.
He will be understanding the lesson.

هِيَ لَنْ تَفْهَمَ ٱلدَّرْس.

hiya lan tafham al-dars

She will not understand the lesson.
She will not be understanding the lesson.

هِيَ سَتَفْهَم ٱلدَّرْس.

hiya sa-tafham al-dars

She will understand the lesson.
She will be understanding the lesson.

هُما لَنْ يَفْهَما ٱلدَّرْس.

homaa lan yafhamaa al-dars

They both will not understand the lesson.
The both will not be understanding the lesson.
(dual, masculine and feminine)

هُما سَيَفْهَمان ٱلدَّرْس.

homaa sa-yafhamaan al-dars

They both will understand the lesson.
The both will be understanding the lesson.
(dual, masculine and feminine)

هُم لَنْ يَفْهَموا ٱلدَّرْس.

hom lan yafhamoo al-dars

They will not understand the lesson.
The will not be understanding the lesson.
(plural, masculine and feminine)

هُم سَيَفْهَمون ٱلدَّرْس.

hom sa-yafhamoon al-dars

They will understand the lesson.
The will be understanding the lesson.
(plural, masculine and feminine)

هُنَّ لَنْ يَفْهَمْنَ ٱلدَّرْس.

honna lan yafhamna al-dars

They will not understand the lesson.
They will not be understanding the lesson.
(plural, feminine)

هُنَّ سَيَفْهَمْنَ ٱلدَّرْس.

honna sa-yafhamna al-dars

They will understand the lesson.
They will be understanding the lesson.
(plural, feminine)

- If the subject of the future verb is (You, singular feminine), the 'n' ن at the end is not commonly pronounced in spoken formal Arabic. Additionally, if the verb is negated, the 'n' ن is dropped in both spoken formal Arabic and classical Arabic. Therefore, the future verb will end with pronouncing the long vowel 'ee' ي, similar to the present verb. Examples:

لَنْ تَفْهَمي	لَنْ تَذْهَبي	لَنْ تَكْتُبي	لَنْ تَدْرُسي	لَنْ تَعيشي
lan tafhamee	lan tadhhabee	lan taktobee	lan tadrosee	lan taA'eeshee
You will not understand..	You will not go..	You will not write..	You will not study..	You will not live..
You will not be under-standing..	You will not be going..	You will not be writing..	You will not be studying..	You will not be living..
(you, singular feminine)	(you, singular feminine)	(you, singular feminine)	(you, singular feminine)	(you, singular feminine)

- If the subject of the future verb is (You, dual or plural, masculine and feminine) or (They, dual or plural, masculine and feminine), the 'n' ن at the end of the future verb is not commonly pronounced in spoken formal Arabic. Furthermore, when the plural or dual verb is negated, the 'n' ن is dropped from both verbs. However, if the subject of the negated verb is (You, plural, or They, masculine and feminine) and not dual, the 'n' ن is replaced with a 'silent alif' ا at the end of the plural future verb, serving as a signal of plurality. Therefore, the future verb ends with pronouncing the long vowel و, similar to the present verb. Examples:

لَنْ تَفْهَموا lan tafhamoo	لَنْ تَذْهَبوا lan tadhhaboo	لَنْ تَكْتُبوا lan taktoboo	لَنْ تَدْرُسوا lan tadrosoo	لَنْ تَعيشوا lan taA'eeshoo
You all will not understand..	You all will not go..	You all will not write..	You all will not study..	You all will not live..
You all will not be under-standing..	You all will not be going..	You all will not be writ-ting..	You all will not be study-ing..	You all will not be living..
(you, plural masculine and feminine)	(you, plural masculine and femi-nine)	(you, plural masculine and feminine)	(you, plural masculine and feminine)	(you, plural masculine and feminine)

لَنْ يَفْهَموا lan yafhamoo	لَنْ يَذْهَبوا lan yadhhaboo	لَنْ يَكْتُبوا lan yaktoboo	لَنْ يَدْرُسوا lan yadrosoo	لَنْ يَعيشوا lan yaA'eeshoo
They will not understand..	They will not go..	They will not write..	They will not study..	They will not live..
They will not be under-standing..	They will not be going..	They will not be writing..	They will not be studying..	They will not be living..
(they, mascu-line and femi-nine)	(they, mascu-line and fem-inine)	(they, mascu-line and femi-nine)	(they, mascu-line and femi-nine)	(they, mascu-line and femi-nine)

- Note, refer to page six for a refresher on the pronunciation system used in this book.

- Please keep in mind that Arabic is a cursive script and it is read and written from right to left while practicing reading.

Lesson Twenty-Seven
The Future Verb with Object Pronouns

The third type of personal pronouns is the object pronouns. These pronouns are attached to the future verb and indicate the object of the verb. They are similar to the possessive pronouns, except for the first possessive pronoun 'me' ـي, where the object pronoun is preceded by the letter 'n' ن before being attached to the verb ـني.

- **In spoken Modern Standard Arabic (MSA), the plural masculine form is commonly used instead of the dual and feminine plural forms. The dual and feminine plural forms are more commonly found in Classical Arabic and are used in formal and poetic contexts.**

Subject pronouns and their corresponding object pronouns are as follows:

Meaning	Object Pronouns	Definition	Subject Pronouns
Me	ـني nee	I	أنا anna
You (masculine)	كَ ka	You (masculine)	أنتَ anta
You (feminine)	كِ ki	You (feminine)	أنتِ anti
You (dual, masculine and feminine)	كُما komaa	You (dual, masculine and feminine)	أنتُما antomaa
You (plural, masculine and feminine)	كُم kom	You (plural, masculine and feminine)	أنتُم antom

Meaning	Object Pronouns	Definition	Subject Pronouns
You (plural, (feminine)	ـكُنَّ konna	You (plural, (feminine)	أَنْتُنَّ antonna
Us masculine and feminine)	ـنا naa	We (masculine and feminine)	نَحْنُ naHno
Him / it	ـهُ ho	He / it	هُوَ howa
Her / it	ـها haa	She / it	هِيَ hiya
Them (dual, masculine and feminine)	هُمَا homaa	They (dual, masculine and feminine)	هُمَا homaa
Them (masculine and feminine)	هُمْ hom	They (masculine and feminine)	هُمْ hom
Them (feminine)	ـهُنَّ honna	They (feminine)	هُنَّ honna

The following tables compare the improper use of subject pronouns with future verbs (a common error among beginners) to the proper use of object pronouns with future verbs in Classical Arabic:

- **The examples in the tables for this lesson are all in spoken Modern Standard Arabic, where the words are not fully vocalized at the end.**

231

The object pronouns with the future verb "to know" سَيَعْرِف.

Meaning	Proper Future Sentences	Improper Future Sentences
Mohammad will know me. Mohammad will recognize me.	مُحَمَّد سَيَعْرِفُنِي moHammad sa-yaA'rifonee	مُحَمَّد سَيَعْرِف أَنا moHammad sa-yaA'rif anaa
Mohammad will know you. Mohammad will recognize you. (singular, masculine)	مُحَمَّد سَيَعْرِفُكَ moHammad sa-yaA'rifoka	مُحَمَّد سَيَعْرِف أَنْتَ moHammad sa-yaA'rif anta
Mohammad will know you. Mohammad will recognize you. (singular, feminine)	مُحَمَّد سَيَعْرِفُكِ moHammad sa-yaA'rifoki	مُحَمَّد سَيَعْرِف أَنْتِ moHammad sa-yaA'rif anti
Mohammad will know both of you. Mohammad will recognize both of you. (dual, masculine and feminine)	مُحَمَّد سَيَعْرِفُكُما moHammad sa-yaA'rifokomaa	مُحَمَّد سَيَعْرِف أَنْتُما moHammad sa-yaA'rif antomaa
Mohammad will know all of you. Mohammad will recognize all of you. (plural, masculine and feminine)	مُحَمَّد سَيَعْرِفُكم moHammad sa-yaA'rifokom	مُحَمَّد سَيَعْرِف أَنْتُم moHammad sa-yaA'rif antom
Mohammad will know all of you. Mohammad will recognize all of you. (plural, feminine)	مُحَمَّد سَيَعْرِفُكن moHammad sa-yaA'rifokonna	مُحَمَّد سَيَعْرِف أَنْتُنْ moHammad sa-yaA'rif antonna
Mohammad will know us. Mohammad will recognize us.	مُحَمَّد سَيَعْرِفُنا moHammad sa-yaA'rifonaa	مُحَمَّد سَيَعْرِف نَحْنُ moHammad sa-yaA'rif naHno

Meaning	Proper Future Sentences	Improper Future Sentences
Mohammad will know him. Mohammad will recognize him.	مُحَمَّد سَيَعْرِفُهُ moHammad sa-yaA'rifoho	مُحَمَّد سَيَعْرِف هُوَ moHammad sa-yaA'rif howa
Mohammad will know her. Mohammad will recognize her.	مُحَمَّد سَيَعْرِفُها moHammad sa-yaA'rifoha	مُحَمَّد سَيَعْرِف هِيَ moHammad sa-yaA'rif hiya
Mohammad will know both of them. Mohammad will recognize both of them. (dual, masculine and feminine)	مُحَمَّد سَيَعْرِفُهُما moHammad sa-yaA'rifohomaa	مُحَمَّد سَيَعْرِف هُما moHammad sa-yaA'rif homaa
Mohammad will know them. Mohammad will recognize them. (plural, masculine and feminine)	مُحَمَّد سَيَعْرِفُهُم moHammad sa-yaA'rifohom	مُحَمَّد سَيَعْرِف هُم moHammad sa-yaA'rif hom
Mohammad will know them. Mohammad will recognize them. (plural, feminine)	مُحَمَّد سَيَعْرِفُهُنَّ moHammad sa-yaA'rifohonna	مُحَمَّد سَيَعْرِف هُنَّ moHammad sa-yaA'rif honna

The object pronouns with the future verb "to talk" سَيُكَلِّم.

Meaning	Proper Future Sentences	Improper Future Sentences
Ahmad will talk to me. Ahmad will speak to me.	أَحْمَد سَيُكَلِّمُنِي aHmad sa-yokallimonee	أَحْمَد سَيُكَلِّم أَنا aHmad sa-yokallim anaa

Meaning	Proper Future Sentences	Improper Future Sentences
Ahmad will talk to you. Ahmad will speak to you. (singular, masculine)	أَحْمَد سَيُكَلِّمُكَ aHmad sa-yokallimoka	أَحْمَد سَيُكَلِّم أَنْتَ aHmad sa-yokallim anta
Ahmad will talk to you. Ahmad will speak to you. (singular, feminine)	أَحْمَد سَيُكَلِّمُكِ aHmad sa-yokallimoki	أَحْمَد سَيُكَلِّم أَنْتِ aHmad sa-yokallim anti
Ahmad will talk to both of you. Ahmad will speak to both of you. (dual, masculine and feminine)	أَحْمَد سَيُكَلِّمُكُما aHmad sa-yokallimokomaa	أَحْمَد سَيُكَلِّم أَنْتُما aHmad sa-yokallim an-tomaa
Ahmad will talk to all of you. Ahmad will speak to all of you. (plural, masculine and feminine)	أَحْمَد سَيُكَلِّمُكم aHmad sa-yokallimokom	أَحْمَد سَيُكَلِّم أَنْتُم aHmad sa-yokallim an-tom
Ahmad will talk to all of you. Ahmad will speak to all of you. (plural, feminine)	أَحْمَد سَيُكَلِّمُكنّ aHmad sa-yokallimokonna	أَحْمَد سَيُكَلِّم أَنْتُنَّ aHmad sa-yokallim an-tonna
Ahmad will talk to us. Ahmad will speak to us.	أَحْمَد سَيُكَلِّمُنا aHmad sa-yokallimon-aa	أَحْمَد سَيُكَلِّم نَحْنُ aHmad sa-yokallim naHno
Ahmad will talk to him. Ahmad will speak to him.	أَحْمَد سَيُكَلِّمُه aHmad sa-yokallimoho	أَحْمَد سَيُكَلِّم هُوَ aHmad sa-yokallim howa
Ahmad will talk to her. Ahmad will speak to her.	أَحْمَد سَيُكَلِّمُها aHmad sa-yokallimo-haa	أَحْمَد سَيُكَلِّم هِيَ aHmad sa-yokallim hiya

Meaning	Proper Future Sentences	Improper Future Sentences
Ahmad will talk to both of them. Ahmad will speak to both of them. (dual, masculine and feminine)	أَحْمَد سَيُكَلِّمُهُما aHmad sa-yokallimhomaa	أَحْمَد سَيُكَلِّم هُما aHmad sa-yokallim homa
Ahmad will talk to them. Ahmad will speak to them. (plural, masculine and feminine)	أَحْمَد سَيُكَلِّمُهُم aHmad sa-yokallimo-hom	أَحْمَد سَيُكَلِّم هُم aHmad sa-yokallim hom
Ahmad will talk to them. Ahmad will speak to them. (plural, feminine)	أَحْمَد سَيُكَلِّمُهُنَّ aHmad sa-yokallimo-honna	أَحْمَد سَيُكَلِّم هُنَّ aHmad sa-yokallim honna

The object pronouns with the future verb "to teach" يُدَرِّس :

Meaning	Proper Future Sentences	Improper Future Sentences
The teacher will be teaching me.	الأُسْتاذ سَيُدَرِّسُنِي al-ostaadh sa-yodar-risonee	الأُسْتاذ سَيُدَرِّس أنا al-ostaadh sa-yodarris anaa
The teacher will be teaching you. (singular, masculine)	الأُسْتاذ سَيُدَرِّسُكَ al-ostaadh sa-yodar-risoka	الأُسْتاذ سَيُدَرِّس أنتَ al-ostaadh sa-yodarris anta
The teacher will be teaching you. (singular, feminine)	الأُسْتاذ سَيُدَرِّسُكِ al-ostaadh sa-yodar-risoki	الأُسْتاذ سَيُدَرِّس أنتِ al-ostaadh sa-yodarris anti

Meaning	Proper Future Sentences	Improper Future Sentences
The teacher will be teaching both of you. (dual, masculine and feminine)	الْأُسْتاذ سَيُدَرِّسُكُما al-ostaadh sa-yodar-risokomaa	الْأُسْتاذ سَيُدَرِّس أَنْتُما al-ostaadh sa-yodarris an-tomaa
The teacher will be teaching all of you. (plural, masculine and feminine)	الْأُسْتاذ سَيُدَرِّسُكم al-ostaadh sa-yodar-risokom	الْأُسْتاذ سَيُدَرِّس أَنْتُم al-ostaadh sa-yodarris an-tom
The teacher will be teaching all of you. (plural, feminine)	الْأُسْتاذ سَيُدَرِسُكُنَّ al-ostaadh sa-yodarris okonna	الْأُسْتاذ سَيُدَرِّس أَنْتُنَّ al-ostaadh sa-yodarris an-tonna
The teacher will be teaching us.	الْأُسْتاذ سَيُدَرِّسُنا al-ostaadh sa-yodar-risonaa	الْأُسْتاذ سَيُدَرِّس نَحْنُ al-ostaadh sa-yodarris naHno
The teacher will be teaching him.	الْأُسْتاذ سَيُدَرِّسُهُ al-ostaadh sa-yodar-risoho	الْأُسْتاذ سَيُدَرِّس هُوَ al-ostaadh sa-yodarris howa
The teacher will be teaching her.	الْأُسْتاذ سَيُدَرِّسُها al-ostaadh sa-yodar-risohaa	الْأُسْتاذ سَيُدَرِّس هِيَ al-ostaadh sa-yodarris hiya
The teacher will be teaching both of them. (dual, masculine and feminine)	الْأُسْتاذ سَيُدَرِّسُهُما al-ostaadh sa-yodarris ohomaa	الْأُسْتاذ سَيُدَرِّس هُما al-ostaadh sa-yodarris homaa
The teacher will be teaching them. (plural, masculine and feminine)	الْأُسْتاذ سَيُدَرِّسُهُم al-ostaadh sa-yodar-risohom	الْأُسْتاذ سَيُدَرِّس هُم al-ostaadh sa-yodarris hom
The teacher will be teaching them. (plural, feminine)	الْأُسْتاذ سَيُدَرِسُهُنَّ al-ostaadh sa-yodar-risohonna	الْأُسْتاذ سَيُدَرِّس هُنَّ al-ostaadh sa-yodarris honna

The object pronouns with the future verb "to ask" يَسْأَل :

Meaning	Proper Future Sentences	Improper Future Sentences
The teacher will be asking me.	الأُسْتاذَة سَتَسْأَلُني al-ostaadha sa-tas,alonee	الأُسْتاذَة سَتَسْأَل أنا al-ostaadha sa-tas,al anaa
The teacher will be asking you. (singular, masculine)	الأُسْتاذَة سَتَسْأَلُكَ al-ostaadha sa-tas,alo-ka	الأُسْتاذَة سَتَسْأَل أنْتَ al-ostaadha sa-tas,al anta
The teacher will be asking you. (singular, feminine)	الأُسْتاذَة سَتَسْأَلُكِ al-ostaadha sa-tas,alo-ki	الأُسْتاذَة سَتَسْأَل أنْتِ al-ostaadha sa-tas,al anti
The teacher will be asking both of you. (dual, masculine and feminine)	الأُسْتاذَة سَتَسْأَلُكُما al-ostaadha sa-tas,alokomaa	الأُسْتاذَة سَتَسْأَل أنْتُما al-ostaadha sa-tas,al an-tomaa
The teacher will be asking all of you. (plural, masculine and feminine)	الأُسْتاذَة سَتَسْأَلُكُم al-ostaadha sa-tas,alokom	الأُسْتاذَة سَتَسْأَل أنْتُم al-ostaadha sa-tas,al an-tom
The teacher will be asking all of you. (plural, feminine)	الأُسْتاذَة سَتَسْأَلُكُنَّ al-ostaadha sa-tas,alokonna	الأُسْتاذَة سَتَسْأَل أنْتُنَّ al-ostaadha sa-tas,al an-tonna
The teacher will be asking us.	الأُسْتاذَة سَتَسْأَلُنا al-ostaadha sa-tas,alonaa	الأُسْتاذَة سَتَسْأَل نَحْنُ al-ostaadha sa-tas,al naH-no
The teacher will be asking him.	الأُسْتاذَة سَتَسْأَلُه al-ostaadha sa-tas,alo-ho	الأُسْتاذَة سَتَسْأَل هُوَ al-ostaadha sa-tas,al howa

Meaning	Proper Future Sentences	Improper Future Sentences
The teacher will be asking her.	الأُسْتاذَة سَتَسْأَلُها al-ostaadha sa-tas,alo-haa	الأُسْتاذَة سَتَسْأَلَ هِيَ al-ostaadha sa-tas,al hiya
The teacher will be asking both of them. (dual, masculine and feminine)	الأُسْتاذَة سَتَسْأَلُهُما al-ostaadha sa-tas,alo-homaa	الأُسْتاذَة سَتَسْأَلَهُما al-ostaadha sa-tas,al homaa
The teacher will be asking them. (plural, masculine and feminine)	الأُسْتاذَة سَتَسْأَلُهُم al-ostaadha sa-tas,alo-hom	الأُسْتاذَة سَتَسْأَلَ هُم al-ostaadha sa-tas,al hom
The teacher will be asking them. (plural, feminine)	الأُسْتاذَة سَتَسْأَلُهُنَّ al-ostaadha sa-tas,alo-honna	الأُسْتاذَة سَتَسْأَلَ هُنَّ al-ostaadha sa-tas,al hon-na

The object pronouns with the future verb "to understand" يَفْهَم.

Meaning	Proper Sentences	Improper Sentences
He will understand me.	هُوَ سَيَفْهَمُني howa sa-yafhamonee	هُوَ سَيَفْهَمْ أَنا howa sa-yafham anaa
He will understand you. (singular, masculine)	هُوَ سَيَفْهَمُكَ howa sa-yafhamoka	هُوَ سَيَفْهَمْ أَنتَ howa sa-yafham anta
He will understand you. (singular, feminine)	هُوَ سَيَفْهَمُكِ howa sa-yafhamoki	هُوَ سَيَفْهَمْ أَنتِ howa sa-yafham anti
He will understand both of you. (dual, masculine and feminine)	هُوَ سَيَفْهَمُكُما howa sa-yafhamoko-maa	هُوَ سَيَفْهَمْ أَنتُما howa sa-yafham antomaa

Meaning	Proper Sentences	Improper Sentences
He will understand all of you. (plural, masculine and feminine)	هُوَ سَيَفْهَمُكَم howa sa-yafhamokom	هُوَ سَيَفْهَم أَنْتُم howa sa-yafham antom
He will understand all of you. (plural, feminine)	هُوَ سَيَفْهَمُكُنَّ howa sa-yafhamokonna	هُوَ سَيَفْهَم أَنْتُنَّ howa sa-yafham antonna
He will understand us.	هُوَ سَيَفْهَمُنا howa sa-yafhamonaa	هُوَ سَيَفْهَم نَحنُ howa sa-yafham naHno
He will understand him.	هُوَ سَيَفْهَمُه howa sa-yafhamoho	هُوَ سَيَفْهَم هُوَ howa sa-yafham howa
He will understand her.	هُوَ سَيَفْهَمُها howa sa-yafhamoha	هُوَ سَيَفْهَم هِي howa sa-yafham hiya
He will understand both of them. (dual, masculine and feminine)	هُوَ سَيَفْهَمُهُما howa sa-yafhamo-homaa	هُوَ سَيَفْهَم هُما howa sa-yafham homaa
He will understand them. (plural, masculine and feminine)	هُوَ سَيَفْهَمُهُم howa sa-yafhamohom	هُوَ سَيَفْهَم هُم howa sa-yafham hom
He will understand them. (plural, feminine)	هُوَ سَيَفْهَمُهِنَّ howa sa-yafhamohonna	هُوَ سَيَفْهَم هُنَّ howa sa-yafham honna

• Reminder to review page six, for the rules regarding the pronunciation system used in this book.

• Keep in mind that while practicing reading, Arabic is cursive and is read and written from right to left.

Lesson Twenty-Eight
Simple Past Tense

The past tense in Arabic refers to actions or events that have already been completed in the past.

Arabic language follows a root system where words are derived from a three-letter core. Each word family shares the same root consisting of three letters. To expand the word family, additional letters known as "letters of increase" are added to the core.

There are a total of nine letters of increase and a symbol called "shaddeh" used in this process.

The letters of increase are:

| shaddeh | t | t | n | s | m | ee/y | oo/w | aa | a |

Out of these nine letters, five are utilized to construct the past tense. These letters are as follows:

| a | oo | m | n | t |

These letters are attached to the root of the word to create the past tense, while also functioning as the subject of the verb. As a result, the subject is integrated into the past verb word and linked to it.

When forming a simple past verb and its subject, one or more of these five letters are added only after the three-letter root. As a result, the root remains intact and in the same order. However, there are exceptions:

• If the subject of the verb is the second person and the letter 'y' ي is one of the three

root letters, appearing in the middle of the root, it is replaced with a 'kasrah' vowel.

- In another scenario, if the subject of the verb is the feminine plural 'they', the 'y' ي is also replaced with a 'kasrah' ِ vowel.

- Lastly, if the subject of the verb is a third person, the 'y' ي can be replaced with a long vowel 'alif' ا.

- **In spoken Modern Standard Arabic (MSA), the plural masculine form is commonly used instead of the dual and feminine plural forms. The dual and feminine plural forms are more commonly found in Classical Arabic and are used in formal and poetic contexts.**

- The examples given in the tables for this lesson are in spoken Modern Standard Arabic. In this form, the words do not have vowels marked at the end.

The conjugations of the verb "to live" in the past tense with the root ع ي ش :

تُ (to)	Is added to the end of the root and it represents the subject of the verb 'I', (عِشْتُ / I lived).
تَ (ta)	Is added to the end of the root and it represents the subject of the verb (you, masculine), (عِشْتَ / you lived).
تِ (ti)	Is added to the end of the root and it represents the subject of the verb (you, feminine), (عِشْتِ / you lived).
تُمَا (tomaa)	Is added to the end of the root and it represents the dual subject of the verb (you, dual masculine and feminine), (عِشْتُمَا / you both lived).

تُم (tom)	Is added to the end of the root and it represents the plural subject of the verb (you, plural masculine and feminine), (عِشتُم / you lived).
تُنَّ (tonna)	Is added to the end of the root and it represents the plural subject of the verb (you, plural feminine), (عِشتُنَّ / you lived).
نا (naa)	Is added to the end of the root and it represents the plural subject of the verb 'we' (عِشنا / we lived).
	The 'fatHa' vowel is added to the end of the root, which is the sound of short 'a' to refer to the subject of the verb 'he' (عاش / he lived).
تْ (t)	Is added to the end of the root and it represents the subject of the verb 'she' (عاشتْ / she lived).
ا (aa)	Is added to the end of the root and it represents the dual subject of the verb (they, dual masculine and feminine) (عاشا / they both lived).
وا (w)	Is added to the end of the root and it represents the plural subject of the verb (they, plural masculine and feminine), (عاشوا / they lived).
نَ (na)	Is added to the end of the root and it represents the plural subject of the verb (they, plural feminine (عِشنَ / they lived).

- When the subject of the past tense is 'He', only the 'fatHa' vowel is added to the root of the word to form the past verb.

- The 'aa' ا at the end of (they, plural masculine and feminine) is a silent alif.

The conjugations of the verb "to study" in the past tense with the root د ر س :

Meaning	Simple Past Tense	Subject Pronoun	
I studied.	أَنا دَرَسْتُ anaa darasto	I	أَنا anaa
You studied.	أَنتَ دَرَسْتَ anta darasta	You (masculine)	أَنتَ anta
You studied.	أَنتِ دَرَسْتِ anti darasti	You (feminine)	أَنتِ anti
You both studied.	أَنْتُما دَرَسْتُما antomaa darastomaa	You (dual, masculine and feminine)	أَنْتُما antomaa
You all studied.	أَنْتُم دَرَسْتُم antom darastom	You (plural, masculine and feminine)	أَنْتُم antom
You all studied.	أَنْتُنَّ دَرَسْتُنَّ antonna darastonna	You (plural feminine)	أَنْتُنَّ antonna
We studied.	نَحْنُ دَرَسْنا naHno darasnaa	We (masculine and feminine)	نَحْنُ naHno
He studied.	هُوَ دَرَسَ howa darasa	He/it	هُوَ howa
She studied.	هِيَ دَرَسَتْ hiya darasat	She/it	هِيَ hiya
They both studied.	هُما دَرَسَا homaa darasaa	They (dual, masculine and feminine)	هُما homaa

Meaning	Simple Past Tense	Subject Pronoun
They studied.	هُم دَرَسوا hom darasoo	They (plural, masculine and feminine) هُم hom
They studied.	هُنَّ دَرَسْنَ honna darasna	They (plural feminine) هُنَّ honna

The conjugations of the verb "to write" in the past tense with the root: ك ت ب :

Meaning	Simple Past Tense	Subject Pronoun
I wrote.	أَنا كَتَبْتُ anaa katabto	I أَنا anaa
You wrote.	أَنتَ كَتَبْتَ anta katabta	You (masculine) أَنتَ anta
You wrote.	أَنتِ كَتَبْتِ anti katabti	You (feminine) أَنتِ anti
You both wrote.	أَنْتُما كَتَبْتُما antomaa katabtomaa	You (dual, masculine and feminine) أَنْتُما antomaa
You all wrote.	أَنْتُم كَتَبْتُم antom katabtom	You (plural, masculine and feminine) أَنْتُم antom
You all wrote.	أَنْتُنَّ كَتَبْتُنَّ antonna katabtonna	You (plural feminine) أَنْتُنَّ antonna

Meaning	Simple Past Tense	Subject Pronoun	
We wrote.	نَحْنُ كَتَبْنا naHno katabnaa	We (masculine and feminine)	نَحْنُ naHno
He wrote.	هُوَ كَتَبَ howa kataba	He/it	هُوَ howa
She wrote.	هِيَ كَتَبَتْ hiya katabat	She/it	هِيَ hiya
They both wrote.	هُما كَتَبَا homaa katabaa	They (dual, masculine and feminine)	هُما homaa
They wrote.	هُم كَتَبوا hom kataboo	They (plural, masculine and feminine)	هُم hom
They wrote.	هُنَّ كَتَبْنَ honna katabna	They (plural feminine)	هُنَّ honna

The conjugations of the verb "to go" in the past tense with the root ذ هـ ب :

Meaning	Simple Past Tense	Subject Pronoun	
I went.	أَنا ذَهَبْتُ anaa dhahbto	I	أَنا anaa
You went.	أنتَ ذَهَبْتَ anta dhahabta	You (masculine)	أنتَ anta
You went.	أنتِ ذَهَبْتِ anti dhahabti	You (feminine)	أنتِ anti

Meaning	Simple Past Tense	Subject Pronoun	
You both went.	أَنْتُما ذَهَبْتُما antomaa dha-habtomaa	You (dual, masculine and feminine)	أَنْتُما antomaa
You all went.	أَنْتُم ذَهَبْتُم antom dhahabtom	You (plural, masculine and feminine)	أَنْتُم antom
You all went.	أَنْتُنَّ ذَهَبْتُنَّ antonna dhahabtonna	You (plural feminine)	أَنْتُنَّ antonna
We went.	نَحْنُ ذَهَبْنا naHno dhahabnaa	We (masculine and feminine)	نَحْنُ naHno
He went.	هُوَ ذَهَبَ howa dhahaba	He/it	هُوَ howa
She went.	هِيَ ذَهَبَتْ hiya dhahabat	She/it	هِيَ hiya
They both went.	هُما ذَهَبا homaa dhahabaa	They (dual, masculine and feminine)	هُما homaa
They went.	هُم ذَهَبُوا hom dhahaboo	They (plural, masculine and feminine)	هُم hom
They went.	هُنَّ ذَهَبْنَ honna dhahabna	They (plural feminine)	هُنَّ honna

The conjugations of the verb "to understand" in the past tense with the root ف ه م

Meaning	Simple Past Tense	Subject Pronoun
I understood.	أَنَا فَهِمْتُ anna fahimto	أَنَا anaa I
You understood.	أَنتَ فَهِمْتَ anta fahimta	أَنتَ anta You (masculine)
You understood.	أَنتِ فَهِمْتِ anti fahimti	أَنتِ anti You (feminine)
You both under-stood.	أَنتُما فَهِمْتُما antomaa fahimtomaa	أَنْتُما antomaa You (dual, masculine and fem-inine)
You all understood.	أَنتُم فَهِمْتُم antom fahimtom	أَنْتُم antom You (plural, masculine and fem-inine)
You all understood.	أَنْتُنَّ فَهِمْتُنَّ antonna fahimtonna	أَنْتُنَّ antonna You (plural, feminine)
We understood.	نَحْنُ فَهِمْنا naHno fahimnaa	نَحْنُ naHno We (masculine and feminine)
He understood.	هُوَ فَهِمَ howa fahima	هُوَ howa He/it
She understood.	هِيَ فَهِمَتْ hiya fahimat	هِيَ hiya She/it

Meaning	Simple Past Tense		Subject Pronoun	
They both understood.	هُمَا فَهِمَا homaa fahimaa		They (dual, masculine and feminine)	هُمَا homaa
They understood.	هُم فَهِمُوا hom fahimoo		They (plural, masculine and feminine)	هُم hom
They understood.	هُنَّ فَهِمْنَ honna fahimna		They (plural feminine)	هُنَّ honna

- In spoken Arabic, if the subject of the past verb is (you, plural), the 'm' مـ at the end is not commonly pronounced, and it is replaced with a long vowel 'oo' و and silent 'alif' ا 'a' as a signal of the plural verb. Examples:

أَنْتُم فَهِمْتُوا antom fahim-too You all understood..	أَنْتُم ذَهَبْتُوا antom dha-habtoo You all went..	أَنْتُم كَتَبْتُوا antom katabtoo You all wrote..	أَنْتُم دَرَسْتُوا antom daras-too You all studied..	أَنْتُم عِشْتُوا antom Aish-too You all lived..

- In most classical and formal spoken Arabic, if the subject of the past verb is (you, plural), and the verb is followed by the object pronoun (he/it) هـ, the 'm' مـ is replaced with the long vowel 'oo' و before adding the object pronoun هـ to make the pronunciation easier. Examples:

أَنْتُمْ فَهِمْتُوهُ	أَنْتُمْ أَكَلْتُوهُ	أَنْتُمْ كَتَبْتُوهُ	أَنْتُمْ دَرَسْتُوهُ	أَنْتُمْ عِشْتُوهُ
antom fahim-tooho	antom akaltooho	antom katabtooho	antom daras-tooho	antom Aish-tooho
You all under-stood it.	You all ate it.	You all wrote it.	You all studied it.	You all lived it.

- In the past tense, when the subject pronoun is "they" (plural), the final 'alif' at the end of the verb is not pronounced. It is merely a spelling convention to indicate a plural verb. However, this 'alif' is dropped when an object pronoun is added to the end of the verb. Examples:

هُمْ فَهِموهُ	هُمْ أَكَلوهُ	هُمْ كَتَبوهُ	هُمْ دَرَسوهُ	هُمْ عاشوهُ
hom fahi-mooho	hom akalooho	hom kata-booho	hom dara-sooho	hom Aashooho
They under-stood it.	They ate it.	They wrote it.	They studied it.	They lived it.

- Note, refer to page six for a refresher on the pronunciation system used in this book.

- Note: In order to emphasize the grammar rules presented in the lesson, most of the words in this textbook have not been marked with vowels at the end.

- Please keep in mind that Arabic is a cursive script and it is read and written from right to left while practicing reading.

Lesson Twenty-Nine
Negating the Simple Past Tense

There are two methods of negating the past tense in Arabic. The first method involves using the word 'maa' ما, which is placed directly before the past verb. The second method involves adding 'lam' لَمْ to the present verb. This style of negating the past tense is similar to the way it is done in the English language.

- The examples given in the tables for this lesson are in spoken Modern Standard Arabic. In this form, the words do not have vowels marked at the end.

- **In spoken Modern Standard Arabic (MSA), the plural masculine form is commonly used instead of the dual and feminine plural forms. The dual and feminine plural forms are more commonly found in Classical Arabic and are used in formal and poetic contexts.**

First Style: Negating the past tense using 'maa' ما:

Negating the verb 'to live' in the past tense. The root for this verb is ع ي ش:

Negating Simple Past Tense Modern Standard Arabic	Simple Past Tense Modern Standard Arabic
أَنا ما عِشْتُ في كَليفورنيا. anaa maa A'ishto fee california I did not live in California.	أَنا عِشْتُ في كَليفورنيا. anaa A'ishto fee california I lived in California.
أَنْتَ ما عِشْتَ في كَليفورنيا. anta maa A'ishta fee california You did not live in California. (singular, masculine)	أَنْتَ عِشْتَ في كَليفورنيا. anta A'ishta fee california You lived in California. (singular, masculine)

250

Negating Simple Past Tense Modern Standard Arabic	Simple Past Tense Modern Standard Arabic
أَنْتِ ما عِشْتِ في كَليفورنيا.	أَنْتِ عِشْتِ في كَليفورنيا.
anti maa A'ishti fee california You did not live in California. (singular, feminine)	anti A'ishti fee california You lived in California. (singular, feminine)
أَنْتُما ما عِشْتُما في كَليفورنيا.	أَنْتُما عِشْتُما في كَليفورنيا.
antomaa maa A'ishtomaa fee california You both did not live in California. (dual, masculine and feminine)	antomaa A'ishtomaa fee california You both lived in California. (dual, masculine and feminine)
أَنْتُم ما عِشْتُم في كَليفورنيا.	أَنْتُم عِشْتُم في كَليفورنيا.
antom maa A'ishtom fee california You all did not live in California. (plural, masculine and feminine)	antom A'ishtom fee california You all lived in California. (plural, masculine and feminine)
أَنْتُنَّ ما عِشْتُنَّ في كَليفورنيا.	أَنْتُنَّ عِشْتُنَّ في كَليفورنيا.
antonna maa A'ishtonna fee california You all did not live in California. (plural, feminine)	antonna A'ishtonna fee california You all lived in California. (plural, feminine)
نَحْنُ ما عِشْنا في كَليفورنيا.	نَحْنُ عِشْنا في كَليفورنيا.
naHno maa A'ishnaa fee california We did not live in California. (masculine and feminine)	naHno A'ishnaa fee california We lived in California. (masculine and feminine)
هُوَ ما عاشَ في كَليفورنيا.	هُوَ عاشَ في كَليفورنيا.
howa maa A'asha fee california He did not live in California.	howa A'asha fee california He lived in California.
هِيَ ما عاشَتْ في كَليفورنيا.	هِيَ عاشَتْ في كَليفورنيا.
hiya maa A'ashat fee california She did not live in California.	hiya A'ashat fee california She lived in California.

Negating Simple Past Tense Modern Standard Arabic	Simple Past Tense Modern Standard Arabic
هُما ما عاشَا في كَليفورنيا.	هُما عاشَا في كَليفورنيا.
homaa maa A'ashaa fee california They both did not live in California. (dual, masculine and feminine)	homaa A'ashaa fee california They both lived in California. (dual, masculine and feminine)
هُم ما عاشوا في كَليفورنيا.	هُم عاشوا في كَليفورنيا.
hom maa A'ashoo fee california They did not live in California. (plural, masculine and feminine)	hom A'ashoo fee california They lived in California. (plural, masculine and feminine)
هُنَّ ما عِشْنَ في كَليفورنيا.	هُنَّ عِشْنَ في كَليفورنيا.
honna maa A'ishna fee california They did not live in California. (plural, feminine)	honna A'ishna fee california They lived in California. (plural, feminine)

Negating the verb 'to study' in the past tense. The root for this verb is د ر س:

Negating Simple Past Tense Modern Spoken Standard Arabic	Simple Past Tense Modern Spoken Standard Arabic
أنا ما دَرَسْتُ في ٱلمَكْتَبَة.	أنا دَرَسْتُ في ٱلمَكْتَبَة.
anaa maa darasto fee al-maktaba I did not study at the library.	anaa darasto fee al-maktaba I studied at the library.
أنْتَ ما دَرَسْتَ في ٱلمَكْتَبَة.	أنْتَ دَرَسْتَ في ٱلمَكْتَبَة.
anta maa darasta fee al-maktaba You did not study at the library. (singular, masculine)	anta darasta fee al-maktaba You studied at the library. (singular, masculine)
أنْتِ ما دَرَسْتِ في ٱلمَكْتَبَة.	أنْتِ دَرَسْتِ في ٱلمَكْتَبَة.
anti maa darasti fee al-maktaba You did not study at the library. (singular, feminine)	anti darasti fee al-maktaba You studied at the library. (singular, feminine)

Negating Simple Past Tense Modern Spoken Standard Arabic	Simple Past Tense Modern Spoken Standard Arabic
أَنْتُما ما دَرَسْتُما في ٱلْمَكْتَبَة.	أَنْتُما دَرَسْتُما في ٱلْمَكْتَبَة.
antomaa maa darastomaa fee al-mak-taba **You both did not study at the library.** **(dual, masculine and feminine)**	antomaa darastomaa fee al-maktaba **You both studied at the library.** **(dual, masculine and feminine)**
أَنْتُم ما دَرَسْتُم في ٱلْمَكْتَبَة.	أَنْتُم دَرَسْتُم في ٱلْمَكْتَبَة.
antom maa darastom fee al-maktaba **You all did not study at the library.** **(plural, masculine and feminine)**	antom darastom fee al-maktaba **You all studied at the library.** **(plural, masculine and feminine)**
أَنْتُنَّ ما دَرَسْتُنَّ في ٱلْمَكْتَبَة.	أَنْتُنَّ دَرَسْتُنَّ في ٱلْمَكْتَبَة.
antonna maa darastonna fee al-mak-taba **You all did not study at the library.** **(plural, feminine)**	antonna darastonna fee al-maktaba **You all studied at the library.** **(plural, feminine)**
نَحْنُ ما دَرَسْنا في ٱلْمَكْتَبَة.	نَحْنُ دَرَسْنا في ٱلْمَكْتَبَة.
naHno maa darasnaa fee al-maktaba **We did not study at the library.** **(masculine and feminine)**	naHno darasnaa fee al-maktaba **We studied at the library.** **(masculine and feminine)**
هُوَ ما دَرَسَ في ٱلْمَكْتَبَة.	هُوَ دَرَسَ في ٱلْمَكْتَبَة.
howa maa darasa fee al-maktaba **He did not study at the library.**	howa darasa fee al-maktaba **He studied at the library.**
هِيَ ما دَرَسَتْ في ٱلْمَكْتَبَة.	هِيَ دَرَسَتْ في ٱلْمَكْتَبَة.
hiya maa darasat fee al-maktaba **She did not study at the library.**	hiya darasat fee al-maktaba **She studied at the library.**
هُما ما دَرَسا في ٱلْمَكْتَبَة.	هُما دَرَسا في ٱلْمَكْتَبَة.
homaa maa darasaa fee al-maktaba **They both did not study at the library.** **(dual, masculine and feminine)**	homaa darasaa fee al-maktaba **They both studied at the library.** **(dual, masculine and feminine)**

Negating Simple Past Tense Modern Spoken Standard Arabic	Simple Past Tense Modern Spoken Standard Arabic
هُمْ ما دَرَسوا في ٱلْمَكْتَبَة.	هُمْ دَرَسوا في ٱلْمَكْتَبَة.
hom maa darasoo fee al-maktaba They did not study at the library. (plural, masculine and feminine)	hom darasoo fee al-maktaba They studied at the library. (plural, masculine and feminine)
هُنَّ ما دَرَسْنَ في ٱلْمَكْتَبَة.	هُنَّ دَرَسْنَ في ٱلْمَكْتَبَة.
honna maa darasna fee al-maktaba They did not study at the library. (plural, feminine)	honna darasna fee al-maktaba They studied at the library. (plural, feminine)

Negating the verb 'to write' in the past tense. The root for this verb is ك ت ب:

Negating Simple Past Tense Modern Standard Arabic	Simple Past Tense Modern Standard Arabic
أنا ما كَتَبْتُ رِسالَة.	أنا كَتَبْتُ رِسالَة.
anaa maa katabto risaala I did not write a letter.	anaa katabto risaala I wrote a letter.
أنْتَ ما كَتَبْتَ رِسالَة.	أنْتَ كَتَبْتَ رِسالَة.
anta maa katabta risaala You did not write a letter. (singular, masculine)	anta katabta risaala You wrote a letter. (singular, masculine)
أنْتِ ما كَتَبْتِ رِسالَة.	أنْتِ كَتَبْتِ رِسالَة.
anti maa katabti risaala You did not write a letter. (singular, feminine)	anti katabti risaala You wrote a letter. (singular, feminine)
أنْتُما ما كَتَبْتُما رِسالَة.	أنْتُما كَتَبْتُما رِسالَة.
antomaa maa katabtomaa risaala You both did not write a letter. (dual, masculine and feminine)	antomaa katabtomaa risaala You both wrote a letter. (dual, masculine and feminine)

Negating Simple Past Tense Modern Standard Arabic	Simple Past Tense Modern Standard Arabic
أَنْتُمْ ما كَتَبْتُمْ رِسالَة.	أَنْتُمْ كَتَبْتُمْ رِسالَة.
antom maa katabtom risaala	antom katabtom risaala
You all did not write a letter. (plural, masculine and feminine)	You all wrote a letter. (plural, masculine and feminine)
أَنْتُنَّ ما كَتَبْتُنَّ رِسالَة.	أَنْتُنَّ كَتَبْتُنَّ رِسالَة.
antonna maa katabtonna risaala	antonna katabtonna risaala
You all did not write a letter. (plural, feminine)	You all wrote a letter. (plural, feminine)
نَحْنُ ما كَتَبْنا رِسالَة.	نَحْنُ كَتَبْنا رِسالَة.
naHno maa katabna risaala	naHno katabna risaala
We did not write a letter. (masculine and feminine)	We wrote a letter. (masculine and feminine)
هُوَ ما كَتَبَ رِسالَة.	هُوَ كَتَبَ رِسالَة.
howa maa kataba risaala	howa kataba risaala
He did not write a letter.	He wrote a letter.
هِيَ ما كَتَبَتْ رِسالَة.	هِيَ كَتَبَتْ رِسالَة.
hiya maa katabat risaala	hiya katabat risaala
She did not write a letter.	She wrote a letter.
هُما ما كَتَبا رِسالَة.	هُما كَتَبا رِسالَة.
homaa maa katabaa risaala	homaa katabaa risaala
They both did not write a letter. (dual, masculine and feminine)	They both wrote a letter. (dual, masculine and feminine)
هُمْ ما كَتَبوا رِسالَة.	هُمْ كَتَبوا رِسالَة.
hom maa kataboo risaala	hom kataboo risaala
They did not write a letter. (plural, masculine and feminine)	They wrote a letter. (plural, masculine and feminine)

Negating Simple Past Tense Modern Standard Arabic	Simple Past Tense Modern Standard Arabic
هُنَّ ما كَتَبْنَ رِسالَة.	هُنَّ كَتَبْنَ رِسالَة.
honna maa katabna risaala They did not write a letter. (plural, feminine)	honna katabna risaala They wrote a letter. (plural, feminine)

Negating the verb 'to go' in the past tense. The root for this verb is :

Negating Simple Past Tense Modern Spoken Standard Arabic	Simple Past Tense Modern Spoken Standard Arabic
أنا ما ذَهَبْتُ إلى ٱلْمَدْرَسَة.	أنا ذَهَبْتُ إلى ٱلْمَدْرَسَة.
anaa maa dhahabto ela al-madrasa I did not go to school.	anaa dhahabto ela al-madrasa I went to school.
أنْتَ ما ذَهَبْتَ إلى ٱلْمَدْرَسَة.	أنْتَ ذَهَبْتَ إلى ٱلْمَدْرَسَة.
anta maa dhahabta ela al-madrasa You did not go to school. (singular, masculine)	anta dhahabta ela al-madrasa You went to school. (singular, masculine)
أنتِ ما ذَهَبْتِ إلى ٱلْمَدْرَسَة.	أنتِ ذَهَبْتِ إلى ٱلْمَدْرَسَة.
anti maa dhahabti ela al-madrasa You did not go to school. (singular, feminine)	anti dhahabti ela al-madrasa You went to school. (singular, feminine)
أنتُما ما ذَهَبْتُما إلى ٱلْمَدْرَسَة.	أنتُما ذَهَبْتُما إلى ٱلْمَدْرَسَة.
antomaa maa dhahabtomaa ela al-madrasa You both did not go to school. (dual, masculine and feminine)	antomaa dhahabtomaa ela al-madrasa You both went to school. (dual, masculine and feminine)

Negating Simple Past Tense Modern Spoken Standard Arabic	Simple Past Tense Modern Spoken Standard Arabic
أَنتُم ما ذَهَبْتُم إلى ٱلْمَدْرَسَة. antom maa dhahabtom ela al-madrasa You all did not go to school. (plural, masculine and feminine)	أَنتُم ذَهَبْتُم إلى ٱلْمَدْرَسَة. antom dhahabtom ela al-madrasa You all went to school. (plural, masculine and feminine)
أَنْتُنَّ ما ذَهَبْتُنَّ إلى ٱلْمَدْرَسَة. antonna maa dhahabtonna ela al-madrasa You all did not go to school. (plural, feminine)	أَنْتُنَّ ذَهَبْتُنَّ إلى ٱلْمَدْرَسَة. antonna dhahabtonna ela al-madrasa You all went to school. (plural, feminine)
نَحنُ ما ذَهَبْنا إلى ٱلْمَدْرَسَة. naHno maa dhahabnaa ela al-madrasa We did not go to school. (masculine and feminine)	نَحنُ ذَهَبْنا إلى ٱلْمَدْرَسَة. naHno dhahabnaa ela al-madrasa We went to school. (masculine and feminine)
هُوَ ما ذَهَبَ إلى ٱلْمَدْرَسَة. howa maa dhahaba ela al-madrasa He did not go to school.	هُوَ ذَهَبَ إلى ٱلْمَدْرَسَة. howa dhahaba ela al-madrasa He went to school.
هِيَ ما ذَهَبَتْ إلى ٱلْمَدْرَسَة. hiya maa dhahabat ela al-madrasa She did not go to school.	هِيَ ذَهَبَتْ إلى ٱلْمَدْرَسَة. hiya dhahabat ela al-madrasa She went to school.
هُما ما ذَهَبا إلى ٱلْمَدْرَسَة. homaa maa dhahabaa ela al-madrasa They both did not go to school. (dual, masculine and feminine)	هُما ذَهَبا إلى ٱلْمَدْرَسَة. homaa dhahabaa ela al-madrasa They both went to school. (dual, masculine and feminine)
هُم ما ذَهَبوا إلى ٱلْمَدْرَسَة. hom maa dhahaboo ela al-madrasa They did not go to school. (plural, masculine and feminine)	هُم ذَهَبوا إلى ٱلْمَدْرَسَة. hom dhahaboo ela al-madrasa They went to school. (plural, masculine and feminine)

Negating Simple Past Tense Modern Spoken Standard Arabic	Simple Past Tense Modern Spoken Standard Arabic
هُنَّ ما ذَهَبْنَ إلى ٱلْمَدْرَسَة.	هُنَّ ذَهَبْنَ إلى ٱلْمَدْرَسَة.
honna maa dhahabna ela al-madrasa They did not go to school. (plural, feminine)	honna dhahabna ela al-madrasa They went to school. (plural, feminine)

Negating the verb 'to understand' in the past tense. The root's verb is  :

Negating Simple Past Tense Modern Standard Arabic	Simple Past Tense Modern Standard Arabic
أنا ما فَهِمْتُ ٱلدَّرْس.	أنا فَهِمْتُ ٱلدَّرْس.
anaa maa fahimto al-dars I did not understand the lesson.	anaa fahimto al-dars I understood the lesson.
أنْتَ ما فَهِمْتَ ٱلدَّرْس.	أنْتَ فَهِمْتَ ٱلدَّرْس.
anta maa fahimta al-dars You did not understand the lesson. (singular, masculine)	anta fahimta al-dars You understood the lesson. (singular, masculine)
أنْتِ ما فَهِمْتِ ٱلدَّرْس.	أنْتِ فَهِمْتِ ٱلدَّرْس.
anti maa fahimti al-dars You did not understand the lesson. (singular, feminine)	anti fahimti al-dars You understood the lesson. (singular, feminine)
أنْتُما ما فَهِمْتُما ٱلدَّرْس.	أنْتُما فَهِمْتُما ٱلدَّرْس.
antomaa maa fahimtomaa al-dars You both did not understand the lesson. (dual, masculine and feminine)	antomaa fahimtomaa al-dars You both understood the lesson. (dual, masculine and feminine)

Negating Simple Past Tense **Modern Standard Arabic**	**Simple Past Tense** **Modern Standard Arabic**
أَنْتُم ما فَهِمْتُم ٱلدَّرْس. antom maa fahimtom al-dars You all did not understand the lesson. (plural, masculine and feminine)	أَنْتُم فَهِمْتُم ٱلدَّرْس. antom fahimtom al-dars You all understood the lesson. (plural, masculine and feminine)
أَنْتُنَّ ما فَهِمْتُنَّ ٱلدَّرْس. antonna maa fahimtonna al-dars You all did not understand the lesson. (plural, feminine)	أَنْتُنَّ فَهِمْتُنَّ ٱلدَّرْس. antonna fahimtonna al-dars You all understood the lesson. (plural, feminine)
نَحْنُ ما فَهِمنا ٱلدَّرْس. naHno maa fahimnaa al-dars We did not understand the lesson. (masculine and feminine)	نَحْنُ فَهِمْنا ٱلدَّرْس. naHno fahimnaa al-dars We understood the lesson. (masculine and feminine)
هُوَ ما فَهِمَ ٱلدَّرْس. howa maa fahima al-dars He did not understand the lesson.	هُوَ فَهِمَ ٱلدَّرْس. howa fahima al-dars He understood the lesson.
هِيَ ما فَهِمَتْ ٱلدَّرْس. hiya maa fahimat al-dars She did not understand the lesson.	هِيَ فَهِمَتْ ٱلدَّرْس. hiya fahimat al-dars She understood the lesson.
هُما ما فَهِما ٱلدَّرْس. homaa maa fahimaa al-dars They both did not understand the lesson. (dual, masculine and feminine)	هُما فَهِما ٱلدَّرْس. homaa fahimaa al-dars They both understood the lesson. (dual, masculine and feminine)
هُم ما فَهِموا ٱلدَّرْس. hom maa fahimoo al-dars They did not understand the lesson. (plural, masculine and feminine)	هُم فَهِموا ٱلدَّرْس. hom fahimoo al-dars They understood the lesson. (plural, masculine and feminine)

Negating Simple Past Tense Modern Standard Arabic	Simple Past Tense Modern Standard Arabic
هُنَّ ما فَهِمْنَ ٱلدَّرْس.	هُنَّ فَهِمْنَ ٱلدَّرْس.
honna maa fahimna al-dars	honna fahimna al-dars
They did not understand the lesson. (plural, feminine)	They understood the lesson. (plural, feminine)

Second Style: Negating the past tense using 'lam' لَمْ :

- In spoken Modern Standard Arabic (MSA), the plural masculine form is commonly used instead of the dual and feminine plural forms. The dual and feminine plural forms are more commonly found in Classical Arabic and are used in formal and poetic contexts.

Negating the verb 'to live' in the past tense. The root for this verb is ع ي ش :

Negating the Past Tense Modern Spoken Standard Arabic	Simple Past Tense Modern Spoken Standard Arabic
أنا لَمْ أعيش في كَليفورنيا.	أنا عِشْتُ في كَليفورنيا.
anaa lam aA'eesh fee california	anaa A'ishto fee california
I did not live in California.	I lived in California.
أنْتَ لَمْ تَعيش في كَليفورنيا.	أنْتَ عِشْتَ في كَليفورنيا.
anta lam taA'eesh fee california	anta A'ishta fee california
You did not live in California. (singular, masculine)	You lived in California. (singular, masculine)
أنْتِ لَمْ تَعيشي في كَليفورنيا.	أنْتِ عِشْتِ في كَليفورنيا.
anti lam taA'eeshee fee california	anti A'ishti fee california
You did not live in California. (singular, feminine)	You lived in California. (singular, feminine)

Negating the Past Tense Modern Spoken Standard Arabic	Simple Past Tense Modern Spoken Standard Arabic
أَنْتُما لَمْ تَعِيشا في كَليفورنيا. antomaa lam taA'eeshaa fee california You both did not live in California. (dual, masculine and feminine)	أَنْتُما عِشْتُما في كَليفورنيا. antomaa A'ishtomaa fee california You both lived in California. (dual, masculine and feminine)
أَنْتُم لَمْ تَعِيشوا في كَليفورنيا. antom lam taA'eeshoo fee california You all did not live in California. (plural, masculine and feminine)	أَنْتُم عِشْتُم في كَليفورنيا. antom A'ishtom fee california You all lived in California. (plural, masculine and feminine)
أَنْتُنَّ لَمْ تَعِشْنَ في كَليفورنيا. antonna lam taA'ishna fee california You all did not live in California. (plural, feminine)	أَنْتُنَّ عِشْتُنَّ في كَليفورنيا. antonna A'ishtonna fee california You all lived in California. (plural, feminine)
نَحْنُ لَمْ نَعِيش في كَليفورنيا. naHno lam naA'eesh fee california We did not live in California. (masculine and feminine)	نَحنُ عِشْنا في كَليفورنيا. naHno A'ishnaa fee california We lived in California (masculine and feminine)
هُوَ لَمْ يَعِيش في كَليفورنيا. howa lam yaA'eesh fee california He did not live in California.	هُوَ عاشَ في كَليفورنيا. howa A'asha fee california He lived in California.
هِيَ لَمْ تَعِيش في كَليفورنيا. hiya lam taA'eesh fee california She did not live in California.	هِيَ عاشَتْ في كَليفورنيا. hiya A'ashat fee california She lived in California.
هُما لَمْ يَعِيشا في كَليفورنيا. homaa lam yaA'eeshaa fee california They both did not live in California. (dual, masculine and feminine)	هُما عاشا في كَليفورنيا. homaa A'ashaa fee california They both lived in California. (dual, masculine and feminine)

Negating the Past Tense Modern Spoken Standard Arabic	Simple Past Tense Modern Spoken Standard Arabic
هُمْ لَمْ يَعيشوا في كَليفورنيا.	هُم عاشوا في كَليفورنيا.
hom lam yaA'eeshoo fee california They did not live in California. (plural, masculine and feminine)	hom A'ashoo fee california They lived in California. (plural, masculine and feminine)
هُنَّ لَمْ يَعِشْنَ في كَليفورنيا.	هُنَّ عِشْنَ في كَليفورنيا.
honna lam yaA'ishna fee california They did not live in California. (plural, feminine)	honna A'ishna fee california They lived in a California. (plural, feminine)

Negating the verb 'to study' in the past tense. The root for this verb is د ر س :

Negating the Past Tense Modern Standard Arabic	Simple Past Tense Modern Standard Arabic
أنا لَمْ أدرُس في ٱلمَكْتَبَة.	أنا دَرَسْتُ في ٱلمَكْتَبَة.
anaa lam adros fee al-maktaba I did not study at the library.	anaa darasto fee al-maktaba I studied at the library.
أنْتَ لَمْ تَدْرُس في ٱلمَكْتَبَة.	أنْتَ دَرَسْتَ في ٱلمَكْتَبَة.
anta lam tadros fee al-maktaba You did not study at the library. (singular, masculine)	anta darasta fee al-maktaba You studied at the library. (singular, masculine)
أنْتِ لَمْ تَدْرُسي في ٱلمَكْتَبَة.	أنْتِ دَرَسْتِ في ٱلمَكْتَبَة.
anti lam tadrosee fee al-maktaba You did not study at the library. (singular, feminine)	anti darasti fee al-maktaba You studied at the library. (singular, feminine)

Negating the Past Tense Modern Standard Arabic	Simple Past Tense Modern Standard Arabic
أَنْتُمَا لَمْ تَدْرُسَا فِي ٱلْمَكْتَبَة.	أَنْتُمَا دَرَسْتُمَا فِي ٱلْمَكْتَبَة.
antomaa lam tadrosaa fee al-maktaba You both did not study at the library. (dual, masculine and feminine)	antomaa darastomaa fee al-mak-taba You both studied at the library. (dual, masculine and feminine)
أَنْتُمْ لَمْ تَدْرُسوا فِي ٱلْمَكْتَبَة.	أَنْتُمْ دَرَسْتُمْ فِي ٱلْمَكْتَبَة.
antom lam tadrosoo fee al-maktaba You all did not study at the library. (plural, masculine and feminine)	antom darastom fee al-maktaba You all studied at the library. (plural, masculine and feminine)
أَنْتُنَّ لَمْ تَدْرُسْنَ فِي ٱلْمَكْتَبَة.	أَنْتُنَّ دَرَسْتُنَّ فِي ٱلْمَكْتَبَة.
antonna lam tadrosna fee al-maktaba You all did not study at the library. (plural, feminine)	antonna darastonna fee al-maktaba You all studied at the library. (plural, feminine)
نَحْنُ لَمْ نَدْرُس فِي ٱلْمَكْتَبَة.	نَحْنُ دَرَسْنا فِي ٱلْمَكْتَبَة.
naHno lam nadros fee al-maktaba We did not study at the library. (masculine and feminine)	naHno darasnaa fee al-maktaba We studied at the library. (masculine and feminine)
هُوَ لَمْ يَدْرُس فِي ٱلْمَكْتَبَة.	هُوَ دَرَسَ فِي ٱلْمَكْتَبَة.
howa lam yadros fee al-maktaba He did not study at the library.	howa darasa fee al-maktaba He studied at the library.
هِيَ لَمْ تَدْرُس فِي ٱلْمَكْتَبَة.	هِيَ دَرَسَتْ فِي ٱلْمَكْتَبَة.
hiya lam tadros fee al-maktaba She did not study at the library.	hiya darasat fee al-maktaba She studied at the library.
هُمَا لَمْ يَدْرُسَا فِي ٱلْمَكْتَبَة.	هُمَا دَرَسَا فِي ٱلْمَكْتَبَة.
homaa lam yadrosaa fee al-maktaba They both did not study at the library. (dual, masculine and feminine)	homaa darasaa fee al-maktaba They both studied at the library. (dual, masculine and feminine)

Negating the Past Tense Modern Standard Arabic	Simple Past Tense Modern Standard Arabic
هُمْ لَمْ يَدْرُسوا في ٱلْمَكْتَبَة.	هُمْ دَرَسوا في ٱلْمَكْتَبَة.
hom lam yadrosoo fee al-maktaba They did not study at the library. (plural, masculine and feminine)	hom darasoo fee al-maktaba They studied at the library. (plural, masculine and feminine)
هُنَّ لَمْ يَدْرُسْنَ في ٱلْمَكْتَبَة .	هُنَّ دَرَسْنَ في ٱلْمَكْتَبَة.
honna lam yadrosna fee al-maktaba They did not study at the library. (plural, feminine)	honna darasna fee al-maktaba They studied at the library. (plural, feminine)

Negating the verb 'to write' in the past tense. The root for this verb is كـ تـ بـ:

Negating the Past Tense Modern Spoken Standard Arabic	Simple Past Tense Modern Spoken Standard Arabic
أَنا لَمْ أَكْتُب رِسالَة.	أَنا كَتَبْتُ رِسالَة.
anaa lam aktob risaala I did not write a letter.	anaa katabto risaala I wrote a letter.
أَنْتَ لَمْ تَكْتُب رِسالَة.	أَنْتَ كَتَبْتَ رِسالَة.
anta lam taktob risaala You did not write a letter. (singular, masculine)	anta katabta risaala You wrote a letter. (singular, masculine)
أَنْتِ لَمْ تَكْتُبي رِسالَة.	أَنْتِ كَتَبْتِ رِسالَة.
anti lam taktobee risaala You did not write a letter. (singular, feminine)	anti katabti risaala You wrote a letter. (singular, feminine)
أَنْتُما لَمْ تَكْتُبا رِسالَة.	أَنْتُما كَتَبْتُما رِسالَة.
antomaa lam taktobaa risaala You both did not write a letter. (dual, masculine and feminine)	antomaa katabtomaa risaala You both wrote a letter. (dual, masculine and feminine)

Negating the Past Tense **Modern Spoken Standard Arabic**	**Simple Past Tense** **Modern Spoken Standard Arabic**
أَنْتُمْ لَمْ تَكْتُبوا رِسالَة. antom lam taktoboo risaala You all did not write a letter. (plural, masculine and feminine)	أَنْتُمْ كَتَبْتُمْ رِسالَة. antom katabtom risaala You all wrote a letter. (plural, masculine and feminine)
أَنْتُنَّ لَمْ تَكْتُبْنَ رِسالَة. antonna lam taktobna risaala You all did not write a letter. (plural, feminine)	أَنْتُنَّ كَتَبْتُنَّ رِسالَة. antonna katabtonna risaala You all wrote a letter. (plural, feminine)
نَحْنُ لَمْ نَكْتُب رِسالَة. naHno lam naktob risaala We did not write a letter. (masculine and feminine)	نَحْنُ كَتَبْنا رِسالَة. naHno katabnaa risaala We wrote a letter. (masculine and feminine)
هُوَ لَمْ يَكْتُب رِسالَة. howa lam yaktob risaala He did not write a letter.	هُوَ كَتَبَ رِسالَة. howa kataba risaala He wrote a letter.
هِيَ لَمْ تَكْتُب رِسالَة . hiya lam taktob risaala She did not write a letter.	هِيَ كَتَبَتْ رِسالَة. hiya katabat risaala She wrote a letter.
هُما لَمْ يَكْتُبا رِسالَة. homaa lam yaktobaa risaala They both did not write a letter. (dual, masculine and feminine)	هُما كَتَبا رِسالَة. homaa katabaa risaala They both wrote a letter. (dual, masculine and feminine)
هُم لَمْ يَكْتُبوا رِسالَة. hom lam yaktoboo risaala They did not write a letter. (plural, masculine and feminine)	هُم كَتَبوا رِسالَة. hom kataboo risaala They wrote a letter. (plural, masculine and feminine)

Negating the Past Tense Modern Spoken Standard Arabic	Simple Past Tense Modern Spoken Standard Arabic
هُنَّ لَمْ يَكْتُبْنَ رِسَالَة.	هُنَّ كَتَبْنَ رِسَالَة.
honna lam yaktobna risaala	honna katabna risaala
They did not write a letter. (plural, feminine)	They wrote a letter. (plural, feminine)

Negating the verb 'to go' in the past tense. The root for this verb is :

Negating the Past Tense Modern Spoken Standard Arabic	Simple Past Tense Modern Spoken Standard Arabic
أَنَا لَمْ أَذْهَب إِلَى ٱلْمَدْرَسَة.	أَنَا ذَهَبْتُ إِلَى ٱلْمَدْرَسَة.
anaa lam adh-hab ela al-madrasa	anaa dhahabto ela al-madrasa
I did not go to school.	I went to school.
أَنْتَ لَمْ تَذْهَب إِلَى ٱلْمَدْرَسَة.	أَنْتَ ذَهَبْتَ إِلَى ٱلْمَدْرَسَة.
anta lam tadh-hab ela al-madrasa	anta dhahabta ela al-madrasa
You did not go to school. (singular, masculine)	You went to school. (singular, masculine)
أَنْتِ لَمْ تَذْهَبِي إِلَى ٱلْمَدْرَسَة.	أَنْتِ ذَهَبْتِ إِلَى ٱلْمَدْرَسَة.
anti lam tadh-habee ela al-madrasa	anti dhahabti ela al-madrasa
You did not go to school. (singular, feminine)	You went to school. (singular, feminine)
أَنْتُما لَمْ تَذْهَبا إِلَى ٱلْمَدْرَسَة.	أَنْتُما ذَهَبْتُما إِلَى ٱلْمَدْرَسَة.
antomaa lam tadh-habaa ela al-madrasa	antomaa dhahabtomaa ela al-madrasa
You both did not go to school. (dual, masculine and feminine)	You both went to school. (dual, masculine and feminine)
أَنْتُم لَمْ تَذْهَبوا إِلَى ٱلْمَدْرَسَة.	أَنْتُم ذَهَبْتُم إِلَى ٱلْمَدْرَسَة.
antom lam tadh-haboo ela al-madrasa	antom dhahabtom ela al-madrasa
You all did not go to school. (plural, masculine and feminine)	You all went to school. (plural, masculine and feminine)

Negating the Past Tense Modern Spoken Standard Arabic	Simple Past Tense Modern Spoken Standard Arabic
أَنْتُنَّ لَمْ تَذْهَبْنَ إلى ٱلْمَدْرَسَة.	أَنْتُنَّ ذَهَبْتُنَّ إلى ٱلْمَدْرَسَة.
antonna lam tadh-habna ela al-madrasa **You all did not go to school.** **(plural, feminine)**	antonna dhahabtonna ela al-madrasa **You all went to school.** **(plural, feminine)**
نَحنُ لَمْ نَذْهَب إلى ٱلْمَدْرَسَة.	نَحنُ ذَهَبْنا إلى ٱلْمَدْرَسَة.
naHno lam nadh-hab ela al-madrasa **We did not go to school.** **(masculine and feminine)**	naHno dhahabnaa ela al-madrasa **We went to school.** **(masculine and feminine)**
هُوَ لَمْ يَذْهَب إلى ٱلْمَدْرَسَة.	هُوَ ذَهَبَ إلى ٱلْمَدْرَسَة.
howa lam yadh-hab ela al-madrasa **He did not go to school.**	howa dhahaba ela al-madrasa **He went to school.**
هِيَ لَمْ تَذْهَب إلى ٱلْمَدْرَسَة.	هِيَ ذَهَبَتْ إلى ٱلْمَدْرَسَة.
hiya lam tadh-hab ela al-madrasa **She did not go to school.**	hiya dhahabat ela al-madrasa **She went to school.**
هُما لَمْ يَذْهَبا إلى ٱلْمَدْرَسَة.	هُما ذَهَبا إلى ٱلْمَدْرَسَة.
homaa lam yadh-habaa ela al-madrasa **They both did not go to school.** **(dual, masculine and feminine)**	homaa dhahabaa ela al-madrasa **They both went to school.** **(dual, masculine and feminine)**
هُم لَمْ يَذْهَبوا إلى ٱلْمَدْرَسَة.	هُم ذَهَبوا إلى ٱلْمَدْرَسَة.
hom lam yadh-haboo ela al-madrasa **They did not go to school.** **(plural, masculine and feminine)**	hom dhahaboo ela al-madrasa **They went to school.** **(plural, masculine and feminine)**
هُنَّ لَمْ يَذْهَبْنَ إلى ٱلْمَدْرَسَة.	هُنَّ ذَهَبْنَ إلى ٱلْمَدْرَسَة.
honna lam yadh-habna ela al-madrasa **They did not go to school.** **(plural, feminine)**	honna dhahabna ela al-madrasa **They went to school.** **(plural, feminine)**

Negating the verb 'to understand' in the past tense. The root verb is :

Negating the Past Tense Modern Standard Arabic	Simple Past Tense Modern Standard Arabic
أَنا لَمْ أَفْهَم ٱلدَّرْس.	أَنا فَهِمْتُ ٱلدَّرْس.
anaa lam afham al-dars	anaa fahimto al-dars
I did not understand the lesson.	I understood the lesson.
أَنْتَ لَمْ تَفْهَم ٱلدَّرْس.	أَنْتَ فَهِمْتَ ٱلدَّرْس.
anta lam tafham al-dars	anta fahimta al-dars
You did not understand the lesson. (singular, masculine)	You understood the lesson. (singular, masculine)
أَنْتِ لَمْ تَفْهَمِي ٱلدَّرْس.	أَنْتِ فَهِمْتِ ٱلدَّرْس.
anti lam tafhamee al-dars	anti fahimti al-dars
You did not understand the lesson. (singular, feminine)	You understood the lesson. (singular, feminine)
أَنْتُما لَمْ تَفْهَما ٱلدَّرْس.	أَنْتُما فَهِمْتُما ٱلدَّرْس.
antomaa lam tafhamaa al-dars	antomaa fahimtomaa al-dars
You both did not understand the lesson. (dual, masculine and feminine)	You both understood the lesson. (dual, masculine and feminine)
أَنْتُم لَمْ تَفْهموا ٱلدَّرْس.	أَنْتُم فَهِمْتُم ٱلدَّرْس.
antom lam tafhamoo al-dars	antom fahimtom al-dars
You all did not understand the lesson. (plural, masculine and feminine)	You all understood the lesson. (plural, masculine and feminine)
أَنْتُنَّ لَمْ تَفْهَمْنَ ٱلدَّرْس.	أَنْتُنَّ فَهِمْتُنَّ ٱلدَّرْس.
antonna lam tafhamna al-dars	antonna fahimtonna al-dars
You all did not understand the lesson. (plural, feminine)	You all understood the lesson. (plural, feminine)

Negating the Past Tense Modern Standard Arabic	Simple Past Tense Modern Standard Arabic
نَحْنُ لَمْ نَفْهَم ٱلدَّرْس.	نَحنُ فَهِمْنا ٱلدَّرْس.
naHno lam nafham al-dars	naHno fahimnaa al-dars
We did not understand the lesson. (masculine and feminine)	We understood the lesson. (masculine and feminine)
هُوَ لَمْ يَفْهَم ٱلدَّرْس.	هُوَ فَهِمَ ٱلدَّرْس.
howa lam yafham al-dars	howa fahima al-dars
He did not understand the lesson.	He understood the lesson.
هِيَ لَمَ تَفْهَم ٱلدَّرْس.	هِيَ فَهِمَتْ ٱلدَّرْس.
hiya lam tafham al-dars	hiya fahimat al-dars
She did not understand the lesson.	She understood the lesson.
هُمَا لَمْ يَفْهَما ٱلدَّرْس.	هُمَا فَهِما ٱلدَّرْس.
homaa lam yafhamaa al-dars	homaa fahimaa al-dars
They both did not understand the lesson.	They both understood the lesson. (dual, masculine and feminine)
هُمْ لَمْ يَفْهَموا ٱلدَّرْس.	هُمْ فَهِموا ٱلدَّرْس.
hom lam yafhamoo al-dars	hom fahimoo al-dars
They did not understand the lesson. (plural, masculine and feminine)	They understood the lesson. (plural, masculine and feminine)
هُنَّ لَمْ يَفْهَمْنَ ٱلدَّرْس.	هُنَّ فَهِمْنَ ٱلدَّرْس.
honna lam yafhamna al-dars	honna fahimna al-dars
They did not understand the lesson. (plural, feminine)	They understood the lesson. (plural, feminine)

- Note, refer to page six for a refresher on the pronunciation system used in this book.

- Please keep in mind that Arabic is a cursive script and it is read and written from right to left while practicing reading.

Lesson Thirty
Simple Past Tense with Object Pronouns

The third and final type of personal pronouns in Arabic are the object pronouns, which are attached to present, past, or future verbs to indicate the object of the verb. They function similarly to possessive pronouns, except for the first possessive pronoun

'my' (ـي). In the case of object pronouns, the pronoun is preceded by the letter

'n' (ن) before being attached to the verb. The subject pronouns and their corresponding object pronouns are as follows:

- **In spoken Modern Standard Arabic (MSA), the plural masculine form is commonly used instead of the dual and feminine plural forms. The dual and feminine plural forms are more commonly found in Classical Arabic and are used in formal and poetic contexts.**

Meaning	Object Pronouns	Meaning	Subject Pronouns
Me	نِي nee	I	أَنَا anna
You (masculine)	كَ ka	You (masculine)	أَنتَ anta
You (feminine)	كِ ki	You (feminine)	أَنتِ anti
You (dual, masculine and feminine)	كُمَا komaa	You (dual, masculine and feminine)	أَنْتُمَا antomaa
You (plural, masculine and feminine)	كُم kom	You (plural, masculine and feminine)	أَنتُم antom

Meaning	Object Pronouns	Meaning	Subject Pronouns
You (plural, (feminine)	كُنَّ konna	You (plural, feminine)	أَنْتُنَّ antonna
Us (masculine and feminine)	نـا naa	We (masculine and feminine)	نَحْنُ naHno
Him / it	ـهُ ho	He / it	هُوَ howa
Her / it	ـها haa	She / it	هِيَ hiya
Them (dual, masculine and feminine)	هُمَا homaa	They (dual, masculine and feminine)	هُمَا homaa
Them (masculine and feminine)	هُمْ hom	They (masculine and feminine)	هُمْ hom
Them (feminine)	هُنَّ honna	They (feminine)	هُنَّ honna

- The tables below demonstrate common errors beginners make when using subject pronouns with past verbs, instead of using object pronouns with past verbs. The first column shows the incorrect usage, while the second column displays the correct usage of object pronouns with past verbs in Classical Arabic and Spoken Formal Arabic.

The object pronouns with the past verb 'to know' عَرَفَ :

Meaning	Proper Simple Sentences	Improper Sentences
Mohammad knew me.	مُحَمَّد عَرَفَنِي moHammad A'arafanee	مُحَمَّد عَرَفَ أَنَا moHammad A'arafa anaa
Mohammad knew you. (masculine)	مُحَمَّد عَرَفَكَ moHammad A'arafaka	مُحَمَّد عَرَفَ أَنْتَ moHammad A'arafa anta
Mohammad knew you. (feminine)	مُحَمَّد عَرَفَكِ moHammad A'arafaki	مُحَمَّد عَرَفَ أَنْتِ moHammad A'arafa anti
Mohammad knew both of you. (dual, masculine and feminine)	مُحَمَّد عَرَفَكُمَا moHammad A'arafako-maa	مُحَمَّد عَرَفَ أَنْتُمَا moHammad A'arafa an-tomaa
Mohammad knew all of you. (plural, masculine and feminine)	مُحَمَّد عَرَفَكُم moHammad A'arafakom	مُحَمَّد عَرَفَ أَنْتُم moHammad A'arafa an-tom
Mohammad knew all of you. (plural, feminine)	مُحَمَّد عَرَفَكُنَّ moHammad A'arafakon-na	مُحَمَّد عَرَفَ أَنْتُنَّ moHammad A'arafa an-tonna
Mohammad knew us.	مُحَمَّد عَرَفَنَا moHammad A'arafanaa	مُحَمَّد عَرَفَ نَحْنُ moHammad A'arafa naHno
Mohammad knew him.	مُحَمَّد عَرَفَهُ moHammad A'arafaho	مُحَمَّد عَرَفَ هُوَ moHammad A'arafa howa

Meaning	Proper Simple Sentences	Improper Sentences
Mohammad knew her.	مُحَمَّد عَرَفَها moHammad A'arafahaa	مُحَمَّد عَرَفَ هِيَ moHammad A'arafa hiya
Mohammad knew both of them. (dual, masculine and feminine)	مُحَمَّد عرَقَهُما moHammad A'arafa-homaa	مُحَمَّد عَرَفَ هُما moHammad A'arafa homaa
Mohammad knew them. (plural, masculine and feminine)	مُحَمَّد عرَقَهُم moHammad A'arafahom	مُحَمَّد عَرَفَ هُم moHammad A'arafa hom
Mohammad knew them. (plural, feminine)	مُحَمَّد عرَقَهُنَّ moHammad A'arafa-honna	مُحَمَّد عَرَفَ هُنَّ moHammad A'arafa honna

The object pronouns with the past verb 'to talk' كَلَّمَ :

Meaning	Proper Sentences	Improper Sentences
Ahmad talked to me.	أَحْمَد كَلَّمَني aHmad kallamanee	أَحْمَد كَلَّمَ أَنا aHmad kallama anaa
Ahmad talked to you. (masculine)	أَحْمَد كَلَّمَكَ aHmad kallamaka	أَحْمَد كَلَّمَ أَنْتَ aHmad kallama anta
Ahmad talked to you. (feminine)	أَحْمَد كَلَّمَكِ aHmad kallamaki	أَحْمَد كَلَّمَ أنْت aHmad kallama anti
Ahmad talked to both of you. (dual, masculine and feminine)	أَحْمَد كَلَّمَكُما aHmad kallamakomaa	أَحْمَد كَلَّمَ أنْتُما aHmad kallama an-tomaa

273

Meaning	Proper Sentences	Improper Sentences
Ahmad talked to all of you. (plural, masculine and feminine)	أَحْمَد كَلَّمَكُم aHmad kallamakom	أَحْمَد كَلَّمَ أَنْتُم aHmad kallama antom
Ahmad talked to all of you. (plural, feminine)	أَحْمَد كَلَّمَكُنَّ aHmad kallamakonna	أَحْمَد كَلَّمَ أَنْتُنَّ aHmad kallama antonna
Ahmad talked to us.	أَحْمَد كَلَّمَنا aHmad kallamanaa	أَحْمَد كَلَّمَ نَحْنُ aHmad kallama naHno
Ahmad talked to him.	أَحْمَد كَلَّمَهُ aHmad kallamaho	أَحْمَد كَلَّمَ هُوَ aHmad kallama howa
Ahmad talked to her.	أَحْمَد كَلَّمَها aHmad kallamahaa	أَحْمَد كَلَّمَ هِيَ aHmad kallama hiya
Ahmad talked to both of them. (dual, masculine and feminine)	أَحْمَد كَلَّمَهُما aHmad kallamahomaa	أَحْمَد كَلَّمَ هُما aHmad kallama homaa
Ahmad talked to them. (plural, masculine and feminine)	أَحْمَد كَلَّمَهُم aHmad kallamahom	أَحْمَد كَلَّمَ هُم aHmad kallama hom
Ahmad talked to them. (them, plural feminine)	أَحْمَد كَلَّمَهُنَّ aHmad kalamahonna	أَحْمَد كَلَّمَ هُنَّ aHmad kallama honna

The object pronouns with the past verb 'to teach' دَرَّسَ :

Meaning	Proper Sentences	Improper Sentences
The teacher taught me.	الأُسْتاذ دَرَّسَني al-ostaadh darrasanee	الأُسْتاذ دَرَّسَ أَنا al-ostaadh darrasa anaa

Meaning	Proper Sentences	Improper Sentences
The teacher taught you. (masculine)	الأُسْتاذ دَرَّسَكَ al-ostaadh darrasaka	الأُسْتاذ دَرَّسَ أَنْتَ al-ostaadh darrasa anta
The teacher taught you. (feminine)	الأُسْتاذ دَرَّسَكِ al-ostaadh darrasaki	الأُسْتاذ دَرَّسَ أَنْتِ al-ostaadh darrasa anti
The teacher taught both of you. (dual, masculine and feminine)	الأُسْتاذ دَرَّسَكُما al-ostaadh darrasako-maa	الأُسْتاذ دَرَّسَ أَنْتُما al-ostaadh darrasa an-toma
The teacher taught all of you. (plural, masculine and feminine)	الأُسْتاذ دَرَّسَكم al-ostaadh darrasakom	الأُسْتاذ دَرَّسَ أَنْتُم al-ostaadh darrasa an-tom
The teacher taught all of you. (plural, feminine)	الأُسْتاذ دَرَّسَكُنَّ al-ostaadh darrasakon-na	الأُسْتاذ دَرَّسَ أَنْتُنَّ al-ostaadh darrasa an-tonna
The teacher taught us.	الأُسْتاذ دَرَّسَنا al-ostaadh darrasanaa	الأُسْتاذ دَرَّسَ نَحْنُ al-ostaadh darrasa naHno
The teacher taught him.	الأُسْتاذ دَرَّسَهُ al-ostaadh darrasaho	الأُسْتاذ دَرَّسَ هُوَ al-ostaadh darrasa howa
The teacher taught her.	الأُسْتاذ دَرَّسَها al-ostaadh darrasahaa	الأُسْتاذ دَرَّسَ هِيَ al-ostaadh darrasa hiya
The teacher taught both of them. (dual, masculine and feminine)	الأُسْتاذ دَرَّسَهُما al-ostaadh darrasa-homa	الأُسْتاذ دَرَّسَ هُما al-ostaadh darrasa homa

Meaning	Proper Sentences	Improper Sentences
The teacher taught them. (plural, masculine and feminine)	الأُسْتاذ دَرَّسَهُم al-ostaadh darrasahom	الأُسْتاذ دَرَّسَ هُم al-ostaadh darrasa hom
The teacher taught them. (plural, feminine)	الأُسْتاذ دَرَّسَهُنَّ al-ostaadh darrasahonna	الأُسْتاذ دَرَّسَ هُنَّ al-ostaadh darrasa honna

The object pronouns with the past verb 'to ask' سَأَلَ :

Meaning	Proper Sentences	Improper Sentences
The teacher asked me.	الأُسْتاذَة سَأَلَتْني al-ostaadha sa,alatnee	الأُسْتاذَة سَأَلَتْ أَنا al-ostaadha sa,alat anaa
The teacher asked you. (masculine)	الأُسْتاذَة سَأَلَتْكَ al-ostaadha sa,alatka	الأُسْتاذَة سَأَلَتْ أَنْتَ al-ostaadha sa,alat anta
The teacher asked you. (feminine)	الأُسْتاذَة سَأَلَتْكِ al-ostaadha sa,alatki	الأُسْتاذَة سَأَلَتْ أَنْتِ al-ostaadha sa,alat anti
The teacher asked both of you. (dual, masculine and feminine)	الأُسْتاذَة سَأَلَتْكُما al-ostaadha sa,alatkomaa	الأُسْتاذَة سَأَلَتْ أَنْتُما al-ostaadha sa,alat an-tomaa
The teacher asked all of you. (plural, masculine and feminine)	الأُسْتاذَة سَأَلَتْكُم al-ostaadha sa,alatkom	الأُسْتاذَة سَأَلَتْ أَنْتُم al-ostaadha sa,alat an-tom
The teacher asked all of you. (plural, feminine)	الأُسْتاذَة سَأَلَتْكُنَّ al-ostaadha sa,alatkonna	الأُسْتاذَة سَأَلَتْ أَنْتُنَّ al-ostaadha sa,alat an-tonna

Meaning	Proper Sentences	Improper Sentences
The teacher asked us.	الأُسْتاذَة سَأَلَتْنا al-ostaadha sa,alatnaa	الأُسْتاذَة سَأَلَتْ نَحْنُ al-ostaadha sa,alat naH-no
The teacher asked him.	الأُسْتاذَة سَأَلَتْهُ al-ostaadha sa,alatho	الأُسْتاذَة سَأَلَتْ هُوَ al-ostaadha sa,alat howa
The teacher asked her.	الأُسْتاذَة سَأَلَتْها al-ostaadha sa,alathaa	الأُسْتاذَة سَأَلَتْ هِيَ al-ostaadha sa,alat hiya
The teacher asked both of them. (dual, masculine and feminine)	الأُسْتاذَة سَأَلَتْهُما al-ostaadha sa,alath-oma	الأُسْتاذَة سَأَلَتْ هُما al-ostaadha sa,alat homa
The teacher asked them. (plural, masculine and feminine)	الأُسْتاذَة سَأَلَتْهُم al-ostaadha sa,alath-om	الأُسْتاذَة سَأَلَتْ هُم al-ostaadha sa,alat hom
The teacher asked them. (plural, feminine)	الأُسْتاذَة سَأَلَتْهُنَّ al-ostaadha sa,alathonna	الأُسْتاذَة سَأَلَتْ هُنَّ al-ostaadha sa,alat hon-na

The object pronouns with the past verb 'to understand' فَهِمَ :

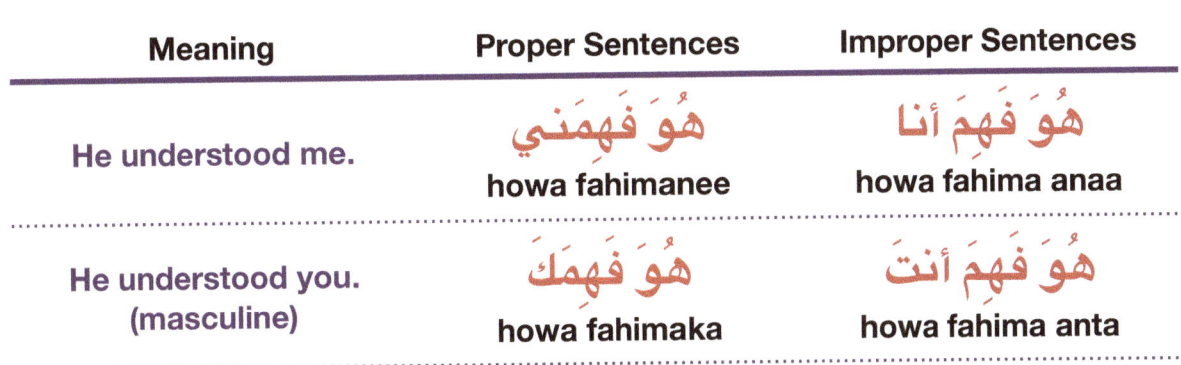

Meaning	Proper Sentences	Improper Sentences
He understood me.	هُوَ فَهِمَني howa fahimanee	هُوَ فَهِمَ أنا howa fahima anaa
He understood you. (masculine)	هُوَ فَهِمَكَ howa fahimaka	هُوَ فَهِمَ أنتَ howa fahima anta

Meaning	Proper Sentences	Improper Sentences
He understood you. (feminine)	هُوَ فَهِمَكِ howa fahimaki	هُوَ فَهِمَ أَنتِ howa fahima anti
He understood both of you. (dual, masculine and feminine)	هُوَ فَهِمَكُما howa fahimakoma	هُوَ فَهِمَ أَنتُما howa fahima antoma
He understood all of you. (plural, masculine and feminine)	هُوَ فَهِمَكُم howa fahimakom	هُوَ فَهِمَ أَنْتُم howa fahima antom
He understood all of you. (plural, feminine)	هُوَ فَهِمَكُنَّ howa fahimakonna	هُوَ فَهِمَ أَنْتُنَّ howa fahima antonna
He understood us.	هُوَ فَهِمَنا howa fahimanaa	هُوَ فَهِمَ نَحْنُ howa fahima naHno
He understood him.	هُوَ فَهِمَهُ howa fahimaho	هُوَ فَهِمَ هُوَ howa fahima howa
He understood her.	هُوَ فَهِمَها howa fahimaha	هُوَ فَهِمَ هِيَ howa fahima hiya
He understood both of them. (dual, masculine and feminine)	هُوَ فَهِمَهُما howa fahimahoma	هُوَ فَهِمَ هُما howa fahima homa
He understood them. (plural, masculine and feminine)	هُوَ فَهِمَهُم howa fahimahom	هُوَ فَهِمَ هُم howa fahima hom
He understood them. (plural, feminine)	هُوَ فَهِمَهُنَّ howa fahimahonna	هُوَ فَهِمَ هُنَّ howa fahima honna

Lesson Thirty-One
Past Continuous Tense

The past continuous tense in Arabic is used to describe an ongoing event that took place in the past and persisted for a period of time. It is formed by adding the verb "kana" (كان) before the present continuous tense verb, indicating the continuous nature of the action in the past. It is important to note that both the simple present tense and the present continuous tense are expressed similarly in Arabic. Example:

Present Continuous: "He is studying." (howa yadros هو يدرس)

Past Continuous: "He was studying." (kana yadros كان يدرس)

The sentence "He was studying" can be translated as "kana yadros" (كان يدرس). However, it is possible to add emphasis by including the pronoun "howa" (هو) in the sentence, resulting in "howa kana yadros" (هو كان يدرس). This form highlights the subject and reinforces the idea that it was indeed "he" who was studying.

In Arabic, the subject is already incorporated within the verb itself, making the addition of the pronoun "howa" (هو) optional for emphasis. The verb form alone is sufficient to indicate the subject. To summarize:

• Present Continuous: "He is studying" is translated as "howa yadros" (هو يدرس).

• Past Continuous: "He was studying" is translated as "kana yadros" (كان يدرس).

• Emphasized Past Continuous: "He was studying" (with emphasis on "he") is translated as "howa kana yadros" (هو كان يدرس).

The verb "kana" كانَ takes the same suffix as other past verbs, adapting to the subject of the sentence.

To negate the past continuous tense in Arabic, you use the same method as negating the simple past tense. The word 'maa' (ما) appears directly before the verb "kana" (كانَ), just as it does when negating any other verb in the simple past tense.

- In spoken Modern Standard Arabic (MSA), the plural masculine form is commonly used instead of the dual and feminine plural forms. The dual and feminine plural forms are more commonly found in Classical Arabic and are used in formal and poetic contexts.

The table below shows all the different forms of "kana" كانَ and the negation of "kana" with different subject pronouns in spoken Modern Standard Arabic and Classical Arabic:

Negating كانَ	Forms of كانَ	Subject Pronouns
أنا ما كُنْتُ anaa maa konto I was not	أنا كُنْتُ anaa konto I was	أنا anaa I
أنتَ ما كُنْتَ anta maa konta You were not	أنتَ كُنْتَ anta konta You were	أنتَ anta You (singular, masculine)
أنتِ ما كُنْتِ anti maa konti You were not	أنتِ كُنْتِ anti konti You were	أنتِ anti You (singular, feminine)
أنتُما ما كُنْتُما antoma maa kontoma You both were not	أنتُما كُنْتُما antoma kontoma You both were	أنْتُما antoma You (dual, masculine and feminine)
أنتُم ما كُنْتُم antom maa kontom You all were not	أنتُم كُنْتُم antom kontom You all were	أنْتُم antom You (plural, masculine and feminine)
أنتُنَّ ما كُنْتُنَّ antonna maa kontonna You all were not	أنتُنَّ كُنْتُنَّ antonna kontonna You all were	أنْتُنَّ antonna You (plural, feminine)

Negating كانَ	Forms of كانَ	Subject Pronouns
نَحْنُ ما كُنّا naHno maa konnaa We were not	نَحْنُ كُنّا naHno konnaa We were	نَحْنُ naHno We (masculine and feminine)
هُوَ ما كان howa maa kana He was not	هُوَ كانَ howa kana He was	هُوَ howa He/it
هِيَ ما كانَتْ hiya maa kanat She was not	هِيَ كانَتْ hiya kanat She was	هِيَ hiya She/it
هُما ما كانا homaa maa kanaa They both were not	هُما كانا homaa kanaa They both were	هُما homaa They (dual, masculine and feminine)
هُم ما كانوا hom maa kanoo They were not	هُم كانوا hom kanoo They were	هُم hom They (plural, masculine and feminine)
هُنَّ ما كُنَّ honna maa konna They were not	هُنَّ كُنَّ honna konna They were	هُنَّ honna They (plural, feminine)

- The examples provided in the tables for this lesson are all in spoken Modern Standard Arabic, which means that the words do not have vowels marked at the end.

The past continuous tense for the verb 'to live'. The root for this verb is  ش ي ع :

Past Continuous Tense Modern Standard Arabic	Present Tense Modern Standard Arabic
أَنا كُنْتُ أَعيش في كَليفورنيا.	أَنا أَعيش في كَليفورنيا.
anaa konto aA'eesh fee california **I was living in California.**	anaa aA'eesh fee california **I am living in California.**
أَنْتَ كُنْتَ تَعيش في كَليفورنيا.	أَنْتَ تَعيش في كَليفورنيا.
anta konta taA'eesh fee california **You were living in California.** **(singular, masculine)**	anta taA'eesh fee california **You are living in California.** **(singular, masculine)**
أَنْتِ كُنْتِ تَعيشي في كَليفورنيا.	أَنْتِ تَعيشين في كَليفورنيا.
anti konti taA'eeshee fee california **You were living in California.** **(singular, feminine)**	anti taA'eesheen fee california **You are living in California.** **(singular, feminine)**
أَنْتُما كُنْتُما تَعيشا في كَليفورنيا.	أَنْتُما تَعيشان في كَليفورنيا.
antomaa kontoma taA'eesha fee california **You both were living in California.** **(dual, masculine and feminine)**	antomaa taA'eeshan fee california **You both are living in California.** **(dual, masculine and feminine)**
أَنْتُم كُنْتُم تَعيشوا في كَليفورنيا.	أَنْتُم تَعيشون في كَليفورنيا.
antom kontom taA'eeshoo fee california **You all were living in California.** **(plural, masculine and feminine)**	antom taA'eeshoon fee california **You all are living in California.** **(plural, masculine and feminine)**
أَنْتُنَّ كُنْتُنَّ تَعِشْنَ في كَليفورنيا.	أَنْتُنَّ تَعِشْنَ في كَليفورنيا.
antonna kontonna taA'ishna fee california **You all were living in California** **(plural, feminine)**	antonna taA'ishna fee california **You all are living in California.** **(plural, feminine)**

Past Continuous Tense Modern Standard Arabic	Present Tense Modern Standard Arabic

نَحْنُ كُنّا نَعيش في كَليفورنيا.

naHno konna naA'eesh fee california
We were living in California.
(masculine and feminine)

نَحْنُ نَعيش في كَليفورنيا.

naHno naA'eesh fee california
We are living in California.
(masculine and feminine)

هُوَ كانَ يَعيش في كَليفورنيا.

howa kana yaA'eesh fee california
He was living in California.

هُوَ يَعيش في كَليفورنيا.

howa yaA'eesh fee california
He is living in California.

هِيَ كانَتْ تَعيش في كَليفورنيا.

hiya kanat taA'eesh fee california
She was living in California.

هِيَ تَعيش في كَليفورنيا.

hiya taA'eesh fee california
She is living in California.

هُما كانا يَعيشا في كَليفورنيا.

homaa kana yaA'eeshaa fee california
They both were living in California.
(dual, masculine and feminine)

هُما يَعيشان في كَليفورنيا.

homaa yaA'eeshan fee california
They both are living in California.
(dual, masculine and feminine)

هُم كانوا يَعيشوا في كَليفورنيا.

hom kanoo yaA'eeshoo fee california
They were living in California.
(plural, masculine and feminine)

هُم يَعيشون في كَليفورنيا.

hom yaA'eeshoon fee california
They are living in California.
(plural, masculine and feminine)

هُنَّ كُنَّ يَعِشْنَ في كَليفورنيا.

honna konna yaA'ishna fee california
They were living in California.
(plural, feminine)

هُنَّ يَعِشْنَ في كَليفورنيا.

honna yaA'ishna fee california
They are living in California.
(plural, feminine)

The past continuous tense for the verb "to study". The root for this verb is  د ر س :

Past Continuous Tense Modern Standard Arabic	Present Tense Modern Standard Arabic
أَنَا كُنْتُ أَدرُس فِي ٱلْمَكْتَبَة. **anaa konto adros fee al-maktaba** I was studying at the library.	أَنَا أَدرُس فِي ٱلْمَكْتَبَة. **anaa adros fee al-maktaba** I am studying at the library.
أَنْتَ كُنْتَ تَدْرُس فِي ٱلْمَكْتَبَة. **anta konta tadros fee al-maktaba** You were studying at the library. (singular, masculine)	أَنْتَ تَدْرُس فِي ٱلْمَكْتَبَة. **anta tadros fee al-maktaba** You are studying at the library. (singular, masculine)
أَنْتِ كُنْتِ تَدْرُسِي فِي ٱلْمَكْتَبَة. **anti konti tadrosee fee al-maktaba** You were studying at the library. (singular, feminine)	أَنْتِ تَدْرُسِين فِي ٱلْمَكْتَبَة. **anti tadroseen fee al-maktaba** You are studying at the library. (singular, feminine)
أَنْتُما كُنْتُما تَدْرُسا فِي ٱلْمَكْتَبَة **antomaa kontomaa tadrosaa fee al-maktaba** You both were studying at the library. (dual, masculine and feminine)	أَنْتُما تَدْرُسان فِي ٱلْمَكْتَبَة. **antomaa tadrosaan fee al-maktaba** You both are studying at the library. (dual, masculine and feminine)
أَنْتُم كُنْتُم تَدْرُسوا فِي ٱلْمَكْتَبَة. **antom kontom tadrosoo fee al-mak-taba** You all were studying at the library. (plural, masculine and feminine)	أَنْتُم تَدْرُسون فِي ٱلْمَكْتَبَة. **antom tadrosoon fee al-maktaba** You all are studying at the library. (plural, masculine and feminine)
أَنْتُنَّ كُنْتُنَّ تَدْرُسْنَ فِي ٱلْمَكْتَبَة. **antonna kontonna tadrosna fee al-maktaba** You all were studying at the library. (plural, feminine)	أَنْتُنَّ تَدْرُسْنَ فِي ٱلْمَكْتَبَة. **antonna tadrosna fee al-maktaba** You all are studying at the library. (plural, feminine)

Past Continuous Tense Modern Standard Arabic	Present Tense Modern Standard Arabic
نَحنُ كُنّا نَدرُس في ٱلمَكتَبَة.	نَحنُ نَدرُس في ٱلمَكتَبَة.
naHno konna nadros fee al-maktaba We were studying at the library. (masculine and feminine)	naHno nadros fee al-maktaba We are studying at the library. (masculine and feminine)
هُوَ كانَ يَدرُس في ٱلمَكتَبَة.	هُوَ يَدرُس في ٱلمَكتَبَة.
howa kana yadros fee al-maktaba He was studying at the library.	howa yadros fee al-maktaba He is studying at the library.
هِيَ كانَتْ تَدرُس في ٱلمَكتَبَة.	هِيَ تَدرُس في ٱلمَكتَبَة.
hiya kanat tadros fee al-maktaba She was studying at the library.	hiya tadros fee al-maktaba She is studying at the library.
هُما كانا يَدرُسا في ٱلمَكتَبَة.	هُما يَدرُسان في ٱلمَكتَبَة.
homaa kanaa yadrosaa fee al-makta-ba They both were studying at the library. (dual, masculine and feminine)	homaa yadrosaan fee al-maktaba They both are studying at the library. (dual, masculine and feminine)
هُم كانوا يَدرُسوا في ٱلمَكتَبَة.	هُم يَدرُسون في ٱلمَكتَبَة.
hom kano yadrosoo fee al-maktaba They were studying at the library. (plural, masculine and feminine)	hom yadrosoon fee al-maktaba They are studying at the library. (plural, masculine and feminine)
هُنَّ كُنَّ يَدرُسنَ في ٱلمَكتَبَة.	هُنَّ يَدرُسنَ في ٱلمَكتَبَة.
honna konna yadrosna fee al-makta-ba They were studying at the library. (plural, feminine)	honna yadrosna fee al-maktaba They are studying at the library. (plural, feminine)

The past continuous tense for the verb "to write". The root is  ك ت ب:

Past Continuous Tense Modern Standard Arabic	Present Tense Modern Standard Arabic
أَنا كُنْتُ أَكْتُب رِسالَة.	أَنا أَكْتُب رِسالَة.
anaa konto aktob risaala I was writing a letter.	**anaa aktob risaala** I am writing a letter.
أَنْتَ كُنْتَ تَكْتُب رِسالَة.	أَنْتَ تَكْتُب رِسالَة.
anta konta taktob risaala You were writing a letter. (singular, masculine)	**anta taktob risaala** You are writing a letter. (singular, masculine)
أَنْتِ كُنْتِ تَكْتُبي رِسالَة.	أَنْتِ تَكْتُبين رِسالَة.
anti konti taktobee risaala You were writing a letter. (singular, feminine)	**anti taktobeen risaala** You are writing a letter. (singular, feminine)
أَنْتُما كُنْتُما تَكْتُبا رِسالَة.	أَنْتُما تَكْتُبان رِسالَة.
antomaa kontomaa taktobaa risaala You both were writing a letter. (dual, masculine and feminine)	**antomaa taktobaan risaala** You both are writing a letter. (dual, masculine and feminine)
أَنْتُم كُنْتُم تَكْتُبوا رِسالَة.	أَنْتُم تَكْتُبون رِسالَة.
antom kontom taktoboo risaala You all were writing a letter. (plural, masculine and feminine)	**antom taktoboon risaala** You all are writing a letter. (plural, masculine and feminine)

Past Continuous Tense **Modern Standard Arabic**	**Present Tense** **Modern Standard Arabic**

أَنْتُنَّ كُنْتُنَّ تَكْتُبْنَ رِسالَة.	أَنْتُنَّ تَكْتُبْنَ رِسالَة.
antonna kontonna taktobna risaala You all were writing a letter. (plural, feminine)	**antonna taktobna risaala** You all are writing a letter. (plural, feminine)

نَحْنُ كُنَّا نَكْتُب رِسالَة.	نَحْنُ نَكْتُب رِسالَة.
naHno konna naktob risaala We were writing a letter. (masculine and feminine)	**naHno naktob risaala** We are writing a letter. (masculine and feminine)

هُوَ كانَ يَكْتُب رِسالَة.	هُوَ يَكْتُب رِسالَة.
howa kana yaktob risaala He was writing a letter.	**howa yaktob risaala** He is writing a letter.

هِيَ كانَتْ تَكْتُب رِسالَة.	هِيَ تَكْتُب رِسالَة.
hiya kanat taktob risaala She was writing a letter.	**hiya taktob risaala** She is writing a letter.

مُحَمَّد كانَ يَكْتُب رِسالَة.	مُحَمَّد يَكْتُب رِسالَة.
moHammad kana yaktob risaala Mohammad was writing a letter.	**moHammad yaktob risaala** Mohammad is writing a letter.

فاطِمَة كانَتْ تَكْتُب رِسالَة.	فاطِمَة تَكْتُب رِسالَة.
faTima kanat taktob risaala Fatima was writing a letter.	**faTima taktob risaala** Fatima is writing a letter.

Past Continuous Tense Modern Standard Arabic	Present Tense Modern Standard Arabic
 هُما كانا يَكْتُبا رسالَة. **homaa kanaa yaktobaa risaala** They both were writing a letter. (dual, masculine and feminine)	 هُما يَكْتُبان رسالَة. **homaa yaktobaan risaala** They both are writing a letter. (dual, masculine and feminine)
هُم كانوا يَكْتُبوا رِسالَة. **hom kano yaktoboo risaala** They were writing a letter. (plural, masculine and feminine)	 هُم يَكْتُبون رِسالَة. **hom yaktoboon risaala** They are writing a letter. (plural, masculine and feminine)
هُنَّ كُنَّ يَكْتُبْنَ رِسالَة. **honna konna yaktobna risaala** They were writing a letter. (plural, feminine)	هُنَّ يَكْتُبْنَ رِسالَة. **honna yaktobna risaala** They are writing a letter. (plural, feminine)

The past continuous tense for the verb 'to go' the root for this verb is ذ هـ ب :

Past Continuous Tense Modern Standard Arabic	Present Tense Modern Standard Arabic
 أَنا كُنْتُ أَذْهَب إلى ٱلْمَدْرَسَة. **anaa konto adh-hab ilaa al-madrasa** I was going to school.	 أَنا أَذْهَب إلى ٱلْمَدْرَسَة. **anaa adh-hab ilaa al-madrasa** I'm going to school.
 أَنْتَ كُنْتَ تَذْهَب إلى ٱلْمَدْرَسَة. **anta konta tadh-hab illa al-madrasa** You were going to school. (singular, masculine)	 أَنْتَ تَذْهَب إلى ٱلْمَدْرَسَة. **anta tadh-hab illa al-madrasa** You are going to school. (singular, masculine)

Past Continuous Tense Modern Standard Arabic	Present Tense Modern Standard Arabic
أَنْتِ كُنْتِ تَذْهَبِي إلى ٱلْمَدْرَسَة. **anti konti tadh-habee illa al-madrasa** You were going to school. (singular, feminine)	أَنْتِ تَذْهَبِين إلى ٱلْمَدْرَسَة. **anti tadh-habeen illa al-madrasa** You are going to school. (singular, feminine)
أَنْتُما كُنْتُما تَذْهَبا إلى ٱلْمَدْرَسَة. **antomaa kontoma tadh-habaa illa al-madrasa** You both were going to school. (dual, masculine and feminine)	أَنْتُما تَذْهَبان إلى ٱلْمَدْرَسَة. **antomaa tadh-habaan illa al-madrasa** You both are going to school. (dual, masculine and feminine)
أَنْتُم كُنْتُم تَذْهَبوا إلى ٱلْمَدْرَسَة. **antom kontom tadh-haboo illa al-madrasa** You all were going to school. (plural, masculine and feminine)	أَنْتُم تَذْهَبون إلى ٱلْمَدْرَسَة. **antom tadh-haboon illa al-madrasa** You all are going to school. (plural, masculine and feminine)
أَنْتُنَّ كُنْتُنَّ تَذْهَبْنَ إلى ٱلْمَدْرَسَة. **antonna kontonna tadh-habna illa al-madrasa** You all were going to school. (plural, feminine)	أَنْتُنَّ تَذْهَبْنَ إلى ٱلْمَدْرَسَة. **antonna tadh-habna illa al-madrasa** You all are going to school. (plural, feminine)
نَحْنُ كُنّا نَذْهَب إلى ٱلْمَدْرَسَة. **naHno konna nadh-hab illa al-madrasa** We were going to school. (masculine and feminine)	نَحْنُ نَذْهَب إلى ٱلْمَدْرَسَة. **naHno nadh-hab illa al-madrasa** We are going to school. (masculine and feminine)
هُوَ كانَ يَذْهَب إلى ٱلْمَدْرَسَة. **howa kana yadh-hab illa al-madrasa** He was going to school.	هُوَ يَذْهَب إلى ٱلْمَدْرَسَة. **howa yadh-hab illa al-madrasa** He is going to school.

Past Continuous Tense Modern Standard Arabic	Present Tense Modern Standard Arabic
هِيَ كانَتْ تَذْهَب إلى ٱلْمَدْرَسَة.	هِيَ تَذْهَب إلى ٱلْمَدْرَسَة.
hiya kanat tadh-hab illa al-madrasa She was going to school.	hiya tadh-hab illa al-madrasa She is going to school.
مُحَمَّد كانَ يَذْهَب إلى ٱلْمَدْرَسَة.	مُحَمَّد يَذْهَب إلى ٱلْمَدْرَسَة.
moHammad kana yadh-hab illa al-madrasa Mohammad was going to school.	moHammad yadh-hab illa al-madrasa Mohammad is going to school.
فاطِمَة كانَتْ تَذْهَب إلى ٱلْمَدْرَسَة.	فاطِمَة تَذْهَب إلى ٱلْمَدْرَسَة.
faTima kanat tadh-hab illa al-madrasa Fatima was going to school.	faTima tadh-hab illa al-madrasa Fatima is going to school.
هُما كانا يَذْهَبا إلى ٱلْمَدْرَسَة.	هُما يَذْهَبان إلى ٱلْمَدْرَسَة.
homaa kanaa yadh-habaa illa al-madrasa They both were going to school. (dual, masculine and feminine)	homaa yadh-habaan illa al-madrasa They both are going to school. (dual, masculine and feminine)
هُم كانوا يَذْهَبوا إلى ٱلْمَدْرَسَة.	هُم يَذْهَبون إلى ٱلْمَدْرَسَة.
hom kano yadh-haboo illa al-madrasa They were going to school. (plural, masculine and feminine)	hom yadh-haboon illa al-madrasa They are going to school. (plural, masculine and feminine)
هُنَّ كُنَّ يَذْهَبْنَ إلى ٱلْمَدْرَسَة.	هُنَّ يَذْهَبْنَ إلى ٱلْمَدْرَسَة.
honna konna yadh-habna illa al-madrasa They were going to school. (plural, feminine)	honna yadh-habna illa al-madrasa They are going to school. (plural, feminine)

The past continuous tense for the verb "to understand". The root is  :

Past Continuous Tense Modern Standard Arabic	Present Tense Modern Standard Arabic
أَنَا كُنْتُ أَفْهَم ٱلدَّرْس. **anaa konto afham al-dars** I was understanding the lesson.	أَنَا أَفْهَم ٱلدَّرْس. **anaa afham al-dars** I am understanding the lesson.
أَنْتَ كُنْتَ تَفْهَم ٱلدَّرْس. **anta konta tafham al-dars** You were understanding the lesson. (singular, masculine)	أَنْتَ تَفْهَم ٱلدَّرْس. **anta tafham al-dars** You are understanding the lesson. (singular, masculine)
أَنْتِ كُنْتِ تَفْهَمي ٱلدَّرْس. **anti konti tafhamee al-dars** You were understanding the lesson. (singular, feminine)	أَنْتِ تَفْهَمين ٱلدَّرْس. **anti tafhameen al-dars** You are understanding the lesson. (singular, feminine)
أَنْتُمَا كُنْتُمَا تَفْهَما ٱلدَّرْس. **antomaa kontomaa tafhamaa al-dars** You both were understanding the lesson. (dual, masculine and feminine)	أَنْتُمَا تَفْهَمان ٱلدَّرْس. **antomaa tafhamaan al-dars** You both are understanding the les- son. (dual, masculine and feminine)
أَنْتُم كُنْتُم تَفْهَموا ٱلدَّرْس. **antom kontom tafhamoo al-dars** You all were understanding the lesson. (plural, masculine and feminine)	أَنْتُم تَفْهَمون ٱلدَّرْس. **antom tafhamoon al-dars** You all are understanding the lesson. (plural, masculine and feminine)

Past Continuous Tense Modern Standard Arabic	Present Tense Modern Standard Arabic
أَنْتُنَّ كُنْتُنَّ تَفْهَمْنَ ٱلدَّرْس.	أَنْتُنَّ تَفْهَمْنَ ٱلدَّرْس.
antonna kontonna tafhamna al-dars You all were understanding the lesson. (plural, feminine)	antonna tafhamna al-dars You all are understanding the lesson. (plural, feminine)
نَحنُ كُنَّا نَفْهَم ٱلدَّرْس.	نَحنُ نَفْهَم ٱلدَّرْس.
naHno konna nafham al-dars We were understanding the lesson. (masculine and feminine)	naHno nafham al-dars We are understanding the lesson. (masculine and feminine)
هُوَ كانَ يَفْهَم ٱلدَّرْس.	هُوَ يَفْهَم ٱلدَّرْس.
howa kana yafham al-dars He was understanding the lesson.	howa yafham al-dars He is understanding the lesson.
هِيَ كانَتْ تَفْهَم ٱلدَّرْس.	هِيَ تَفْهَم ٱلدَّرْس.
hiya kanat tafham al-dars She was understanding the lesson.	hiya tafham al-dars She is understanding the lesson.
هُما كانا يَفْهَما ٱلدَّرْس.	هُما يَفْهَمان ٱلدَّرْس.
homaa kanaa yafhamaa al-dars They both were understanding the lesson. (dual, masculine and feminine)	homaa yafhamaan al-dars They both are understanding the lesson. (dual, masculine and feminine)
هُمْ كانوا يَفْهَموا ٱلدَّرْس.	هُمْ يَفْهَمون ٱلدَّرْس.
hom kano yafhamoo al-dars They were understanding the lesson. (plural, masculine and feminine)	hom yafhamoon al-dars They are understanding the lesson. (plural, masculine and feminine)
هُنَّ كُنَّ يَفْهَمْنَ ٱلدَّرْس.	هُنَّ يَفْهَمْنَ ٱلدَّرْس.
honna konna yafhamna al-dars They were understanding the lesson. (plural, feminine)	honna yafhamna al-dars They are understanding the lesson. (plural, feminine)

Lesson Thirty-Two
Past Perfect Tense

The past perfect tense, is used to express an action that occurred before another past action or time reference. In Arabic, it is formed by adding the verb "kana" (كانَ), which means "was / were / had / used to," to the simple past sentence.

This construction signifies that the action described by the verb "kana" (كانَ) was completed before the action or time reference mentioned in the simple past sentence.

The verb "kana" (كانَ) is conjugated according to the subject pronoun, just like any other verb in the past tense in Arabic.

To negate the past perfect tense, which is formed by adding "kana" (كانَ) to the simple past tense, the same method can be used. You would add the word "maa" (ما) before "kana" (كانَ) to indicate negation. This is similar to negating any other verb in the simple past tense or past continuous tense.

- **In spoken Modern Standard Arabic (MSA), the plural masculine form is commonly used instead of the dual and feminine plural forms. The dual and feminine plural forms are more commonly found in Classical Arabic and are used in formal and poetic contexts.**

Here are the forms of "kana" (كانَ) in the past tense and their corresponding subject pronouns, including the negated forms:

Negating كانَ	Forms of كانَ	Subject Pronouns
أَنا ما كُنْتُ anaa maa konto I was not	أَنا كُنْتُ anaa konto I was	أَنا anaa I

293

Negating كانَ	Forms of كانَ	Subject Pronouns
أنتَ ما كُنْتَ anta maa konta You were not	أنتَ كُنْتَ anta konta You were	أنتَ anta You (singular, masculine)
أنتِ ما كُنْتِ anti maa konti You were not	أنتِ كُنْتِ anti konti You were	أنتِ anti You (singular, feminine)
أنتُما ما كُنْتُما antoma maa kontoma You both were not	أنتُما كُنْتُما antoma kontoma You both were	أنتُما antoma You (dual, masculine and feminine)
أنتُم ما كُنْتُم antom maa kontom You all were not	أنتُم كُنْتُم antom kontom You all were	أنتُم antom You (plural, masculine and feminine)
أنْتُنَّ ما كُنْتُنَّ antonna maa kontonna You all were not	أنْتُنَّ كُنْتُنَّ antonna kontonna You all were	أنْتُنَّ antonna You (plural, feminine)
نَحنُ ما كُنّا naHno maa konnaa We were not	نَحنُ كُنّا naHno konnaa We were	نَحنُ naHno We (masculine and feminine)
هُوَ ما كانَ howa maa kana He was not	هُوَ كانَ howa kana He was	هُوَ howa He/it
هِيَ ما كانَتْ hiya maa kanat She was not	هِيَ كانَتْ hiya kanat She was	هِيَ hiya She/it

Negating كانَ	Forms of كانَ	Subject Pronouns
هُما ما كانا homaa maa kanaa They both were not	هُما كانا homaa kanaa They both were	هُما homaa They (dual, masculine and feminine)
هُم ما كانوا hom maa kanoo They were not	هُم كانوا hom kanoo They were	هُم hom They (plural, masculine and feminine)
هُنَّ ما كنَّ honna maa konna They were not	هُنَّ كنَّ honna konna They were	هُنَّ honna They (plural, feminine)

Forming the past perfect tense from simple past tense:

The past perfect tense, is used to express an action that occurred before another past action or a specific point in the past. In Arabic, the past perfect tense is formed by adding the verb "kana" كان, which means "was / were / had / used to," to the simple past verb. This combination creates a compound verb that represents the completed action before a reference point in the past.

The past perfect tense in Arabic provides a way to indicate the sequence of events in the past and establish a temporal relationship between two past actions or events. By using "kana" كان with the simple past verb, you create a compound verb that conveys the idea of a completed action that took place before another past event or a specific point in the past.

- **The examples given in the tables for this lesson are in spoken Modern Standard Arabic. In this form, the words do not have vowels marked at the end.**

The past perfect tense of the verb "to live" with the root ع ي ش:

Past Perfect Tense Modern Standard Arabic	Simple Past Tense Modern Standard Arabic
أَنا كُنْتُ عِشْتُ في كَليفورنيا. anaa konto A'ishto fee california I had lived in California.	أَنا عِشْتُ في كَليفورنيا. anaa A'ishto fee california I lived in California.
أَنْتَ كُنْتَ عِشْتَ في كَليفورنيا. anta konta A'ishta fee california You had lived in California. (singular, masculine)	أَنْتَ عِشْتَ في كَليفورنيا. anta A'ishta fee california You lived in California. (singular, masculine)
أَنْتِ كُنْتِ عِشْتِ في كَليفورنيا. anti konti A'ishti fee california You had lived in California. (singular, feminine)	أَنْتِ عِشْتِ في كَليفورنيا. anti A'ishti fee california You lived in California. (singular, feminine)
أَنْتُما كُنْتُما عِشْتُما في كَليفورنيا. antomaa kontoma A'ishtomaa fee california You both had lived in California. (dual, masculine and feminine)	أَنْتُما عِشْتُما في كَليفورنيا. antomaa A'ishtomaa fee california You both lived in California. (dual, masculine and feminine)
أَنْتُم كُنْتُم عِشْتُم في كَليفورنيا. antom kontom A'ishtom fee california You all had lived in California. (plural, masculine and feminine)	أَنْتُم عِشْتُم في كَليفورنيا. antom A'ishtom fee california You all lived in California. (plural, masculine and feminine)
أَنْتُنَّ كُنْتُنَّ عِشْتُنَّ في كَليفورنيا. antonna kontonna A'ishtonna fee california You all had lived in California. (plural, feminine)	أَنْتُنَّ عِشْتُنَّ في كَليفورنيا. antonna A'ishtonna fee california You all lived in California. (plural, feminine)

Past Perfect Tense Modern Standard Arabic	Simple Past Tense Modern Standard Arabic
نَحْنُ كُنّا عِشْنا في كَليفورنيا.	نَحنُ عِشْنا في كَليفورنيا.
naHno konna A'ishna fee california We had lived in California. (masculine and feminine)	naHno A'ishnaa fee california We lived in California. (masculine and feminine)
هُوَ كانَ عاشَ في كَليفورنيا.	هُوَ عاشَ في كَليفورنيا.
howa kana A'asha fee california He had lived in California.	howa A'asha fee california He lived in California.
هِيَ كانَتْ عاشَتْ في كَليفورنيا.	هِيَ عاشَتْ في كَليفورنيا.
hiya kanat A'ashat fee california She had lived in California.	hiya A'ashat fee california She lived in California.
هُما كانَا عاشَا في كَليفورنيا.	هُما عاشَا في كَليفورنيا.
homaa kanaa A'ashaa fee california They both had lived in California. (dual, masculine and feminine)	homaa A'ashaa fee california They both lived in California. (dual, masculine and feminine)
هُمْ كانوا عاشوا في كَليفورنيا.	هُمْ عاشوا في كَليفورنيا.
hom kanoo A'ashoo fee california They had lived in California. (plural, masculine and feminine)	hom A'ashoo fee california They lived in California. (plural, masculine and feminine)
هُنَّ كُنَّ عِشْنَ في كَليفورنيا.	هُنَّ عِشْنَ في كَليفورنيا.
honna konna A'ishna fee california They had lived in California. (plural, feminine)	honna A'ishna fee california They lived in a California. (plural, feminine)

The past perfect tense of the verb "to study" with the root  د ر س :

Past Perfect Tense Sentences Modern Spoken Standard Arabic	Simple Past Tense Modern Standard Arabic
أَنَا كُنْتُ دَرَسْتُ فِي ٱلْمَكْتَبَةِ.	أَنَا دَرَسْتُ فِي ٱلْمَكْتَبَةِ.
anaa konto darasto fee al-maktaba I had studied at the library.	anaa darasto fee al-maktaba I studied at the library.
أَنْتَ كُنْتَ دَرَسْتَ فِي ٱلْمَكْتَبَةِ.	أَنْتَ دَرَسْتَ فِي ٱلْمَكْتَبَةِ.
anta konta darasta fee al-maktaba You had studied at the library. (singular, masculine)	anta darasta fee al-maktaba You studied at the library. (singular, masculine)
أَنْتِ كُنْتِ دَرَسْتِ فِي ٱلْمَكْتَبَةِ.	أَنْتِ دَرَسْتِ فِي ٱلْمَكْتَبَةِ.
anti konti darasti fee al-maktaba You had studied at the library. (singular, feminine)	anti darasti fee al-maktaba You studied at the library. (singular, feminine)
أَنْتُمَا كُنْتُمَا دَرَسْتُمَا فِي ٱلْمَكْتَبَةِ.	أَنْتُمَا دَرَسْتُمَا فِي ٱلْمَكْتَبَةِ.
antoma kontoma darastoma fee al-mak-taba You both had studied at the library. (dual, masculine and feminine)	antoma darastoma fee al-mak-ba You both studied at the library. (dual, masculine and feminine)
أَنْتُمْ كُنْتُمْ دَرَسْتُمْ فِي ٱلْمَكْتَبَةِ.	أَنْتُمْ دَرَسْتُمْ فِي ٱلْمَكْتَبَةِ.
antom kontom darastom fee al-maktaba You all had studied at the library. (plural, masculine and feminine)	antom darastom fee al-maktaba You all studied at the library. (plural, masculine and feminine)
أَنْتُنَّ كُنْتُنَّ دَرَسْتُنَّ فِي ٱلْمَكْتَبَةِ.	أَنْتُنَّ دَرَسْتُنَّ فِي ٱلْمَكْتَبَةِ.
antonna kontonna darastonna fee al-maktaba You all had studied at the library. (plural, feminine)	antonna darastonna fee al-mak-taba You all studied at the library. (plural, feminine)

Past Perfect Tense Sentences Modern Spoken Standard Arabic	Simple Past Tense Modern Standard Arabic
نَحْنُ كُنّا دَرَسْنا في ٱلمَكْتَبَة. **naHno konna darasnaa fee al-maktaba** We had studied at the library. (masculine and feminine)	نَحْنُ دَرَسْنا في ٱلمَكْتَبَة. **naHno darasnaa fee al-maktaba** We studied at the library. (masculine and feminine)
هُوَ كانَ دَرَسَ في ٱلمَكْتَبَة. **howa kana darasa fee al-maktaba** He had studied at the library.	هُوَ دَرَسَ في ٱلمَكْتَبَة. **howa darasa fee al-maktaba** He studied at the library.
هِيَ كانَتْ دَرَسَتْ في ٱلمَكْتَبَة. **hiya kanat darasat fee al-maktaba** She had studied at the library.	هِيَ دَرَسَتْ في ٱلمَكْتَبَة. **hiya darasat fee al-maktaba** She studied at the library.
هُمَا كانا دَرَسَا في ٱلمَكْتَبَة. **homaa kanaa darasaa fee al-maktaba** They both had studied at the library. (dual, masculine and feminine)	هُمَا دَرَسَا في ٱلمَكْتَبَة. **homaa darasaa fee al-maktaba** They both studied at the library. (dual, masculine and feminine)
هُمْ كانوا دَرَسوا في ٱلمَكْتَبَة. **hom kanoo darasoo fee al-maktaba** They had studied at the library. (plural, masculine and feminine)	هُمْ دَرَسوا في ٱلمَكْتَبَة. **hom darasoo fee al-maktaba** They studied at the library. (plural, masculine and feminine)
هُنَّ كُنَّ دَرَسْنَ في ٱلمَكْتَبَة. **honna konna darasna fee al-maktaba** They had studied at the library. (plural, feminine)	هُنَّ دَرَسْنَ في ٱلمَكْتَبَة. **honna darasna fee al-maktaba** They studied at the library. (plural, feminine)

The past perfect tense of the verb "to write" with the root  :

Past Perfect Tense Modern Standard Arabic	Simple Past Tense Modern Standard Arabic
أَنا كُنْتُ كَتَبْتُ رِسالَة.	أَنا كَتَبْتُ رِسالَة.
anaa konto katabto risaala I had written a letter.	anaa katabto risaala I wrote a letter.
أَنْتَ كُنْتَ كَتَبْتَ رِسالَة.	أَنْتَ كَتَبْتَ رِسالَة.
anta konta katabta risaala You had written a letter. (singular, masculine)	anta katabta risaala You wrote a letter. (singular, masculine)
أَنْتِ كُنْتِ كَتَبْتِ رِسالَة.	أَنْتِ كَتَبْتِ رِسالَة.
anti konti katabti risaala You had written a letter. (singular, feminine)	anti katabti risaala You wrote a letter. (singular, feminine)
أَنْتُما كُنْتُما كَتَبْتُما رِسالَة.	أَنْتُما كَتَبْتُما رِسالَة.
antomaa kontomaa katabtomaa risaala You both had written a letter. (dual, masculine and feminine)	antomaa katabtomaa risaala You both wrote a letter. (dual, masculine and feminine)
أَنْتُم كُنْتُم كَتَبْتُم رِسالَة.	أَنْتُم كَتَبْتُم رِسالَة.
antom kontom katabtom risaala You all had written a letter. (plural, masculine and feminine)	antom katabtom risaala You all wrote a letter. (plural, masculine and feminine)
أَنْتُنَّ كُنْتُنَّ كَتَبْتُنَّ رِسالَة.	أَنْتُنَّ كَتَبْتُنَّ رِسالَة.
antonna kontonna katabtonna risaala You all had written a letter. (plural, feminine)	antonna katabtonna risaala You all wrote a letter. (plural, feminine)

Past Perfect Tense Modern Standard Arabic	Simple Past Tense Modern Standard Arabic
نَحْنُ كُنَّا كَتَبْنا رِسالَة.	نَحْنُ كَتَبْنا رِسالَة.
naHno konna katabnaa risaala We had written a letter. (masculine and feminine)	naHno katabnaa risaala We wrote a letter. (masculine and feminine)
هُوَ كانَ كَتَبَ رِسالَة.	هُوَ كَتَبَ رِسالَة.
howa kana kataba risaala He had written a letter.	howa kataba risaala He wrote a letter.
هِيَ كانَتْ كَتَبَتْ رِسالَة.	هِيَ كَتَبَتْ رِسالَة.
hiya kanat katabat risaala She had written a letter.	hiya katabat risaala She wrote a letter.
هُما كانا كَتَبا رِسالَة.	هُما كَتَبا رِسالَة.
homaa kanaa katabaa risaala They both had written a letter. (dual, masculine and feminine)	homaa katabaa risaala They both wrote a letter. (dual, masculine and feminine)
هُم كانوا كَتَبوا رِسالَة.	هُم كَتَبوا رِسالَة.
hom kano kataboo risaala They had written a letter. (plural, masculine and feminine)	hom kataboo risaala They wrote a letter. (plural, masculine and feminine)
هُنَّ كُنَّ كَتَبْنَ رِسالَة.	هُنَّ كَتَبْنَ رِسالَة.
honna konna katabna risaala They had written a letter. (plural, feminine)	honna katabna risaala They wrote a letter. (plural, feminine)

The past perfect tense of the verb "to go" with the root ذ ـ هـ ـ ب :

Past Perfect Tense Modern Spoken Standard Arabic	Simple Past Tense Modern Spoken Standard Arabic
أَنا كُنْتُ ذَهَبْتُ إِلَى ٱلْمَدْرَسَة. anaa konto dhahabto ela al-madrasa I had gone to school.	أَنا ذَهَبْتُ إِلَى ٱلْمَدْرَسَة. anaa dhahabto ela al-madrasa I went to school.
أَنْتَ كُنْتَ ذَهَبْتَ إِلَى ٱلْمَدْرَسَة. anta konta dhahabta ela al-madrasa You had gone to school. (singular, masculine)	أَنْتَ ذَهَبْتَ إِلَى ٱلْمَدْرَسَة. anta dhahabta ela al-madrasa You went to school. (singular, masculine)
أنتِ كُنْتِ ذَهَبْتِ إِلَى ٱلْمَدْرَسَة. anti konti dhahabti ela al-madrasa You had gone to school. (singular, feminine)	أنتِ ذَهَبْتِ إِلَى ٱلْمَدْرَسَة. anti dhahabti ela al-madrasa You went to school. (singular, feminine)
أنتُما كُنْتُما ذَهَبْتُما إِلَى ٱلْمَدْرَسَة antomaa kontoma dhahabtomaa ela al-madrasa You both had gone to school. (dual, masculine and feminine)	أنتُما ذَهَبْتُما إِلَى ٱلْمَدْرَسَة. antomaa dhahabtomaa ela al-madrasa You both went to school. (dual, masculine and feminine)
أنتُم كُنْتُم ذَهَبْتُم إِلَى ٱلْمَدْرَسَة. antom kontom dhahabtom ela al-madrasa You all had gone to school. (plural, masculine and feminine)	أنتُم ذَهَبْتُم إِلَى ٱلْمَدْرَسَة. antom dhahabtom ela al-madrasa You all went to school. (plural, masculine and feminine)
أَنْتُنَّ كُنْتُنَّ ذَهَبْتُنَّ إِلَى ٱلْمَدْرَسَة. antonna kontonna dhahabtonna ela al-madrasa You all had gone to school. (plural, feminine)	أَنْتُنَّ ذَهَبْتُنَّ إِلَى ٱلْمَدْرَسَة. antonna dhahabtonna ela al-madrasa You all went to school. (plural, feminine)

Past Perfect Tense **Modern Spoken Standard Arabic**	**Simple Past Tense** **Modern Spoken Standard Arabic**
نَحْنُ كُنَّا ذَهَبْنا إلى ٱلْمَدْرَسَة. naHno konna dhahabnaa ela al-madrasa We had gone to school. (masculine and feminine)	نَحْنُ ذَهَبْنا إلى ٱلْمَدْرَسَة. naHno dhahabnaa ela al-madrasa We went to school. (masculine and feminine)
هُوَ كانَ ذَهَبَ إلى ٱلْمَدْرَسَة. howa kana dhahaba ela al-madrasa He had gone to school.	هُوَ ذَهَبَ إلى ٱلْمَدْرَسَة. howa dhahaba ela al-madrasa He went to school.
هِيَ كانَتْ ذَهَبَتْ إلى ٱلْمَدْرَسَة. hiya kanat dhahabat ela al-madrasa She had gone to school.	هِيَ ذَهَبَتْ إلى ٱلْمَدْرَسَة. hiya dhahabat ela al-madrasa She went to school.
هُما كانا ذَهَبا إلى ٱلْمَدْرَسَة. homaa kanaa dhahabaa ela al-madrasa They both had gone to school. (dual, masculine and feminine)	هُما ذَهَبا إلى ٱلْمَدْرَسَة. homaa dhahabaa ela al-madrasa They both went to school. (dual, masculine and feminine)
هُمْ كانوا ذَهَبوا إلى ٱلْمَدْرَسَة. hom kano dhahaboo ela al-madrasa They had gone to school. (plural, masculine and feminine)	هُمْ ذَهَبوا إلى ٱلْمَدْرَسَة. hom dhahaboo ela al-madrasa They went to school. (plural, masculine and feminine)
هُنَّ كُنَّ ذَهَبْنَ إلى ٱلْمَدْرَسَة. honna konna dhahabna ela al-madrasa They had gone to school. (plural, feminine)	هُنَّ ذَهَبْنَ إلى ٱلْمَدْرَسَة. honna dhahabna ela al-madrasa They went to school. (plural, feminine)

The past perfect tense of the verb "to understand" with the root  :

Past Perfect Tense Modern Standard Arabic	Simple Past Tense Modern Standard Arabic
أَنَا كُنْتُ فَهِمْتُ ٱلدَّرْسَ. anaa konto fahimto al-dars I had understood the lesson.	أَنَا فَهِمْتُ ٱلدَّرْسَ. anaa fahimto al-dars I understood the lesson.
أَنْتَ كُنْتَ فَهِمْتَ ٱلدَّرْسَ. anta konta fahimta al-dars You had understood the lesson. (singular, masculine)	أَنْتَ فَهِمْتَ ٱلدَّرْسَ. anta fahimta al-dars You understood the lesson. (singular, masculine)
أَنْتِ كُنْتِ فَهِمْتِ ٱلدَّرْسَ. anti konti fahimti al-dars You had understood the lesson. (singular, feminine)	أَنْتِ فَهِمْتِ ٱلدَّرْسَ. anti fahimti al-dars You understood the lesson. (singular, feminine)
أَنْتُما كُنْتُما فَهِمْتُما ٱلدَّرْسَ. antomaa kontomaa fahimtomaa al-dars You both had understood the lesson. (dual, masculine and feminine)	أَنْتُما فَهِمْتُما ٱلدَّرْسَ. antomaa fahimtomaa al-dars You both understood the lesson. (dual, masculine and feminine)
أَنْتُم كُنْتُم فَهِمْتُم ٱلدَّرْسَ. antom kontom fahimtom al-dars You all had understood the lesson. (plural, masculine and feminine)	أَنْتُم فَهِمْتُم ٱلدَّرْسَ. antom fahimtom al-dars You all understood the lesson. (plural, masculine and feminine)
أَنْتُنَّ كُنْتُنَّ فَهِمْتُنَّ ٱلدَّرْسَ. antonna kontonna fahimtonna al-dars You all had understood the lesson. (plural, feminine)	أَنْتُنَّ فَهِمْتُنَّ ٱلدَّرْسَ. antonna fahimtonna al-dars You all understood the lesson. (plural, feminine)

Past Perfect Tense Modern Standard Arabic	Simple Past Tense Modern Standard Arabic
نَحْنُ كُنَّا فَهِمْنا ٱلدَّرْس.	نَحْنُ فَهِمْنا ٱلدَّرْس.
naHno konna fahimnaa al-dars We had understood the lesson. (masculine and feminine)	naHno fahimnaa al-dars We understood the lesson. (masculine and feminine)
هُوَ كانَ فَهِمَ ٱلدَّرْس.	هُوَ فَهِمَ ٱلدَّرْس.
howa kana fahima al-dars He had understood the lesson.	howa fahima al-dars He understood the lesson.
هِيَ كانَتْ فَهِمَتْ ٱلدَّرْس.	هِيَ فَهِمَتْ ٱلدَّرْس.
hiya kanat fahimat al-dars She had understood the lesson.	hiya fahimat al-dars She understood the lesson.
هُما كانا فَهِما ٱلدَّرْس.	هُما فَهِما ٱلدَّرْس.
homaa kana fahimaa al-dars They both had understood the lesson. (dual, masculine and feminine)	homaa fahimaa al-dars They both understood the lesson. (dual, masculine and feminine)
هُمْ كانوا فَهِموا ٱلدَّرْس.	هُمْ فَهِموا ٱلدَّرْس.
hom kano fahimoo al-dars They had understood the lesson. (plural, masculine and feminine)	hom fahimoo al-dars They understood the lesson. (plural, masculine and feminine)
هُنَّ كُنَّ فَهِمْنَ ٱلدَّرْس.	هُنَّ فَهِمْنَ ٱلدَّرْس.
honna konna fahimna al-dars They had understood the lesson. (plural, feminine)	honna fahimna al-dars They understood the lesson. (plural, feminine)

- Note, refer to page six for a refresher on the pronunciation system used in this book.

- Note: In order to emphasize the grammar rules presented in the lesson, most of the words in this textbook have not been marked with vowels at the end.

Lesson Thirty-Three
The Imperative or Command Verb

The imperative or command verb is used to express requests or orders to do something. It is specifically used with second person pronouns ("You") in singular, dual, or plural forms. Therefore, there are only five conjugations for the command verb, which also depend on the gender and number of the second person.

In both Classical Arabic and spoken Modern Standard Arabic, the common indicator

for the command verb is the addition of the letter "alif hamzah" (أ) before the first root

of the word, carrying a fatHah, Dammeh, or kasrah vowel.

The grammar rules for the command verb are numerous and can be challenging to remember, even for native Arabic speakers. Therefore, we will study this verb by focusing on recognizing the most common groups and patterns of command verbs. Every word in the Arabic language, including the command verb, belongs to a family or group of words that follow the same pattern. This similarity creates a rhyme due to the shared short and long vowels. The Arabic language has many patterns and groups of words, but we will concentrate on the most common ones.

The negated command verb is formed by adding the word 'laa' لا (don't) to the

present form of the verb, specifically for the second person pronouns 'You' (singular, dual, or plural) in both masculine and feminine.

- **In spoken Modern Standard Arabic (MSA), the plural masculine form is commonly used instead of the dual and feminine plural forms. The dual and feminine plural forms are more commonly found in Classical Arabic and are used in formal and poetic contexts.**

- Examples of the most common patterns of the command verbs in Arabic. Keep in mind, the examples given in the tables for this lesson are in the spoken Modern Standard Arabic (MSA):

First Pattern:

Command verbs are formed by adding an 'alif hamzah' with a 'fatHa' vowel أَ before

the first root, adding 'sukoon' to the first root, adding 'kasrah' vowel to the second root, and adding 'sukoon' to the last root if it's not connected to a pronoun.

Command verb 'Hurry up!' with the pronoun 'You'. The root verb is س ر ع :

Negated Command	Command Verb	Pronoun 'You'	
لا تُسْرِعْ ! laa tosriA' Do not hurry!	أَسْرِعْ ! asriA' Hurry up!	You (masculine)	أَنتَ anta
لا تُسْرِعي ! laa tosriA'ee Do not hurry!	أَسْرِعي ! asriA'ee Hurry up!	You (feminine)	أَنتِ anti
لا تُسْرِعا ! laa tosriA'a Do not hurry, both of you!	أَسْرِعا ! asriA'a Hurry up, both of you!	You (dual, masculine and feminine)	أَنتُما antomaa
لا تُسْرِعوا ! laa tosriA'oo Do not hurry, all of you!	أَسْرِعوا ! asriA'oo Hurry up, all of you!	You (plural, masculine and feminine)	أَنتُم antom
لا تُسْرِعْنَ ! laa tosriA'na Do not hurry, all of you!	أَسْرِعْنَ ! asriA'na Hurry up, all of you!	You (plural, feminine)	أَنْتُنَّ antonna

Command verb 'Tell!' with the pronoun 'You', the root of the verb is خ ب ر:

Negated Command	Command Verb	Pronoun 'You'	
لا تُخْبِرْ ! laa toKHbir Do not tell..!	أَخْبِرْ ! aKHbir Tell..!	You (masculine)	أنتَ anta
لا تُخْبِري ! laa toKHbiree Do not tell..!	أَخْبِري ! aKHbiree Tell..!	You (feminine)	أنتِ anti
لا تُخْبِرا ! laa toKHbiraa Do not tell..both of you!	أَخْبِرا ! aKHbiraa Tell..both of you!	You (dual, masculine and feminine)	أنتُما antomaa
لا تُخْبِروا ! laa toKHbiroo Do not tell..all of you!	أَخْبِروا ! aKHbiroo Tell..all of you!	You (plural, masculine and feminine)	أنتُم antom
لا تُخْبِرْنَ ! laa toKHbirna Do not tell..all of you!	أَخْبِرْنَ ! aKHbirna Tell..all of you!	You (plural, feminine)	أنْتُنَّ antonna

Command verb 'Continue!' with the pronoun 'You'. The root is ك م ل:

Negated Command	Command Verb	Pronoun 'You'	
لا تُكْمِل ! laa tokmil Do not continue..!	أكْمِل ! akmil Continue!	You (masculine)	أنتَ anta

Negated Command	Command Verb	Pronoun 'You'	
لا تُكْمِلِي ! laa tokmilee Do not continue..!	أَكْمِلِي ! akmilee Continue!	You (feminine)	أنتِ anti
لا تُكْمِلا ! laa tokmilaa Do not continue.. both of you!	أَكْمِلا ! akmilaa Continue, both of you!	You (dual, masculine and feminine)	أنتُما antomaa
لا تُكْمِلوا ! laa tokmiloo Do not continue..all of you!	أَكْمِلوا ! akmiloo Continue, all of you!	You (plural, masculine and feminine)	أنتُم antom
لا تُكْمِلْنَ ! laa tokmilna Do not continue..all of you!	أَكْمِلْنَ ! akmilna Continue, all of you!	You (plural, feminine)	أنْتُنَّ antonna

Command verb 'Warn!' with the pronoun 'You'. The root of the verb is ن ذ ر :

Negated Command	Command Verb	Pronoun 'You'	
لا تُنْذِرْ ! laa tondhir Do not warn!	أَنْذِرْ ! andhir Warn!	You (masculine)	أنتَ anta
لا تُنْذِري ! laa tondhiree Do not warn!	أَنْذِري ! andhiree Warn!	You (feminine)	أنتِ anti

Negated Command	Command Verb	Pronoun 'You'	
لا تُنْذِرا ! laa tondhiraa Do not warn, both of you!	أَنْذِرا ! andhiraa Warn, both of you!	You (dual, masculine and feminine)	أنتُما antomaa
لا تُنْذِروا ! laa tondhiroo Do not warn, all of you!	أَنْذِروا ! andhiroo Warn, all of you!	You (plural, mascu- line and femi- nine)	أنتُم antom
لا تُنْذِرْنَ ! laa tondhirna Do not warn, all of you!	أَنْذِرْنَ ! andhirna Warn, all of you!	You (plural, feminine)	أنْتُنَّ antonna

Second Pattern:

In the second pattern, command verbs are formed by adding an 'alif hamzah' with a 'Dammah' vowel أ before the first root, adding 'sukoon' to the first root, adding a 'Dammah' vowel to the second root, and adding 'sukoon' to the last root if it's not connected to a pronoun.

Command verb 'Study!' with the pronoun 'You'. The root of the verb is د ر س :

Negated Command	Command Verb	Pronoun 'You'	
لا تَدْرُسْ! laa tadros Do not study!	أُدْرُسْ! odros Study!	You (masculine)	أنتَ anta
لا تَدْرُسي! laa tadrosee Do not study!	أُدْرُسي! odrosee Study!	You (feminine)	أنتِ anti

Negated Command	Command Verb	Pronoun 'You'
لا تَدْرُسا! laa tadrosaa Do not study, both of you!	أُدْرُسا! odrosaa Study, both of you!	You (dual, masculine and feminine) أَنْتُما antomaa
لا تَدْرُسوا! laa tadrosoo Do not study, all of you!	أُدْرُسوا! odrosoo Study, all of you!	You (plural, (masculine and feminine) أَنْتُم antom
لا تَدْرُسْنَ ! laa tadrosna Do not study, all of you!	أُدْرُسْنَ ! odrosna Study, all of you!	You (plural, feminine) أَنْتُنَّ antonna

Command verb 'Look!' with the pronoun 'You'. The root of the verb is ن ظ ر:

Negated Command	Command Verb	Pronoun 'You'
لا تَنْظُرْ ! laa tanDHor Do not look!	أُنْظُرْ ! onDHor Look!	You (masculine) أَنْتَ anta
لا تَنْظُرِي ! laa tanDHoree Do not look!	أُنْظُرِي ! onDHoree Look!	You (feminine) أَنْتِ anti
لا تَنْظُرا ! laa tanDHoraa Do not look, both of you!	أُنْظُرا ! onDHoraa Look, both of you!	You (dual, masculine and feminine) أَنْتُما antomaa

Negated Command	Command Verb	Pronoun 'You'	
لا تَنْظُروا ! **laa tanDHoroo** Do not look, all of you!	أُنْظُروا ! **onDHoroo** Look, all of you!	You (plural, mascu- line and femi- nine)	أَنْتُم **antom**
لا تَنْظُرْنَ ! **laa tanDHorna** Do not look, all of you!	أُنْظُرْنَ ! **onDHorna** Look, all of you!	You (plural, feminine)	أَنْتُنَّ **antonna**

Command verb 'Write!' with the pronoun 'You'. The root of the verb is ك ت ب :

Negated Command	Command Verb	Pronoun 'You'	
لا تَكْتُبْ! **laa taktob** Do not write!	أُكْتُبْ! **oktob** Write!	You (masculine)	أَنْتَ **anta**
لا تَكْتُبي! **laa taktobee** Do not write!	أُكْتُبي! **oktobee** Write!	You (feminine)	أَنْتِ **anti**
لا تَكْتُبا! **laa taktobaa** Do not write, both of you!	أُكْتُبا! **oktobaa** Write, both of you!	You (dual, mascu- line and femi- nine)	أَنْتُما **antomaa**
لا تَكْتُبوا! **laa taktoboo** Do not write, all of you!	أُكْتُبوا! **oktoboo** Write, all of you!	You (plural, mascu- line and femi- nine)	أَنْتُم **antom**
لا تَكْتُبْنَ ! **laa taktobna** Do not write, all of you!	أُكْتُبْنَ ! **oktobna** Write, all of you!	You (plural, feminine)	أَنْتُنَّ **antonna**

Command verb 'Run!' with the pronoun 'You'. The root of the verb is ر ك ض :

Negated Command	Command Verb		Pronoun 'You'
لا تَركُضْ ! laa tarkoD Do not run!	أُركُضْ ! orkoD Run!	You (masculine)	أنتَ anta
لا تَركُضي ! laa tarkoDee Do not run!	أُركُضي ! orkoDee Run!	You (feminine)	أنتِ anti
لا تَركُضا ! laa tarkoDaa Do not run, both of you!	أُركُضا ! orkoDaa Run, both of you!	You (dual, masculine and feminine)	أنتُما antomaa
لا تَركُضوا ! laa tarkoDoo Do not run, all of you	أُركُضوا ! orkoDoo Run, all of you!	You (plural, mascu- line and femi- nine)	أنتُم antom
لا تَركُضْنَ ! laa tarkoDna Do not run, all of you!	أُركُضْنَ ! orkoDna Run, all of you!	You (plural, feminine)	أنتُنَّ antonna

Third Pattern:

In the third pattern, command verbs are formed by adding an 'alif hamza' with the 'kasrah' vowel إ before the first root, adding a 'sukoon' to the first root, adding a 'fatHah' vowel to the second root, and adding a 'sukoon' to the last root if it's not connected to a pronoun.

Command verb 'Go!' with the pronoun 'You'. The root of the verb is ذ ـ هـ ـ ب:

Negated Command	Command Verb	Pronoun 'You'	
لا تَذْهَبْ! laa tadh-hab Do not go!	إذْهَبْ! idhhab Go!	You (masculine)	أنتَ anta
لا تَذْهَبي! laa tadh-habee Do not go!	إذْهَبي! idhhabee Go!	You (feminine)	أنتِ anti
لا تَذْهَبا! laa tadh-habaa Do not go, both of you!	إذْهَبا! idhhabaa Go, both of you!	You (dual, masculine and feminine)	أنتُما antomaa
لا تَذْهَبوا! laa tadh-haboo Do not go, all of you	إذْهَبوا! idhhaboo Go, all of you!	You (plural, mascu- line and femi- nine)	أنتُم antom
لا تَذْهَبْنَ ! laa tadh-habna Do not go, all of you!	إذْهَبْنَ ! Idhhabna Go, all of you!	You (plural, feminine)	أنتُنَّ antonna

Command verb 'Work!' with pronoun 'You', the root of the verb is ع م ل:

Negated Command	Command Verb	Pronoun 'You'	
لا تَعْمَلْ! laa taA'mal Do not work! Do not make..!	إعْمَلْ! iA'mal Work! Make..!	You (masculine)	أنتَ anta

Negated Command	Command Verb	Pronoun 'You'	
لا تَعْمَلي! laa taA'malee Do not work! Do not make..!	إعْمَلي! iA'malee Work! Make..!	You (feminine)	أنتِ anti
لا تَعْمَلا! laa taA'malaa Do not work, both of you! Do not make..both of you!	إعْمَلا! iA'malaa Work, both of you! Make..both of you!	You (dual, masculine and feminine)	أنتُما antomaa
لا تَعْمَلوا! laa taA'maloo Do not work, all of you! Do not make..all of you!	إعْمَلوا! iA'maloo Work, all of you! Make..all of you!	You (plural, masculine and feminine)	أنتُم antom
لا تَعْمَلْنَ ! laa taA'malna Do not work, all of you! Do not make..all of you!	إعْمَلْنَ ! iA'malna Work, all of you! Make..all of you!	You (plural, feminine)	أنْتُنَّ antonna

Command verb 'Understand!' with the pronoun 'You', the root of the verb is ف هـ م:

Negated Command	Command Verb	Pronoun 'You'	
لا تَفْهَم خَطَأً! laa tafham khaTa,a Do not understand wrong!	إفْهَمْ! ifham Understand!	You (masculine)	أنتَ anta
لا تَفْهَمي خَطَأً! laa tafhamee khaTa,a Do not understand wrong!	إفْهَمي! ifhamee Understand!	You (feminine)	أنتِ anti

Negated Command	Command Verb	Pronoun 'You'	
لا تَفْهَما خَطَأً! laa tafhamaa khaTa,a Do not understand wrong, both of you!	إفْهَما! ifhamaa Understand, both of you!	You (dual, masculine and feminine)	أنتُما antomaa
لا تَفْهَموا خَطَأً! laa tafhamoo khaTa,a Do not understand wrong, all of you!	إفْهَموا! ifhamoo Understand, all of you!	You (plural, masculine and feminine)	أنتُم antom
لا تَفْهَمْنَ خَطَأً! laa tafhamna khaTa,a Do not understand wrong, all of you!	إفْهَمْنَ! ifhamna Understand, all of you!	You (plural, feminine)	أنْتُنَّ antonna

Command verb 'Listen!' with the pronoun 'You'. The root of the verb is ع م س:

Negated Command	Command Verb	Pronoun 'You'	
لا تَسْمَع! laa tasmaA' Do not listen!	إسْمَع! ismaA' Listen!	You (masculine)	أنتَ anta
لا تَسْمَعي! laa tasmaA'ee Do not listen!	إسْمَعي! ismaA'ee Listen!	You (feminine)	أنتِ anti
لا تَسْمَعا! laa tasmaA'aa Do not listen, both of you!	إسْمَعا! ismaA'aa Listen, both of you!	You (dual, masculine and feminine)	أنتُما antomaa

Negated Command	Command Verb	Pronoun 'You'	
لا تَسْمَعوا! laa tasmaA'oo Do not listen, all of you!	إسْمَعوا! ismaA'oo Listen, all of you!	You (plural, mascu- line and femi- nine)	أنْتُم antom
لا تَسْمَعنَ ! laa tasmaA'na Do not listen, all of you!	إسْمَعْنَ ! ismaA'na Listen, all of you!	You (plural, femi- nine)	أنْتُنَّ antonna

Command verb 'Ask!' with the pronoun 'You'. The root of the verb is س ء ل:

Negated Command	Command Verb	Pronoun 'You'	
لا تَسْأَلْ! laa tas,al Do not ask!	إسْأَلْ! is,al Ask!	You (masculine)	أنتَ anta
لا تَسْأَلي! laa tas,alee Do not ask!	إسْأَلي! is,alee Ask!	You (feminine)	أنتِ anti
لا تَسْأَلا! laa tas,alaa Do not ask, both of you!	إسْأَلا! is,alaa Ask, both of you!	You (dual, mascu- line and femi- nine)	أنتُما antomaa
لا تَسْأَلوا! laa tas,aloo Do not ask, all of you!	إسْأَلوا! is,aloo Ask, all of you!	You (plural, mascu- line and femi- nine)	أنْتُم antom
لا تَسْأَلْنَ ! laa tas,alna Do not ask, all of you!	إسْأَلْنَ ! is,alna Ask, all of you!	You (plural, femi- nine)	أنْتُنَّ antonna

Command verb 'Open!' with the pronoun 'You'. The root of the verb is ف ت ح

Negated Command	Command Verb	Pronoun 'You'	
لا تَفْتَحْ! laa taftaH Do not open!	إفْتَحْ! iftaH Open!"	You (masculine)	أنتَ anta
لا تَفْتَحِي! laa taftaHee Do not open!	إفْتَحِي! iftaHee Open!"	You (feminine)	أنتِ anti
لا تَفْتَحَا! laa taftaHaa Do not open, both of you!	إفْتَحَا! iftaHaa Open, both of you!	You (dual, masculine and feminine)	أنتُما antomaa
لا تَفْتَحُوا! laa taftaHoo Do not open, all of you!	إفْتَحُوا! iftaHoo Open, all of you!	You (plural, masculine and feminine)	أنتُم antom
لا تَفْتَحْنَ! laa taftaHna Do not open, all of you!	إفْتَحْنَ! iftaHna Open, all of you!	You (plural, feminine)	أنْتُنَّ antonna

Command verb 'Gather!' with the pronoun 'You'. The root of the verb is ج م ع

Negated Command	Command Verb	Pronoun 'You'	
لا تَجْمَعْ! laa tajmaA' Do not gather!	إجْمَعْ! ijmaA' Gather!	You (masculine)	أنتَ anta

Negated Command	Command Verb	Pronoun 'You'	
لا تَجْمَعِي! laa ijmaA'ee Do not gather!	إِجْمَعِي! ijmaA'ee Gather!	You (feminine)	أَنْتِ anti
لا تَجْمَعَا! laa tajmaA'a Do not gather, both of you!	إِجْمَعَا! ijmaA'a Gather, both of you!	You (dual, mascu-line and femi-nine)	أَنْتُمَا antomaa
لا تَجْمَعُوا! laa tajmaA'oo Do not gather, all of you!	إِجْمَعُوا! ijmaA'oo Gather, all of you!	You (plural, mas-culine and feminine)	أَنْتُم antom
لا تَجْمَعْنَ! laa tajmaA'na Do not gather, all of you!	إِجْمَعْنَ! ijmaA'na Gather, all of you!	You (plural, feminine)	أَنْتُنَّ antonna

Fourth Pattern:

Command verbs in the fourth pattern are formed by adding the 'fatHah' vowel to the first root, adding 'kasrah' vowel with 'shaddah' to the second root, and adding 'sukoon' to the last root if it's not connected to a pronoun.

Command verb 'Talk!' with the pronoun 'You'. The root of the verb is م ل ك :

Negated Command	Command Verb	Pronoun 'You'	
لا تُكَلِّمْ! laa tokallim Do not talk to..!	كَلِّمْ! kallim Talk to..!	You (masculine)	أَنْتَ anta

Negated Command	Command Verb	Pronoun 'You'	
لا تُكَلِّمي ! laa tokallimee Do not talk to..!	كَلِّمي ! kallimee Talk to..!	You (feminine)	أنتِ anti
لا تُكَلِّما! laa tokallimaa Both of you, do not talk to..!	كَلِّما! kallimaa Both of you, talk to..!	You (dual, masculine and feminine)	أنتُما antomaa
لا تُكَلِّموا! laa tokallimoo All of you, do not talk to..!	كَلِّموا! kallimoo All of you, talk to..!	You (plural, masculine and feminine)	أنتُم antom
لا تُكَلِّمْنَ ! laa tokallimna All of you, do not talk to..!	كَلِّمْنَ ! kallimna All of you, talk to..!	You (plural, feminine)	أنْتُنَّ antonna

Command verb 'Teach!' with the pronoun 'You'. The root of the verb is د ر س :

Negated Command	Command Verb	Pronoun 'You'	
لا تُدَرِّسْ ! laa todarris Do not teach!	دَرِّسْ ! darris Teach!	You (masculine)	أنتَ anta
لا تُدَرِّسي ! laa todarrisee Do not teach!	دَرِّسي ! darrisee Teach!	You (feminine)	أنتِ anti

Negated Command	Command Verb	Pronoun 'You'	
لا تُدَرِّسا ! laa todarrisaa Do not teach, both of you!	دَرِّسا ! darrisaa Teach, both of you!	You (dual, masculine and feminine)	أنتُما antomaa
لا تُدَرِّسوا ! laa todarrisoo Do not teach, all of you!	دَرِّسوا ! darrisoo Teach, all of you!	You (plural, masculine and feminine)	أنتُم antom
لا تُدَرِّسْنَ ! laa todarrisna Do not teach, all of you!	دَرِّسْنَ ! darrisna Teach, all of you!	You (plural, feminine)	أنْتُنَّ antonna

Command verb 'Collect!' with the pronoun 'You'. The root of the verb is ع م ج :

Negated Command	Command Verb	Pronoun 'You'	
لا تُجَمِّعْ ! laa tojammiA' Do not collect!	جَمِّعْ ! jammiA' Collect!	You (masculine)	أنتَ anta
لا تُجَمِّعي ! laa tojammiA'ee Do not collect!	جَمِّعي ! jammiA'ee Collect!	You (feminine)	أنتِ anti
لا تُجَمِّعا ! laa tojammiA'a Do not collect, both of you!	جَمِّعا ! jammiA'a Collect, both of you!	You (dual, masculine and feminine)	أنتُما antomaa
لا تُجَمِّعوا ! laa tojammiA'oo Do not collect, all of you!	جَمِّعوا ! jammiA'oo Collect, all of you!	You (plural, masculine and feminine)	أنتُم antom

Negated Command	Command Verb	Pronoun 'You'	
لَا تُجَمِّعْنَ ! laa tojammiA'na Do not collect, all of you!	جَمِّعْنَ ! jammiA'na Collect, all of you!	You (plural, feminine)	أَنْتُنَّ antonna

Command verb 'Educate!' with the pronoun 'You'. The root of the verb is ث ق ف :

Negated Command	Command Verb	Pronoun 'You'	
لا تُثَقِّفْ ! laa tothaCCif Do not educate..!	ثَقِّفْ ! thaCCif Educate!	You (masculine)	أَنتَ anta
لا تُثَقِّفي ! laa tothaCCifee Do not educate..!	ثَقِّفي ! thaCCifee Educate!	You (feminine)	أَنتِ anti
لا تُثَقِّفا ! laa tothaCCifaa Do not educate..both of you!	ثَقِّفا ! thaCCifaa Educate, both of you!	You (dual, masculine and feminine)	أَنتُما antomaa
لا تُثَقِّفوا ! laa tothaCCifoo Do not educate..all of you!	ثَقِّفوا ! thaCCifoo Educate, all of you!	You (plural, masculine and feminine)	أَنتُم antom
لا تُثَقِّفْنَ ! laa tothaCCifna Do not educate..all of you!	ثَقِّفْنَ ! thaCCifna Educate, all of you!	You (plural, feminine)	أَنْتُنَّ antonna

Fifth Pattern:

In the fifth pattern, command verbs are formed by adding the 'Dammah' vowel to the first root, dropping the second root 'و' for the singular masculine and plural feminine forms, and adding a 'sukoon' to the last root if it's not connected to a pronoun.

Command verb 'Get up!' with the pronoun 'You'. The root of the verb is ق و م :

Negated Command	Command Verb		Pronoun 'You'
لا تَقُمْ ! laa taCom Do not get up!	قُمْ ! Com Get up!	You (masculine)	أنتَ anta
لا تَقومي ! laa taCoomee Do not get up!	قُومي ! Coomee Get up!	You (feminine)	أنتِ anti
لا تَقوما ! laa taCoomaa Do not get up, both of you!	قُوما ! Coomaa Get up, both of you!	You (dual, masculine and feminine)	أنتُما antomaa
لا تَقوموا ! laa taCoomoo Do not get up, all of you!	قُوموا ! Coomoo Get up, all of you!	You (plural, masculine and feminine)	أنتُم antom
لا تَقُمْنَ ! laa taComna Do not get up, all of you!	قُمْنَ ! Comna Get up, all of you!	You (plural, feminine)	أنْتُنَّ antonna

Command verb 'Say!' with the pronoun 'You'. The root of the verb is ق و ل:

Negated Command	Command Verb		Pronoun 'You'
لا تَقُلْ ! laa taCol Do not say!	قُلْ ! Col Say!	You (masculine)	أَنتَ anta
لا تَقُولي ! laa taCoolee Do not say!	قُولي ! Colee Say!	You (feminine)	أَنتِ anti
لا تَقُولا ! laa taCoolaa Do not say, both of you!	قُولا ! Colaa Say, both of you!	You (dual, masculine and feminine)	أَنتُما antomaa
لا تَقُولوا ! laa taCooloo Do not say, all of you!	قُولوا ! Coloo Say, all of you!	You (plural, masculine and feminine)	أَنتُم antom
لا تَقُلْنَ ! laa taColna Do not say, all of you!	قُلْنَ ! Colna Say, all of you!	You (plural, feminine)	أَنْتُنَّ antonna

Command verb 'Come back!' with the pronoun 'You'. The root of the verb is ع و د:

Negated Command	Command Verb		Pronoun 'You'
لا تَعُدْ ! laa taA'od Do not come back!	عُدْ ! A'od Come back!	You (masculine)	أَنتَ anta

Negated Command	Command Verb	Pronoun 'You'	
لا تَعُودي ! laa taA'oodee Do not come back!	عُودي ! A'oodee Come back!	You (feminine)	أنتِ anti
لا تَعُودا ! laa taA'oodaa Do not come back, both of you!	عُودا ! A'oodaa Come back, both of you!	You (dual, mascu- line and femi- nine)	أنتُما antomaa
لا تَعُودوا ! laa taA'oodoo Do not come back, all of you!	عُودوا ! A'oodoo Come back, all of you!	You (plural, mas- culine and feminine)	أنتُم antom
لا تَعُدْنَ ! laa taA'odna Do not come back, all of you!	عُدْنَ ! A'odna Come back, all of you!	You (plural, feminine)	أنْتُنَّ antonna

Command verb 'Be!' with the pronoun 'You'. The root of the verb is ك و ن :

Negated Command	Command Verb	Pronoun 'You'	
لا تَكُنْ ! laa takon Do not be..!	كُنْ ! kon Be..!	You (masculine)	أنتَ anta
لا تَكُوني ! laa takoonee Do not be..!	كُوني ! koonee Be..!	You (feminine)	أنتِ anti

Negated Command	Command Verb	Pronoun 'You'	
لا تَكُونا ! laa takoonaa Do not be..both of you!	كُونا ! koonaa Be..both of you!	You (dual, masculine and feminine)	أنتُما antomaa
لا تَكُونوا ! laa takoonoo Do not be..all of you!	كُونوا ! koonoo Be..all of you!	You (plural, masculine and feminine)	أنتُم antom
لا تَكُنَّ ! laa takonna Do not be..all of you!	كُنَّ ! konna Be..all of you!	You (plural, feminine)	أنتُنَّ antonna

Sixth Pattern:

Command verbs in the sixth pattern are formed by adding the 'kasrah' vowel to the

first root, dropping the second root 'ي' for the singular masculine and plural feminine

forms, and adding 'sukoon' to the last root if it's not connected to a pronoun.

Command verb 'Live!' with the pronoun 'You'. The root of the verb is ع ي ش :

Negated Command	Command Verb	Pronoun 'You'	
لا تَعِشْ هُناك! laa taA'ish honaak Do not live there!	عِشْ هُناك! A'ish honaak Live there!	You (masculine)	أنتَ anta
لا تَعيشي هُناك! laa taA'eeshee honaak Do not live there!	عِيشي هُناك! A'eeshee honaak Live there!	You (feminine)	أنتِ anti

Negated Command	Command Verb	Pronoun 'You'	
لا تَعيشا هُناك! laa taA'eeshaa honaak Do not live there, both of you!	عِيشا هُناك! A'eeshaa honaak Live there, both of you!	You (dual, masculine and feminine)	أنتُما antomaa
لا تَعيشوا هُناك! laa taA'eeshoo honaak Do not live there, all of you!	عِيشوا هُناك! A'ishoo honaak Live there, all of you!	You (plural, masculine and feminine)	أنتُم antom
لا تَعِشْنَ هُناك! laa taA'ishna honaak Do not live there, all of you!	عِشْنَ هُناك! A'ishna honaak Live there, all of you!	You (plural, feminine)	أنتْنَّ antonna

Command verb 'Fly!' with the pronoun 'You'. The root of the verb is ط ي ر :

Negated Command	Command Verb	Pronoun 'You'	
لا تَطير ! laa taTeer Do not fly..!	طِرْ ! Tir Fly..!	You (masculine)	أنتَ anta
لا تَطيري ! laa taTeeree Do not fly..!	طِيري ! Teeree Fly..!	You (feminine)	أنتِ anti
لا تَطيرا ! laa taTeeraa Do not fly, both of you!	طِيرا ! Teeraa Fly, both of you!	You (dual, masculine and feminine)	أنتُما antomaa

Negated Command	Command Verb	Pronoun 'You'	
لا تَطيروا ! laa taTeeroo Do not fly, all of you!	طِيروا ! Teeroo Fly, all of you!	You (plural, masculine and feminine)	أَنْتُم antom
لا تَطِرْنَ ! laa taTirna Do not fly, all of you!	طِرْنَ ! Tirnaa Fly, all of you!	You (plural, feminine)	أَنْتُنَّ antonna

Command verb 'Increase!' with the pronoun 'You'. The root is ز ي د :

Negated Command	Command Verb	Pronoun 'You'	
لا تَزِدْ ! laa tazid Do not increase..!	زِدْ ! zid Increase..!	You (masculine)	أَنتَ anta
لا تَزيدي ! laa tazeedee Do not increase..!	زِيدي ! zeedee Increase..!	You (feminine)	أَنتِ anti
لا تَزيدا ! laa tazeedaa Do not increase, both of you!	زِيدا ! zeedaa Increase, both of you	You (dual, masculine and feminine)	أَنتُما antomaa
لا تَزيدوا ! laa tazeedoo Do not increase, all of you!	زِيدوا ! zeedoo Increase, all of you!	You (plural, masculine and feminine)	أَنتُم antom
لا تَزِدْنَ ! laa tazidna Do not increase, all of you!	زِدْنَ ! zidna Increase, all of you!	You (plural, feminine)	أَنْتُنَّ antonna

Command verb 'Wake up!' with the pronoun 'You'. The root of the verb is ف ي ق

(this word is common as an 'informal' verb in spoken Arabic) :

Negated Command	Command Verb	Pronoun 'You'	
لا تَفِقْ ! laa tafiC Do not wake up!	فِقْ ! fiC Wake up!	You (masculine)	أنتَ anta
لا تَفيقي ! laa tafeeCee Do not wake up!	فيقي ! feeCee Wake up!	You (feminine)	أنتِ anti
لا تَفيقا ! laa tafeeCaa Do not wake up, both of you!	فيقا ! feeCaa Wake up, both of you!	You (dual, masculine and feminine)	أنتُما antomaa
لا تَفيقوا ! laa tafeeCoo Do not wake up, all of you!	فيقوا ! feeCoo Wake up, all of you!	You (plural, masculine and feminine)	أنتُم antom
لا تَفِقْنَ ! laa tafiCna Do not wake up, all of you!	فِقْنَ ! fiCna Wake up, all of you!	You (plural, feminine)	أنْتُنَّ antonna

- Keep in mind that while practicing reading Arabic, it is important to remember that Arabic is a cursive script and is read and written from right to left.

- The examples provided in the tables for this lesson are all in spoken Modern Standard Arabic, which means that the words do not have vowels marked at the end of each word.

- Please be aware that the pronunciation system used in this book is explained on page six for your reference.

Building Vocabulary
Common Phrases and Expressions

The vocabulary listed in the last chapter of this book is a combination between Classical Arabic, spoken Modern Standard Arabic (MSA) and common words from the Middle-East dialect.

Meaning	Pronunciation	In Arabic
Hello	marHaba	مَرحَبا
Welcome	ahlan	أهْلاً
How are you? (asking a male)	kayfa Haaloka?	كَيْفَ حالُكَ ؟
How are you? (asking a female)	kayfa Haaloki?	كَيْفَ حالُكِ ؟
Good	bi-khair	بِخير
Good morning	SabaH al-KHair	صَباح الخير
Morning of light (reply to good morning)	SabaH al-noor	صَباح النور
Good evening	Masaa, al-khair	مساء الخير
Evening of light (Reply to good evening)	Masaa, al-noor	مَساء النور
What time is it please? (asking a male)	law samaHt kam al-saA'a	لَو سَمَحت كَم الساعَة؟
What time is it please? (asking a female)	law samaHti kam al-saA'a	لَو سَمَحتِ كَم الساعَة؟
What is your name? (asking a male)	maa ismoka?	ما إسْمُكَ ؟

Meaning	Pronunciation	In Arabic
What is your name? (asking a female)	maa ismoki?	ما إسْمُكِ ؟
My name is ...	ismee...	إسْمي ...
Where are you from? (asking a male)	min ayna anta?	مِنْ أَيْنَ أنْتَ ؟
Where are you from? (asking a female)	min ayna anti?	مِنْ أَيْنَ أنْتِ ؟
I am from...	anaa min...	أنا مِن ...
What is your job? (asking a male)	maathaa taA'-mal?	ماذا تَعْمَل ؟
What is your job? (asking a female)	maathaa taA'-malee?	ماذا تَعْمَلي ؟
Where is the bathroom?	ayna al-Ham-maam?	أيْنَ ٱلحَمّام ؟
I am hungry (male speaking)	anaa jowA'an	أنا جَوْعان
I am hungry (female speaking)	anaa jawA'ana	أنا جَوْعانة
Where is the restaurant?	ayna al-maTA'am?	أيْنَ ٱلمَطْعَم ؟
I am sleepy (male speaking)	anaa naA'saan	أنا نَعْسان
I am sleepy (female speaking)	anaa naA'saana	أنا نَعْسانَة
I am thirsty (male speaking)	anaa A'aTshaan	أنا عَطْشان
I am thirsty (female speaking)	anaa A'aTshaana	أنا عَطْشانَة

Meaning	Pronunciation	In Arabic
Where is the hotel?	ayna al-fondoC?	أَيْنَ ٱلْفُنْدُق ؟
I need a taxi	oreed taxi	أُريد تَكْسي
I need to go to the airport	oreed an adhhab ilaa al-maTaar	أُريد أَنْ أَذْهَب إلى ٱلْمَطار
I need to go to the hotel	oreed an adhhab ilaa al-fondoC	أُريد أن أَذْهَب إلى ٱلْفُنْدُق
How old are you? (asking a male)	kam A'omroka?	كَم عُمْرُكَ ؟
How old are you? (asking a female)	kam A'omroki?	كَم عُمْرُكِ ؟
Are you married? (asking a male)	hal anta mo-tazawwij?	هَل أنْتَ مُتَزَوِّج ؟
Are you married? (asking a female)	hal anti mo-tazawwija?	هَل أنْتِ مُتَزَوِّجَة ؟
Yes	naA'am	نَعَم
No	laa	لا
Help yourself / Go ahead (talking to a male)	tafaDDal	تَفَضَّل
Help yourself / Go ahead (talking to a female)	tafaDDalee	تَفَضَّلي
Please / begging a male	arjook	أَرْجوك..
Please / begging a female	arjooki	أَرْجوكِ..
Please.. (talking to a male) More formal	min faDlak	مِنْ فَضْلَك..

Meaning	Pronunciation	In Arabic
Please.. (talking to a female) More formal	min faDlik	..مِنْ فَضْلِكِ

Daily Informal Expressions

Meaning	Pronunciation	In Arabic
Hello	marHaba	مَرحَبا
Welcome	ahlan	أهْلاً
How are you? (asking a male)	kaif Haalak?	كيف حالَك ؟
How are you? (asking a female)	kaif Haalik?	كيف حالِك ؟
Let's go	yalla	يَلّا
Perfect	tamaam	تَمام
Please.. (talking to a male)	law samaHt	..لَوْ سَمَحْت
Please.. (talking to a female)	law samaHti	..لَوْ سَمَحْتِ
Please / begging someone	rajaa-an	..رَجاءً
I want to go to the market.	,oreed an adhhab ,ila al-sooC	أُرِيد أَنْ أَذهَب إلَى السُّوق
I want to learn the Arabic language.	,oreed an ata-A'alam al-loGHa al-A'arabiya	أُرِيد أَنْ أَتَعَلَّم اللُّغَة العَرَبِيَّة
I want to be a lawyer. (male speaking)	,oreed an akoon moHamee	أُرِيد أَنْ أَكُون مُحامي

Meaning	Pronunciation	In Arabic
I want to be a lawyer. (female speaking)	,oreed an akoon moHamiya	أُرِيد أَنْ أَكُون مُحَامِيَّة
I want to drink a cup of tea.	,oreed an ashrab koob mina al-shaii	أُرِيد أَنْ أَشْرَب كوب مِنَ الشّاي
I want food.	,oreed TaA'am	أُرِيد طَعَام
I want water.	,oreed maa,	أُرِيد مَاء
I want to sleep.	,oreed an anaam	أُرِيد أَنْ أَنَام
I want help / I need help	,oreed mosaA'ada	أُرِيد مُسَاعَدَة
I need a job.	,oreed A'amal	أُرِيد عَمَل
I need to borrow money.	,oreed dayyn	أُرِيد دَيْن
I need an opportunity.	,oreed forSa	أُرِيد فُرْصَة
I want to buy a gift for my brother.	,oreed an ashta-ree hadiya li,aKHee	أُرِيد أَنْ أَشْتَرِي هَدِيَّة لأُخِي
Present / Ok	HaaDir	حَاضِر
Okay / Alright.	maashee	مَاشِي
Okey / I agree	mowafiC	موَافِق

Body Parts

Meaning	Pronunciation	In Arabic
Head	ra,as	رَأس

Meaning	Pronunciation	In Arabic
Hair	shaA'r	شَعر
Ear	odhon	أُذُن
Nose	anf	أنْف
Eyebrows	Hawajib	حَواجِب
Eyelashes	romoosh	رُموش
Skin	jild	جِلْد
Neck	raCaba	رَقَبَة
Hand	yad	يَد
Leg	rejil	رِجِل
Heart	Calb	قَلْب
Chest	SaDir	صَدِر
Abdomen	baTin	بَطِن
Stomach	maA'ida	مَعِدَة
Kidney	kilya	كِلْيَة
Liver	kabid	كَبِد
Hip	KHaSir	خَصِر
Bones	A'iDHaam	عِظام
Muscles	A'aDalaat	عَضَلات
Back	DHahir	ظَهِر
Knee	rokba	رُكْبَة

Nouns of Family Members

Meaning	Pronunciation	In Arabic
Father	waalid	والِد
My father (more formal)	walidee	والِدي
Father	abb	أب
My father	abee	أبي
Dad	baba	بابا
Mother	waalida	والِدَة
My mother (more formal)	walidatee	والِدَتي
Mother	omm	أُم
My mother	ommee	أُمّي
Mom	mama	ماما
Son	ibn	إبْن
Daughter	ibna	إبْنَة
Brother	aKH	أَخ
Sister	oKHt	أُخْت
Husband	zawj	زَوْج
Wife	zawja	زَوْجَة
Uncle (father's side)	A'am	عَم
Aunt (father's side)	A'amma	عَمَّة
Uncle (mother's side)	KHaal	خال

Meaning	Pronunciation	In Arabic
Aunt (mother's side)	KHala	خَالة
Grandfather	jadd	جَدّ
Grandmother	jadda	جَدَّة
Grandson	Hafeed	حَفيد
Granddaughter	Hafeeda	حَفيدَة
Blood relative (male)	Careeb	قَريب
Blood relative (female)	Careeba	قَريبَة
Relative (in-law)	naseeb	نَسيب
Neighbor (male)	jaar	جار
Neighbor (female)	jaara	جارَة
Cousin male (father's side)	ibn A'am	إبْن عَم
Cousin male (mother's side)	ibn Khaal	إبْن خال
Cousin female (father's side)	Ibnat A'am	إبْنَة عَم
Cousin female (mother's side)	Ibnat Khaal	إبْنَة خال
Friend (male)	SadeeC	صَديق
Friend (female)	SadeeCa	صَديقَة

Words of Nature

Meaning	Pronunciation	In Arabic
Tree	shajara	شَجَرَة
Garden	bostaan	بُسْتان
Forest	GHaaba	غابَة
Sky	samaa,	سَماء
Earth	arD	أَرْض
Clouds	GHoyoom	غُيوم
Rain	maTar	مَطَر
Sun	shams	شَمْس
Moon	Camar	قَمَر
Sea	baHr	بَحْر
Ocean	moHeet	مُحيط
Desert	SaHraa,	صَحْراء
Wind	riyaaH	رِياح
Grass	Hasheesh	حَشيش
Flowers	azhaar	أزْهار
Bugs	Hasharaat	حَشَرات
Fog	Dabaab	ضَباب
Stars	nojoom	نُجوم
Space	faDaa,	فَضاء

Meaning	Pronunciation	In Arabic
Thunder	raA'd	رَعْد
Lightening	barC	بَرْق
Cosmos	kawn	كَوْن

Clothing and Accessories

Meaning	Pronunciation	In Arabic
Dress	fostaan	فُسْتان
Pants	sirwaal	سِرْوال
Skirt	tannoora	تَنّورَة
Handkerchief	mindeel	مِنْديل
Hat	TaCiyya	طاقِيَّة
Shoes	Hidhaa,	حِذاء
Shirt	CameeS	قَميص
Jacket	jakait	جاكيت
Suit	badlah	بَدْلَة
Fabric	Cimaash	قِماش
Button	zir	زِرّ
Zipper	saHHaab	سَحّاب
Earring	HalaC	حَلَق
Bracelet	iswaara	إسْوارَة

Meaning	Pronunciation	In Arabic
Eyeglasses	naDHDHara	نَظَّارَة
Ring	KHatim	خاتِم
Wallet	maHfaDHa	مَحْفَظَة
Necklace	TawC	طَوْق
Anklet	KHilKHaal	خِلْخال
Jewelry	mojawharaat	مُجَوْهَرات
Socks	jawaarib	جَوارِب

Household

Meaning	Pronunciation	In Arabic
Chair	korsee	كُرْسي
Table	Tawila	طاوِلَة
Bed	sareer	سَرير
Closet	khazana	خَزانَة
Sofa	kanabaya	كَنَبايَة
Door	baab	باب
Window	shobbak	شُبَّاك
Bathroom	Hammam	حَمَّام
Bedroom	GHorfat nawm	غُرْفَة نَوْم
Dining Room	GHorfat TaA'am	غُرْفَة طَعام

Meaning	Pronunciation	In Arabic
Kitchen	maTbaKH	مَطْبَخ
Family Room	GHorfat joloos	غُرْفَة جُلُوس
Living Room	GHorfat Doyoof	غُرْفَة ضُيوف
Ceiling	saCif	سَقِف
Mattress	farsha	فَرْشَة
Comforter	liHaaf	لِحاف
Blanket	baTTaniya	بَطَّانِيّة
Pillow	maKHadda	مَخَدَّة
Bed Sheet	sharshaf	شَرْشَف
Picture Frame	lawHah	لَوْحَة
Clock	saA'at Haa,iT	ساعَة حائِط

The Kitchen

Meaning	Pronunciation	In Arabic
Refrigerator	thal-laaja	ثَلّاجَة
Oven	foron	فُرُن
Faucet	Hanafiyya	حَنَفِيَّة
Water	maa,	ماء
Plate	SaHin	صَحِن
Plate (another term used)	wiA'a,	وِعاء

Meaning	Pronunciation	In Arabic
Cup	finjaan	فِنْجان
Tray	Seeniyya	صِينِيِّة
Pitcher	ibreeC	إبْرِيق
Food	TaA'am	طَعام
Cooking pot	Tanjara	طَنْجَرة
Sugar	sokkar	سُكَّر
Salt	milH	مِلْح
Bowl	Zobdiy-yi	زُبْدِيِّة
Basket	sal-la	سَلَّة
Spoon	milA'aCa	مِلْعَقة
Fork	shawka	شَوْكَة
Knife	sik-keen	سِكّين
Sink	majlaa	مَجْلى
Spices	bhaaraat	بهارات
Apron	maryool	مَرْيول

Common Produce

Meaning	Pronunciation	In Arabic
Fruit	fakiha	فاكِهَة
Orange	bortoCaal	بُرْتُقال

Meaning	Pronunciation	In Arabic
Banana	mawz	مَوْز
Grapes	A'inab	عِنَب
Pomegranate	romman	رُمّان
Watermelon	baTTeeKH	بطّيخ
Cantaloupe	shommaam	شُمّام
Guava	Jawwafi	جَوّافِه
Apricot	mishmish	مِشْمِش
Peach	dorraC	دُرّاق
Raspberry	toot	توت
Apple	toffaaH	تُفّاح
Strawberry	farawla	فَراولِة
Vegetables	KHoDrawaat	خُضْرَوات
Zucchini / Squash	koosaa	كوسا
Eggplant	bathinjaan	باثِنْجان
Cabbage	malfoof	مَلْفوف
Lettuce	KHas	خَسّ
Lemon	laymoon	لَيْمون
Tomatoes	TamaaTim	طَماطِم
Cucumber	KHiyaar	خِيار

Meaning	Pronunciation	In Arabic
Carrots	jazar	جَزَر
Parsley	baCdoonis	بَقْدونِس
Onion	baSal	بَصَل
Bell Pepper	fifil Hiloo	فِلْفِل حِلو
Jalapeno	filfil HarraC	فِلْفِل حَرّاق
Sweet peas	bazailla	بازيلّا
Green beans	faSoolyaa	فاصوليْا
Okra	bamyaa	باميا

Colors

Meaning	Pronunciation	In Arabic (F)	Pronunciation	In Arabic (M)
Blue	zarCaa,	زَرْقاء	azraC	أزْرَق
Green	KHaDraa,	خَضْراء	aKHDar	أخْضَر
Yellow	Safraa,	صَفْراء	aSfar	أصْفَر
Red	Hamraa,	حَمْراء	aHmar	أحْمَر
White	baiDaa,	بَيْضاء	abyaD	أبْيَض
Black	sawdaa,	سَوْداء	aswad	أسْوَد
Orange	borto-Caaliyya	بُرْتُقاليّة	bortoCaliy	بُرْتُقالِيّ
Violet	banafsajiyya	بَنَفْسَجيّة	banafsajiy	بَنَفْسَجِيّ

Meaning	Pronunciation	In Arabic (F)	Pronunciation	In Arabic (M)
Purple	nahdiyya	نَهْدِيَّة	nahdiy	نَهْدِيّ
Gray	sakaniyya	سَكَنِيَّة	sakaniy	سَكَنِيّ

Things in the street

Meaning	Pronunciation	In Arabic
Car	sayyara	سَيَّارَة
Truck	shaahina	شاحِنَة
Bus	baaS	باص
Street	shaariA'	شارِع
Sidewalk	raSeef	رَصيف
Road	TareeC	طَريق
Exit	maKHraj	مَخْرَج
Entrance	madKHal	مَدْخَل
Traffic light	ishaara Daw,iyya	إشارَة ضَوْئِيَّة
Alley	daKHli	دَخْلة
Uphill	TalA'a	طَلْعَة
Downhill	nazla	نَزْلة
Parking	mawCif	مَوْقِف
Store	dokkaan	دُكّان

Meaning	Pronunciation	In Arabic
Gas station	Kaaziyya	كَازِيَّة
Pole	A'amood	عامود
Stop sign	ishaarat woCoof	إشارة وُقوف
Detour	taHweela	تَحْويلَة
No entry	mamnooA' al-moroor	مَمْنوع المُرور
Yield	intabih	إنْتَبِه

Animals

Meaning	Pronunciation	In Arabic
Dog	kalb	كَلْب
Cat	CiTTa	قِطَّة
Turtle	solHofaa	سُلْحُفاة
Horse	HiSaan	حِصان
Donkey	Himaar	حِمار
Cow	baCara	بَقَرَة
Goat	maaA'iz	ماعِز
Sheep	KHaroof	خَروف
Chicken	dajaaja	دَجاجَة
Rooster	deek	ديك
Fox	thaA'lab	ثَعْلَب

Meaning	Pronunciation	In Arabic
Coyote	waawee	واوي
Wolf	dhi,ib	ذِئِب
Bird	Taa,ir	طائِر
Mouse	fa,ra	فَأْرَة
Frog	DifdaA'	ضِفْدَع
Turkey	Habash	حَبَش
Duck	baTT	بَطّ
Camel	jamal	جَمَل
Crow	GHoraab	غُراب

Professions

Meaning	Pronunciation	In Arabic
King	malik	مَلِك
Prince	ameer	أمير
President	ra,ees	رَئيس
Doctor	Tabeeb	طَبيب
Minister	wazeer	وَزير
Colonel	A'eCeed	عَقيد
Nurse	momarriD	مُمَرِّض
Teacher	modarris	مُدَرِّس

Meaning	Pronunciation	In Arabic
Teacher (another term used)	moA'allim	مُعَلِّم
Engineer	mohandis	مُهَنْدِس
Translator	motarjim	مُتَرْجِم
Actor	momathil	مُمَثِّل
Broadcaster	modheeA'	مُذيع
Principal	modeer	مُدير
Writer	kaatib	كاتِب
Publisher	naashir	ناشِر
Guard	Haaris	حارِس
Worker	A'amil	عامِل
Housekeeper	khaadim	خادِم
Shepherd	raaA'ee	راعي
Driver	saa,iC	سائِق
Scientist	A'aalim	عالِم
Artist	fan-naan	فَنّان
Contractor	ban-naa,	بَنّاء
Artist (painter)	ras-saam	رَسّام
Butcher	laH-Haam	لَحّام
Carpenter	naj-jaar	نَجّار
Blacksmith	Had-daad	حَدّاد

Meaning	Pronunciation	In Arabic
Barber	Hal-laaC	حَلّاق
Tailor	KHay-yaaT	خَيّاط
Cook / Chef	Tab-baaKH	طَبّاخ
Bread-maker	KHab-baaC	خَبّاز
Fisherman	Say-yaad	صَيّاد
Sailor	mal-laaH	مَلّاح
Pilot	Tay-yaar	طَيّار
Governor	moHaafiTH	مُحافِظ
Accountant	moHaasib	مُحاسِب
Farmer	mozaariA'	مُزارِع
Attorney	moHaamee	مُحامي
Dry cleaner	kawwaa	كَوّى
Banker	maSrifiy	مَصْرِفيّ
Nanny	Morab-biya	مُرَبِّية
Employee	mowaDH-DHaf	مُوَظَّف

Countries

Meaning	Pronunciation	In Arabic
Jordan	al-,ordon	الأُردن
Palestine	falasteen	فَلَسْطين

349

Meaning	Pronunciation	In Arabic
Lebanon	lobnaan	لُبنان
Syria	sooryaa	سوريا
Iraq	al-A'iraaC	العِراق
Saudi Arabia	al-saA'oodiy-ya	السَعودِيّة
Kuwait	al-kowait	ألكُويت
Bahrain	al-baHrain	البَحْرين
Qatar	CaTar	قَطَر
United Arab Emirates	al-imaarat al-A'ara-biyya	الإمارات ألعَرَبِيّة
Oman	A'omaan	عُمان
Yaman	al-yaman	أليَمَن
Somalia	aS-Soomaal	الصومال
Egypt	miSir	مِصر
Sudan	as-soodaan	السودان
Libya	leebyaa	ليبيا
Tunisia	toonis	تونِس
Algeria	al-jaza,ir	الجَزائِر
Morocco	al-maGHrib	المَغْرِب
Mauritania	mooritaania	موريتانيا

Shapes and Sizes

Meaning	Pronunciation	In Arabic
Triangle	mothallath	مُثَلَّث
Square	morabaA'	مُرَبَّع
Oval	bayDawee	بَيْضَوي
Heart	Calb	قَلْب
Circle	daa,ira	دائِرَة
Rectangle	mostaTeel	مُسْتَطيل
Crescent	hilaal	هِلال
Star	najma	نَجْمَة
Quarter	roboA'	رُبْع
Half	niSf	نِصْف
One-third	tholth	ثُلْث
Two-third	tholthaan	ثُلْثان

The Four Seasons

Meaning	Pronunciation	In Arabic
Spring	ar-rabeeA'	الرَّبيع
Summer	aS-Sayf	الصَّيْف
Fall	al-KHareef	الخَريف
Winter	ash-shitaa,	الشِتاء

Directions

Meaning	Pronunciation	In Arabic
North	shamaal	شَمال
South	janoob	جَنوب
East	sharC	شَرْق
West	GHarb	غَرْب

Common Arabic Islamic Expressions

Meaning	Pronunciation	In Arabic
In the name of God	bismillah	بِسْمِ ٱللّٰه
By God's will	inshallah	إنْشاءَ ٱللّٰه
"God has willed it" equivalent to "knock on wood"/"bless your heart"	mashallah	ما شاءَ ٱللّٰه
Glory be to God	subHanaallah	سُبْحانَ ٱللّٰه
"Thank God' "Praise be to God"	alhamdulillah	ٱلْحَمْدُ لِلّٰه

Days Of The Week

(In the Arab world, Saturday is the first day of the week.)

Meaning	Pronunciation	In Arabic
Saturday	as-sabt	السَّبت
Sunday	al-,aHad	الأَحَد

Meaning	Pronunciation	In Arabic
Monday	al-,ithnayn	الإثْنَيْن
Tuesday	atholaathaa,	الثُلاثاء
Wednesday	al-arbiA'aa,	الأَرْبعاء
Thursday	al-KHamees	الخَميس
Friday	Aj-jomA'a	الجُمَعَة

Months of the Arab Year
(Solar Months)

Meaning	Pronunciation	In Arabic
January	kaanoon aththaanee	كانون ٱلثاني
February	shobaaT	شُباط
March	aadhaar	آذار
April	neesaan	نيسان
May	ayyaar	أيّار
June	Hozairaan	حُزَيْران
July	tam-mooz	تَمّوز
August	aab	آب
September	aylool	أيْلول
October	tishreen al-awwal	تِشْرين ٱلأوّل
November	tishreen aththaanee	تِشْرين ٱلثاني

Meaning	Pronunciation	In Arabic
December	kanoon al-awal	كانون ٱلأوّل

Months of the Muslim Year
(Lunar Months used in Arab Countries)

Meaning	In Arabic
MoHarram	مُحَرَّم
Safar	صَفَر
RabeeA' al-awal	رَبيع ٱلأوّل
RabeeA' al-ththaanee	رَبيع ٱلثاني
Jamaadee al-awal	جَمادي ٱلأوّل
Jamaadee al-ththaanee	جَمادي ٱلثاني
Rajab	رَجَب
ShaA'baan	شَعْبان
RamaDaan	رَمَضان
Shawwal	شَوّال
dho al-CiA'da	ذو ٱلقِعْدة
dho al-Hija	ذو ٱلحِجّة

• These months follow the lunar months, and are composed of 29 or 30 days. In addition, the lunar year is composed of 355 or 354 days. Therefore, these months vary from year-to-year with their solar month's equivalence.

Counting (1-20)

Meaning	Pronunciation	In Arabic
One	waHid	واحِد
Two	ithnaan	إثْنان
Three	thalatha	ثلاثة
Four	arbaA'a	أربَعة
Five	KHamsa	خَمسَة
Six	sitta	سِتَّة
Seven	sabA'a	سَبْعَة
Eight	thamaniya	ثَمانِيَة
Nine	tisA'a	تِسْعَة
Ten	A'shara	عَشَرَة
Eleven	iHda A'ashar	إحدى عَشَر
Twelve	ithnaa A'ashar	إثنا عَشَر
Thirteen	thalathata A'ashar	ثَلاثَة عَشَر
Fourteen	arbaA'a'ta A'ashar	أربَعَة عَشَر
Fifteen	KHamsata A'ashar	خَمسَة عَشَر
Sixteen	sittata A'ashar	سِتَّة عَشَر
Seventeen	sabA'ta A'ashar	سَبعَة عَشَر
Eighteen	thamaniyata A'ashar	ثَمانِيَة عَشَر

Meaning	Pronunciation	In Arabic
Nineteen	tisA'ata A'ashar	تِسعَةَ عَشَر
Twenty	A'ishroon	عِشرون

Counting in Tens

Meaning	Pronunciation	In Arabic
Ten	A'ashara	عَشرَة
Twenty	A'ishroon	عِشْرون
Thirty	thalathoon	ثَلاثون
Forty	arbaA'oon	أربَعون
Fifty	KHamsoon	خَمسون
Sixty	sittoon	سِتّون
Seventy	sabA'oon	سَبعون
Eighty	thamanoon	ثَمانون
Ninety	tisA'oon	تِسعون
One Hundred	mi,ah	مِئَة

Counting in Hundreds

Meaning	Pronunciation	In Arabic
One Hundred	mi,ah	مِئَة
Two Hundred	mi,ataan	مِئَتان
Three Hundred	thalaatho mi,ah	ثَلاثُ مِئَة
Four Hundred	arbaA'o mi,ah	أربعُ مِئَة
Five Hundred	KHamso mi,ah	خَمسُ مِئَة
Six Hundred	sitto mi,ah	سِتُّ مِئَة
Seven Hundred	sabA'o mi,ah	سَبْعُ مِئَة
Eight Hundred	thamaanee mi,ah	ثَماني مِئَة
Nine Hundred	tisA'o mi,ah	تِسْعُ مِئَة
One Thousand	alf	أَلَف